HISTORY

OF

TENNESSEE

From the Earliest Time to the Present; Together with an Historical
and a Biographical Sketch of Fayette and Harde-
man Counties, Besides a Valuable Fund
of Notes, Original Observations,
Reminiscences, Etc., Etc.

ILLUSTRATED.

Nashville:
THE GOODSPEED PUBLISHING CO.,
1887.

This volume was reproduced from
An 1887 edition located in the
Knoxville Public Library,
Knoxville, Tennessee

All rights reserved. No part of this publication may be reproduced,
stored in a retrieval system, transmitted in any form,
posted on to the web in any form or by any means
without the prior written permission of the publisher.

Please direct all correspondence and orders to:

www.southernhistoricalpress.com
or
SOUTHERN HISTORICAL PRESS, Inc.
PO BOX 1267
375 West Broad Street
Greenville, SC   29601
southernhistoricalpress@gmail.com

Originally published: Nashville, 1887
Reprinted with New Material by:
Southern Historical Press, Inc.
Greenville, SC
New Material Copyright 1979 by
The Rev. Silas Emmett Lucas, Jr.
Easley, SC
ISBN #0-89308-112-4
All rights Reserved.
Printed in the United States of America

PREFACE.

THIS volume has been prepared in response to the prevailing and popular demand for the preservation of local history and biography. The method of preparation followed is the most successful and the most satisfactory yet devised—the most successful in the enormous number of volumes circulated, and the most satisfactory in the general preservation of personal biography and family record conjointly with local history. The number of volumes now being distributed appears fabulous. Within the last four years not less than 20,000 volumes of this class of works have been distributed in Kentucky, and the demand is not half satisfied. Careful estimates place the number circulated in Ohio at 50,000; Pennsylvania, 60,000; New York, 75,000; Indiana, 35,000; Illinois, 40,000; Iowa, 35,000, and every other Northern State at the same proportionate rate. The Southern States, with the exception of Kentucky, Virginia and Georgia, owing mainly to the disorganization succeeding the civil war, yet retain, ready for the publisher, their stories of history and biography. Within the next five years the vast and valuable fund of perishing event in all the Southern States will be rescued from decay, and be recorded and preserved—to be reviewed, studied and compared by future generations. The design of the present extensive historical and biographical research is more to gather and preserve in attractive form while fresh with the evidences of truth, the enormous fund of perishing occurrence, than to abstract from insufficient contemporaneous data remote, doubtful or incorrect conclusions. The true perspective of the landscape of life can only be seen from the distance that lends enchantment to the view. It is asserted that no person is competent to write a philosophical history of his own time—that, owing to conflicting circumstantial evidence that yet conceals the truth, he can not take that luminous, correct, comprehensive, logical and unprejudiced view of passing events that will enable him to draw accurate and enduring conclusions. The duty, then, of a historian of his own time is to collect, classify and preserve the material for the final historian of the future. The present historian deals in fact, the future historian, in conclusion; the work of the former is statistical, of the latter, philosophical.

To him who has not attempted the collection of historical data, the obstacles to be surmounted are unknown. Doubtful traditions, conflicting statements, imperfect records, inaccurate private correspondence, the bias or untruthfulness of informers, and the general obscurity which envelops all events combine to bewilder and mislead. On the contrary, the preparation of statistical history by experienced, unprejudiced and competent workers in specialties; the accomplishment by a union of labor of a vast result that would cost one person the best years of his life and transfer the collection of perishing event beyond the hope of research; the judicious selection of important matter from the general rubbish; and the careful and intelligent revision of all final manuscript by an editor-in-chief, yield a degree of celerity, system, accuracy, comprehensiveness and value unattainable by any other method. The publishers of this volume, fully aware of their inability to furnish a perfect history, an accomplishment vouchsafed only to the dreamer or the theorist, make no pretension of having prepared a work devoid of blemish. They feel assured that all thoughtful people, at present and in future, will recognize and appreciate the importance of their undertaking and the great public benefit that has been accomplished.

In the preparation of this volume the publishers have met with nothing but courtesy and assistance. They acknowledge their indebtedness for valuable favors to the Governor, the State Librarian, the Secretary of the State Historical Society and to more than a hundred of other prominent citizens of Nashville, Memphis, Knoxville, Chattanooga, Jackson, Clarksville and the smaller cities of the State. It is the design of the publishers to compile and issue, in connection with the State history, a brief yet comprehensive historical account of every county in the State, copies of which will be placed in the State Library. In the prosecution of this work they hope to meet with the same cordial assistance extended to them during the compilation of this volume.

THE PUBLISHERS.

NASHVILLE, April, 1887.

CONTENTS.

FAYETTE COUNTY.

	PAGE.
FAYETTE COUNTY	797
Banks, Lodges, etc.	805
Bell County	799
Court Houses and Jails	798–799
County Court, The	800–801
Churches	811–814
County Officers	801–803
Geology and Natural Features	797
La Grange	806
Moscow	807
Merchants	804
Newspapers	805–806
Population and Productions	799–800
Railroads	800
Somerville	803–806
Seat of Justice Located	798
Schools	810–811
Soil and Drainage	797
Settlement, etc.	808–810
Villages	807
War Record	814–817

HARDEMAN COUNTY.

	PAGE.
HARDEMAN COUNTY	818
Banks, Cemetery, etc.	828
Bolivar	826–830
Bench and Bar, The	825–826
County Officers	823–824
Commercial Highways	822–823
County Court and Business	824–825
Education	834–835
Insane Asylum	823
Location of the County Seat	820
Military Exhibit	831–834
Paupers	822
Public Buildings	821–822
Press, The	828
Religion	835–840
Secret Societies	829–830
Small Towns	830–831
Southern Boundary, The	820
Settlers, Industries, etc.	819
Streams and Soil	818
Surface Characteristics	818
Timber, etc.	818

BIOGRAPHICAL APPENDIX.

Fayette County	840
Hardeman County	887

FAYETTE COUNTY.

THE topographical features of Fayette County are not very strongly marked. The northern portion is slightly undulating, the middle and western rather hilly with extended plateaus, the southeast hilly with fertile valleys, and the extreme southern portion an unbroken level, the latter being the Wolf River bottoms.

The formation underlying the surface of the county is, as seen in the bluffs, railroad cuts, washes, etc., generally a stratified mass of sands, more or less argillaceous, which when exposed to the weather, are of red, yellow and orange colors, and is known as the Lagrange sand. This, however, is often concealed by the Orange sand and the drift. No minerals are found.

The soils are generally sandy, with more silicates in those in the southern portion of the county, and a gradual increase of clay in the northern portion. Generally the soils are quick, and produce good crops, the principal ones being wheat, corn, oats, sweet and Irish potatoes, tobacco and cotton. The soil easily washes into gullies, sometimes very large, but this is prevented to a great extent by the horizontilization system of cultivation, which is generally adopted. This system of levels has each row to carry off its own water.

The timber, of which there now remains none for export, was heavy and grew in abundance, consisting of cypress, oak, walnut, poplar, hickory, gum, ash and beech.

The water courses of the county are the Wolf River, the largest, which passes across the entire southern portion of the county; the Loosahatchie, which rises in the eastern part of the county and runs west nearly through its center; the North Fork of Wolf River, which also rises in the eastern part and joins the main stream at Moscow, and Beaver, Bear, Bennett, Bluff, Muddy, Town, Treadwell, Jones, Laurel and Cypress Creeks.

Fayette County is bounded on the north by the counties of Tipton and Haywood, east by Hardeman County, south by the State of Mississippi, west by the counties of Shelby and Tipton, and has an area of about 700 square miles, being one of the largest and best counties in Tennessee. It was named in honor of Gen. LaFayette, who visited the United States about the time of its organization. The General Assembly, in session at Murfreesboro, passed on September 29, 1824, an act "entitled an act to establish the county of Fayette," and on the first Monday in December of that year the new county was formally organized at the house of Robert G. Thornton, on the North Fork of Wolf River, twelve miles southeast from Somerville, and seven miles northwest from LaGrange, in what is now Civil District No. 13. In February, 1825, Benjamin Reynolds, Robert Jetton, James Fentress and William Martin, commissioners appointed by the Legislature to lay off the new county and locate a permanent seat of justice, reported to the county court, in session at Mr. Thornton's, that they had "located the county site upon the lands of George Bowers and James Brown, on both sides of the meridian line dividing the Tenth and Eleventh (Surveyor's) Districts." Messrs. Bowers and Brown each donated the county a tract containing about twenty-five acres of land. The Court then appointed William Owen, Daniel Johnson, Hamilton Thornton, Henry Kirk and John T. Patterson commissioners to lay off the above land into town lots, sell the same at public auction, and with the moneys derived therefrom cause to be erected a temporary log courthouse, jail and other necessary public buildings. The sale of lots occurred September 14, 1825, a large number but by no means a majority of the lots being disposed of. The county seat was given the name it bears in honor of Lieut. Somerville, who fell while fighting under Gen. Jackson in the Creek war in 1814, though for a number of years the town was called Bowersville, in honor of George Bowers, who donated half of the land on which the town stood. Legally, however, Somerville was the name.

By November, 1825, the temporary courthouse was completed and ready for occupancy. It was a twenty-foot square, one story, log building, and stood about fifty feet northeast of the north corner of the present courthouse. In 1833 a two-story brick courthouse, 50x60 feet in size, was erected immediately in the center of the public square, and stood until 1876, when it was removed to make place for the present imposing courthouse, which was erected at a cost of about $45,000, and which is the most beautiful and best arranged courthouse in West Tennessee, if not the State—city buildings not excepted. The building is of brick and galvanized iron, painted a stone color, slate roof, stone floor, with a tower in front, and two smaller ones in the rear; the front tower being surmounted by a statue of Justice, with sword and balance in hand. The lower floor is divided into a county court room and county court clerk's office, chancery court room and clerk and master's office, circuit court clerk, register, trustee and sheriff's offices, while the entire second floor, with the exception of a few small rooms and a hall, is devoted to the handsomest circuit court room in the

State. A large bell clock tells the time of day from the tower. The building is enclosed with a neat iron fence.

In the latter part of 1825 a log jail of the usual pattern and dimensions was completed and was used as a county prison until about 1838, when a substantial brick jail was erected. The latter building, with the aid of numerous repairs, stood until 1873, when a handsome two-story brick, with tin roof, was completed at a cost of about $20,000. This building was set on fire by a negro prisoner on the night of November 26, 1886, and totally destroyed. This is being rebuilt by the Pauley Jail & Manufacturing Co., of St. Louis, at a cost of $8,500. In about 1869 the question of forming a new county out of a narrow strip of country lying between the Memphis & Charleston Railway and the Mississippi line, in the counties of Fayette, Shelby and Hardeman, was raised and agitated with much feeling pro and con. The Legislature passed an act in 1870 authorizing the erection of the new county, and naming the same Bell, in honor of Hon. John Bell, one of Tennessee's most distinguished sons. The question was submitted to the voters in 1871 and carried by a large vote, but lost by a technicality. In 1872 the question was revived, a second act was passed, and a second time was the question submitted to the voters and carried. Fayette County then protested and carried the matter to the supreme court, where a ruling adverse to the proposed county was made, and the matter dropped. Should Bell County have been organized, Fayette would have lost about one-tenth of her territory. In 1825 the population of Fayette County was about 800, in 1830 it was 8,652, in 1840 it was 21,501, in 1850 it was 26,719, in 1860 it was 24,327, in 1870 it was 26,145, in 1880 it was 31,874, and in 1886 it is estimated at about 30,000, showing a decrease since 1880, which is accounted for by the removing in large numbers of the negroes to Arkansas, Texas and other Southern States. The vote of the county, amounting to about 6,000, is divided between the Democratic and Republican parties, in the ratio of three to four, the colored voters all going with the latter party. Though so uneven, the Democrats manage, as a rule, to keep control of the county offices. The products of the county in 1870 were, wheat 11,786 bushels, rye 34 bushels, corn 627,271 bushels, oats 9,450 bushels, potatoes 85,000 bushels, tobacco 840 pounds, cotton 20,131 bales; 1880, wheat 18,004 bushels, rye 316 bushels, corn 1,003,505 bushels, oats 38,129 bushels, potatoes 95,630 bushels, tobacco 20,901 pounds, cotton 35,000 bales; 1886 (estimated), wheat 19,500 bushels, rye 320 bushels, corn 1,000,000 bushels, oats 40,000 bushels, potatoes 90,000 bushels, tobacco 20,000 pounds cotton 30,000 bales.

In 1870 the live stock of the county amounted to 6,912 head of horses and mules, 14,939 head of cattle, 3,828 head of sheep, and 30,762 head of hogs; 1880, 8,631 head of horses and mules, 18,621 head of cattle, 4,360 head of sheep, and 28,536 head of hogs; 1886 (estimated), 8,500 head of horses and mules, 18,000 head of cattle, 4,200 head of sheep, and 28,000 head of hogs. In 1870 there were 438,652 acres assessed for taxation in Fayette County, which were valued at $4,910,805, while the total valuation of taxable property was $6,343,325. The tax duplicate for 1886 shows the number of acres assessed to be 436,786, valued at $2,003,555, the value of town lots to be $253,950, the personal property, less $1,000 to each individual, $134,045, and the total valuation, including real, personal and all other property, $2,391,550, showing a decrease in the total in 16 years of $3,951,775, and during the same time a decrease in the value of acres assessed of $2,907,250. The tax levy for 1886 is, State 30 cents, county 30 cents, school 10 cents, roads 8 cents, poll $1, amounting in the aggregate to, State $7,174.65, county $11,063.65, school $8,672.10, road $1,708.80, poll $3,889; total, $32,508.20.

The county has good railroad facilities. The Memphis & Charleston Railroad passes through the entire southern end of the county and has a branch running from Moscow to Somerville, a distance of about thirteen miles. The Memphis & Louisville Railroad passes through the northwest corner, while the Mississippi Central Railroad runs within a few hundred yards of the southeast corner of the county forming a junction with the Memphis & Charleston at Grand Junction, Hardeman County, three miles east from La Grange, Fayette County. The proposed Nashville, Jackson & Memphis Railroad, as surveyed, will pass through Somerville. In 1835 a charter was granted by the Legislature for a road to run from Memphis to La Grange, to be known as the Memphis & La Grange Railroad. Several miles of roadbed were graded, but from a lack of funds the enterprise proved a failure. The State was to contribute $125,000 stock which was equal to one-half of the individual stock. This was the first road chartered in the State and only six miles of it were ever completed and that was at the end leading into Memphis.

The first county court of Fayette County convened at the house of Robert G. Thornton, the location of which is elsewhere given, on Monday, December 6, 1824, the justices present and holding said court being Henry Kirk, Henry M. Johnson, Daniel Johnson, Robert G. Thornton, Edmund D. Tarver, Lawrence G. Evans, David Jarnigan, Daniel Cleft, William Ramsey and John T. Patterson, all of whom held commissions as magistrates from the governor and were administered the oath of office by Squire John H. Bills, of Hardeman County.

Edmund D. Tarver was chosen chairman of the court, Henry M. Johnson clerk, Samuel B. Harper sheriff, Jarman Koonce register, David Jarnigan trustee, Henry Brooks ranger, and William Owen coroner. The sessions of the court were held at Thornton's until the completion of the courthouse at Somerville in November, 1825, when the records were removed thereto, and the first session held in the new building began November 14 of the above year. Below is given a complete list of the officers of this court together with their terms: Chairman, Edmund D. Tarver, 1824-25; Daniel Johnson, 1825-26; Thomas C. Hudson, 1826-27; Daniel Johnson, 1827-31; John C. Cooper, 1831-32; Daniel Johnson, 1832-33; R. A. Parker, 1833-34; Seton Hudspeth, 1834-35; Jesse Allen, 1835-36; Lewis P. Williams, 1836-37; W. D. Wilkinson, 1837-40; James A. Heaslett, 1840-41; William Burton, 1841-44; William C. Loving, 1844-48; Hardy W. Tharp, 1848-49; Joel Jones, 1849-52; Robert Caldwell, 1852-54; James A. Heaslett, 1854-55; A. M. Shaw, 1855-56; G. W. Adams, 1856-57; John C. Cooper (judge), 1857-58; Charles Lynn, 1858-61; Robert N. Nesbitt, 1861-63; Charles Lynn, 1863-65; Thomas R. Cocke, 1865-83; John J. Steiger, 1883-86 and present.

Clerks: Henry M. Johnson, 1824-28; Thomas C. Hudson, 1828-36; Jarman Koonce, 1836-56; William H. Robertson, 1856-61; William R. Rutledge, 1861-62; William H. Thompson, 1862-65; John C. Reeves, 1865-74; S. H. Morton, 1874-86; John C. Reeves, present.

Sheriffs: Samuel B. Harper, 1824-29; Joel Jones, 1829-36; Nathaniel Atkinson, 1836-42; Seaton Hudspeth, 1842-44; Benj. Trotter, 1844-48; Abe Appleberry, 1848-50; Benj. Branch, 1850-55; John Cloyd, 1855-56; John D. Stanley, 1856-62; J. S. Perry, 1862-68; W. H. Hester, 1868-72; John G. Reeves, 1872-74; Thomas E. Holmes, 1874-74; Nat. Word, 1874-76; D. N. Rieves, 1876-78;* W. C. Rieves, 1878-80, R. E. Steiger, 1880-86; W. A. Koonce, present.

Registers: Jarman Koonce, 1824-36; Simon H. Walker, 1836-62; D. W. Thomas, 1862-65; DeWitt C. Mosbey, 1865-70; Bart. F. Tatum, 1870-71; Edward W. Tatum, 1871-86; A. D. Lewis, present.

Trustees: David Jarnigan, 1824-29; Wm. F. Hodge, 1829-36; John Wilfong, 1836-38; Jerrod Hotchkiss, 1838-42; Samuel O. Ballard, 1842-44; Alex. Provine, 1844-46; John C. Waddell, 1846-48; Martin H. Cablier, 1848-50; Samuel Sneed, 1850-54; Dickason Wyatt, 1854-56; Samuel Sneed, 1856-58; John L. Foote, 1858-60; Robert B. Pickens, 1860-72; J. O. K. Reeves, 1872-73; W. C. Trent, 1873-76; Thomas G. McClelland, 1876-86, and present.

---

*W. S. Latty was elected, but failing to give bonds, the court appointed Rieves.

Chancery court.—This court was organized at Somerville on the first Monday in May, 1836, by Chancellor Pleasant M. Miller, who appointed James F. Ruffin clerk and master. The following is a list of the officers of this court:

Chancellors: Pleasant M. Miller, 1836-38; Milton Brown, 1838-39; George W. Gibbs, 1839-40; Andrew McCampbell, 1840-48; Calvin Jones, 1848-54; Isaac B. Williams, 1854-60; John Somers, 1860; Wm. M. Smith, 1860-62; John W. Harris, 1865-70; James Fentress, 1870-72; Henry J. Livingston, 1872-86; John Somers present.

Clerks and masters: James F. Ruffin, 1836-37; Isaac B. McClelland, 1837-62; Thomas G. McClelland, 1865-70; Andrew J. Peebles, 1870-79; Junius Hobson, 1879-85; Horace P. Hobson, 1885-86 and present.

Circuit court.—Judge Joshua Haskell organized the circuit court of Fayette County at Thornton's house, the meeting being held in open air, in June, 1825. The judge's bench consisted of a split-bottom chair and the jury box of two parallel logs, with seating capacity to accommodate thirteen men. The grand jury was in session for two days, but found no indictments, and in discharging the jury Judge Haskell expressed a devout wish that the work of all subsequent grand juries of the county might be similar to that of the one being addressed. Valentine D. Barry was the solicitor-general of the court, and John Brown was appointed clerk. Upon the completion of the courthouse, the court was removed to Somerville. The following is a list of the officers of this court.

Judges: Joshua Haskell, 1825-36; Austin Miller, 1836-38, Valentine D. Barry, 1838-44; Wm. C. Dunlap, 1844-50; J. C. Humphreys, 1850-62; George W. Reeves, 1865-69; J. T. Swayne, 1869-70; Thomas J. Flippin, 1870-86 and present.

Attorney-generals: Valentine D. Barry, 1825-32; Roger Barton, 1832-38; E. W. King, 1838-46; John P. Caruthers, 1846-48; D. M. Leatherman, 1848-50; J. D. Goodall, 1850-52; John L. T. Sneed, 1852-54; R. V. Richardson, 1854-56; A. B. Harris, 1856-58; William P. Finnie, 1858-62; W. F. Talley, 1865-66; W. G. Reeves, 1866-68; Walker Wood, 1868-70; John J. Dupuy, 1870-86; S. L. Cockroft, present.

Clerks: John Brown, 1825-29; Isaac B. McClelland, 1829-36; W. H. Mitchell, 1836-40; William Burton, 1840-65; R. M. Moore, 1865-78; R. M. Cousar, 1878-86; J. H. Dortch, three months in 1886 by appointment; C. A. F. Shaw, present.

Bar.—John Brown was the pioneer resident member of the Fayette bar, and contemporaneous with him up to 1840 were William

Davis, James F. Ruffin, Henry G. Smith, —— Harris, J. M. Longwell, West H. Humphreys, Calvin Jones, Leven H. Coe and Granville D. Searcy. Those who practiced between 1840 and 1850 were John Brown, Calvin Jones, P. T. Scruggs, Leven H. Coe, James F. Ruffin, Henry G. Smith, West H. Humphreys, Thomas R. Smith, J. M. Williamson and Nicholas Long. Between 1850 and 1860: Calvin Jones, P. D. Glenn, J. C. Humphreys, J. L. Pulliam, C. C. Harris, E. H. Shelton, W. B. Dortch, John Finney, C. C. Moore, Asberry Warren, R. S. Parham, R. C. Williamson, John W. Harris, C. H. Whitmore, T. H. Logwood, W. G. Goodall and Blair Ballard. Between 1860 and 1870: Calvin Jones, J. L. Pulliam, E. H. Shelton, T. J. Flippin, J. L. T. Sneed, W. B. Dortch, W. P. Finney, C. C. Moore, H. C. Moorman and E. R. Scruggs. Between 1870 and 1880; Calvin Jones, George Hardin, J. J. Steiger, W. B. Dortch, E. D. Steiger, J. L. Pulliam, T. J. Shelton, Jr., T. S. Galloway, W. P. Finney, E. H. Shelton, W. A. Milliken, C. A. Stainback, H. C. Moorman, T. K. Riddick, John P. Edmundson, H. P. Hobson, A. B. Humphreys, C. C. Harris, John T. Lattin and E. R. Scruggs. The bar of the present is as follows: Calvin Jones, J. H. Dortch, T. S. Galloway, H. C. Moorman, E. R. Scruggs, C. A. Stainback, T. K. Riddick, E. D. Steiger, Calvin Harris, F. A. Mayo of Somerville, T. J. Shelton, Jr., W. A. Turner of La Grange, and J. J. Steiger of Moscow.

The following are the representatives sent to the General Assembly by Fayette County: West H. Humphreys, 1835-37; Burchet Douglass, 1837-39; L. P. Williamson, 1839-41; Burchet Douglass, 1841-43; George W. Fisher, 1843-47; James M. McCalla, 1847-49; Andrew M. Campbell, 1849-51; Joseph R. Mosbey, 1851-53; W. B. Dortch, 1853-57; William Maric, 1857-59; Robert M. Ingram, 1859-61; Fred B. Ragland, 1861-65; Henry Biggs, 1865-67; James O. K. Reeves, 1867-69; John T. Lattin, 1869-70; Edmund J. Tucker, 1870-72; Charles Lynn, 1872-74; Milton A. Gober, 1874-76; Henry H. Perry, 1876-78; H. B. Ramsey, 1878-80; A. D. Lewis, 1880-82; D. F. Rivers, 1882-84; J. C. Harrell, 1884-86; Monroe Gooden, present.

Towns.—Somerville, the county seat, is situated near the center of the county, at the terminus of the Somerville branch of the Memphis & Charleston Railroad, and has a population of about 1,000. The town was founded in 1825 and named in honor of Lieut. Robert Somerville (who fell at the battle of the Horseshoe, leading a charge in the war of 1812), though for a number of years was called Bowersville in honor of George Bowers, who donated a portion of the land for the town site. Under the original survey and plat the town consisted of 192 lots, which number has been increased from time to time by enlargements and additions. A charter of incorporation was secured January 30, 1836, which was re-issued January 4, 1854, under which the town has since worked.

The first store was opened in Somerville by one Anderson, who was sent with a stock of goods by David Dederick, a merchant of Jonesboro, E. Tenn., in 1825, and the first tavern was opened the same year by Henry M. Johnson. In the course of a year or so the goods of Mr. Dedrick were purchased by Isaac B. McClelland, who was in fact the first local merchant. Col. John Brown afterward became a partner of Mr. McClelland. The next store was opened by Horace Lumas in 1827, who sold goods for a year or two and then mysteriously disappeared and was never heard of again. The third store was opened in 1828 by John Cooper. The above stores were general in character and constituted the commercial portion of the town up to 1830. The merchants of the thirties were Hiram Fain & Co., William S. Gray, Crenshaw & Bacon, Armour, Lake & Co., Owen, Rhodes & Co., Parker & Wert, John C. Spence and W. A. Jones; of the forties: Rhodes & McNutt, Owen & Palmer, W. D. Wilkerson, John A. Stanfield, J. J. Woodfin, Kahn & Co., Marshall & Clark, Armour, Lake & Smith, Key & Holloway, Crenshaw & Son, Ford & Wilfong, Hilliard & Bro., Hiram, Fain & Co., E. & T. L. Dickinson and Cooper & Jones; of the fifties: Key & Holloway, T. G. McClelland, John Wilfong, Hilliard & Bro., E. & T. L. Dickinson, G. W. Bumpass, D. W. Thomas, John C. Cooper, H. S. Dickinson & Son, J. C. Holloman, F. M. Ross, Hill, Dupuy & Co., E. W. Tatum and William S. Rose. The above, with but few exceptions, continued in business until its suspension during the late war. In 1865, at the close of the war, Frank Trimble was the first man to begin business, he opening a large general store during the latter part of that year. From that time until 1870 there was a multiplicity of business houses, the following firms engaging in merchandising: E. & T. L. Dickinson, Scaller & Co., Meriweather & Co., Covington & Co., Boyd, Mosbey & Co., Shaw & Co., W. N. Morgan, W. J. Rivers, Key & Holloway, J. M. Gilliam & Son, Warr & Christian, John E. Logwood, Old & Shaw, Brightwell & Holloway, Wiggins & Son, E. J. Eastham, J. J. Worrell, Bumpass & Hendon, P. H. Bowers, Hawkins Bros. and Thomas & Roberts. Business declined during the ten years following, the number of business firms being materially reduced; the merchants of the seventies were Frank Trimble, E. & T. L. Dickinson, Scaller & Co., Thomas & Collier, Covington & Bailey, Boyd, Mosbey & Co., Shaw & Co. and Hersh Bros. The business of the present is as follows: Scaller & Co., Covington & Co., Hersh Bros., J. S. Carter & Co. and Hull & Bosswell, general mer-

FAYETTE COUNTY.   805

chandise; Wynn & Wilson and M. P. Alexander, drugs; F. Goosman, jewelry; W. H. Leech and Wetzler & Hendon, hardware; D. Worrell and W. T. Hamblett, groceries and confections; C. A. S. Shaw and Conrad & Weatherly, hotels; W. C. Trent, J. B. Love and Finley Bros., livery stables, and James G. Knox, steam-mill and cotton-gin.

The first physician of Somerville was Dr. Henry M. Johnson, the first tavern-keeper, and contemporaneous with him up to 1840 were Drs. Josiah Higgason, Benjamin Gray, Thomas Ivedell, W. A. Ealey and W. A. Booth. The present physicians are W. A. Harris, J. S. Washington, W. A. Ealey, P. T. Jones and C. W. Robertson, of whom Harris, Washington and Ealey have been practicing since about 1860. The dentists are G. B. Yancy and W. A. Small.

In 1837 a branch of the State Bank was established at Somerville, which continued to transact business until the war. Somerville Lodge, No. 73, F. & A. M., was instituted October 9, 1829, and has been in active operation from that time to the present, the lodge having consecutive minutes of its proceedings covering that period. Somerville Lodge, No. 24, I. O. O. F., was instituted in 1846, and continued as an organization until the late war, when it temporarily suspended. In about 1868-69 the lodge was reorganized under the original charter, and this time ran until 1878, when the order again suspended on account of the yellow fever. A third time the lodge was organized about 1881, only to suspend in a short time, since when the order has remained inactive. Loosa-Hatchie Lodge, No. 1299, K. of H., was instituted December 17, 1878, and Azalea Lodge, No. 337, K. & L. of H., was instituted June 25, 1880.

The first newspaper published in Somerville was the Somerville *Reporter*, established by Wm. Lewis in March, 1837. The following December the paper was purchased by John C. Reeves, who conducted the sheet until 1844, and then took as a partner R. J. Yancy, and under this management the *Reporter* continued until 1847, when Mr. Yancy became sole proprietor and ran the paper until 1850, when the plant was purchased by J. W. T. Hilliard, and W. E. Gibson became editor. The *Reporter* suspended in 1856. The second newspaper adventure was the Somerville *Star*, which was established in 1856 by E. B. Hotchkiss, and in 1857 the Somerville *Democrat* was established by C. H. Whitmore, the latter paper being published until 1859, when the material was purchased by the proprietor of the *Democrat*, who continued until about 1861. The Somerville *Falcon* was established in 1866 by S. G. Sparks, and the Somerville *Reporter* in 1880 by S. G. Sparks and R. H. Yancy. The *Falcon* and *Reporter* were consolidated in 1883, Mr.

Sparks becoming proprietor of both papers. The paper is now known as the *Reporter and Falcon*, and is a neat and successful sheet, enjoying a good advertising and subscription patronage. It is Democratic, and the only paper published in the county.

La Grange, the oldest town in the county, lies sixteen miles southeast from Somerville on the M. & C. Ry., forty-nine miles east from Memphis and north of the Mississippi line three miles. The town was founded in about 1826 by Samuel Harper, the first sheriff of the county, who laid off the land into town lots and sold the same about 1828. For a number of years La Grange was quite a trading village for the Indians, who would visit the town regularly to dispose of their game, hides, etc.

The first store was opened in about 1827 by George Gray, and other early merchants from 1830 to 1840 were Jones & Harper, George Cossett, Irish & Bailey, Gray & Macbeth, Glaster & Hackney, Lynn & Davis, Robert Locke, George Shinporch and Nelson & Co. Between 1850 and 1860 the merchants were Wm. R. Baugh, J. S. Day, George P. Shelton, H. H. Falls, B. Houston, C. F. Chapman, Brown Bros., D. T. Fowler, George G. Cossett, A. D. Lewis, Lock & Hasley, John Thompson, and R. W. Smith & Co. Between 1860 and 1862 the merchants were J. T. Foote, George P. Shelton, O. S. Jordan, C. F. Chessman, Cossett, Davis & Bryan, Fowler & Louston, T. S. Parham, R. J. Bass & Co., and John W. Goodwin. Business was suspended from 1862 until the close of the war, and from 1865 until 1870 the merchants were J. T. Bowers, Wm. Frank, King & Fairfield, S. W. Baird, Crenshaw & Denny, Arthur J. Quinn, Pollock & Co., Benj. Word, Adams & Toombs, Day & Proudfit and Curtis & Coolidge. Between 1870 and 1880 the merchants were C. T. Hodges, W. P. Lipscomb, Cowan & Cowan, Jones & Co., Lipscomb & Gibbons, Wright, McNannie & Co., F. L. Adams, J. M. Crenshaw, J. E. Osborn & Son, T. G. Toombs, A. Michaels, Benj. Word, Adams & Moody and J. M. Guthrie. The present business men are Joseph Gibbons & Co., Cowan & Simms, Moody Bros., W. P. Lipscomb, M. Michael, Mrs. Fannie McNance and F. M. McNance, general stores; Jesse Stafford and W. R. Pankey, groceries; T. G. Toombs, drugs; Halton & Anderson, foundry, mill and cotton-gin combined.

La Grange was incorporated January 5, 1836, at about which date the town was enjoying its best and brightest days, having about 1,000 inhabitants, and having the name of being the wealthiest and most cultured town in the South. There are not over 300 inhabitants at the present, while on every hand may be seen evidence of decay of the once flourishing village.

Moscow, with about 200 inhabitants, is situated at the junction of the Memphis & Charleston Railroad and the Somerville branch of the same, 13 miles south from Somerville and 38 miles east from Memphis. The town was founded about 1829, by a company who purchased the land for that purpose from William Head. In 1864 the town was entirely destroyed by fire but was rebuilt at the close of the war, and in 1870 was incorporated.

The first store was opened about 1830 by Mitchell & Co., which firm was soon followed by William Coapwood and Thomas Young, and by those firms was the business principally transacted until about 1840. Between 1840 and 1850 the business men were William Harrell, John Coleman and Winfield Curtise. Between 1850 and 1862: J. W. Dyer, Dickens & Griffin, Beverly Dyer and John W. Goodwin. Between 1862 and the latter part of 1865 business was entirely suspended. Between 1865 and 1870 the merchants were Philip B. Plummer, Davis, McClaren & Co., Steiger Bros., Bailey & Parr and Wheeler Bros. Between 1870 and 1880 the merchants were Samuel Bejach, Hecht & Sturm, Alexander & Abernathy, Steiger Bros., Davis, McClaren & Co., H. J. H. Maas, McClaren & Cossett, Crossett Bros., Brook & Co. and Dowdy Bros. The business men of the present are J. S. R. Cowan and Samuel Bejach, general merchandise; W. H. Clark, drugs; John Owen, lumber; W. L. Davis, livery stable, and B. A. Maas, hotel.

Moscow Lodge, No. 198, F. & A. M., was instituted in 1850; Concordia Lodge, No. 498, K. of H., instituted in 1876; Rebecca Lodge, No. 147, K. & L. of H., instituted in 1879.

Other villages of the county are Macon, situated twelve miles southwest of Somerville, founded in 1835; Rossville, on the Memphis & Charleston Railroad twenty-two miles southwest from Somerville, founded in 1853; Hickory Withe, fifteen miles west from Somerville, founded in 1835; Oakland, ten miles west from Somerville, founded in 1830; Braden, on the Memphis & Louisville Railroad, eighteen miles northwest from Somerville, founded in 1855; Galloway, on the Memphis & Louisville Railroad, twenty miles northwest from Somerville, founded in 1855, and Williston, on the Somerville Branch Railroad, six miles south of Somerville, founded in 1867.

The majority of the settlers of Fayette County came from North Carolina and north Alabama. There were some from Middle Tennessee, some from Virginia, a few from Kentucky, and occasional settlers from the majority of the older Southern States. Each of these brought the peculiar characteristics of his particular neighborhood. These differences, however, were not so great that they did not readily blend into almost one individuality. Fayette County lying, as it does, between the two thoroughfares of travel, the Mississippi and the Tennessee River settlements, did not begin quite so early in that county as in Shelby or Hardin. The first settlers began to arrive within the limits of the county with a view to permanent residence in 1822-23. Thomas J. Cocke, who came from North Carolina, settled in the northwest part of the county in 1823. Robert G. Thornton also came into the county in 1823 and erected a comfortable log house on the North Fork of Wolf River, twelve miles southeast from Somerville and seven miles northwest from La Grange. It was probably from his luxurious accommodations that Henry Kirk, Henry M. Johnson, Daniel Johnson, Robert S. Thornton, David Jarnigan, Daniel Clift, William Ramsey and John J. Patterson met in 1824 to hold the first county court. About the same time also came Joel Langham. The land upon which Somerville stands was entered and owned, at the time of the selection of that place as a seat of justice for the county, by the commissioners selected to choose sites for all the counties in West Tennessee by George Bowers and James Brown. An effort was made to call the place Bowersville but it seems the fates had decreed otherwise. Very little of the timber had been cleared away at that time (1824) and the wild beasts of the forest held high carnival wherever they pleased. James Simpson, one of the first settlers, claimed to have killed a bear near where the courthouse now stands in 1824. Daniel Head was doubtless the first gunsmith ever in the county. The county was settled in neighborhoods frequently several miles apart. The groups or neighbors were usually related to each other or came in colonies from the parent State, and settled near each other for assistance and self-protection. In the neighborhood of La Grange and the vicinity of Thornton there were settled Edmund Tarver, the first chairman of the county court, Samuel B. Harper, the first sheriff of the county, James Titus, Robert Cotton, John Winston, Thomas and Robert Isom, E. W. Harris and others. In the neighborhood of Somerville were Joseph Simpson, before mentioned, John Albright, A. J. Henry, H. M. Johnson; Bowen and Brown as stated above. Others in the county were G. L. Bennett, George W. Bennett, Samuel Cox, William Owen, Marcus Ragan, John Culbertson, Joseph Choat, John Jarnigan, Robert Knox, Samuel House, Andrew Haynes, Squire Simpson, William Adams, Edmund Price, Thomas Langham, Ludwick Kidd, John Howard, Pleasant Ward, George Allen, William Metcalf, Thomas and Joseph Neil, Henry Brooks, Nathan Spurlock, William Isom, Daniel Carter, Alexander and James McKenzie, Alfred Austin,

Thomas Bennett, Horace Loomis, Dr. Smith, Henry Kirk, Amos Koonce, Charles Belvat, Nathan Ragland, Charles Williams, James Kimbrough, H. C. Payne, James Bickerstaff, Zebra Grider, J. R. A. Griffin, F. Bounds, Jesse Simpson, Amasa Spencer, James and Moses Ritchey, Thomas Estel, A. P. Morgan, John Yancey, John Shinault, Samuel Wyatt, C. S. Belvat, J. Pratt, Samuel Cox, J. C. Hudson, J. B. McClellan and W. Oldham. All these were living in settled houses in 1824. The rapid increase in population will be seen from the census as shown in another chapter. Game was there abundant and not only did it enter largely into the support of the whites, but also the Indians frequently came through the county on hunting expeditions. The Indians frequently left their reservations in Mississippi to visit Fayette and adjacent counties on hunting expeditions. La Grange was a favorite trading point with them. They were all at this time peaceable and no trouble between them and the settlers occurred. Persons receiving grants in this county from North Carolina were George Bowers, James Brown, Thomas Person, John Long, Job Garges, Hugh L. Parks, Asa Thompson, Mark Fate, Dempsey Bryan, Louis Wilson, James Galloway, Dixon Marshall, John Brown, Thomas Hunt, Thomas Booth, A. Bryan, John Hain, Jonah Newell, Alex Morghis, John Edgerton, Joseph Bryan, Thomas J. Deverneux, William, Thomas and Samuel Polk, Horace and Robert Burton and W. Reeves. Gideon Pillow, father of Gen. Gideon J. Pillow, purchased 793 acres of land from Robert Brooks for $700 in October, 1827.

The first water-mill for grinding corn was built in 1825 by David Jarnigan and Wm. Owen seven miles south of Somerville on North Fork of Wolf River and the first horse-power corn-mill was built in 1827 by Thomas Cook twelve miles southwest of Somerville. Mathew Spurlock soon after built another mill; the first cotton-gin was built in 1830 by George Bond. The first public road was cut out in 1824 by direction of Robert Cotter, Tobia Grider, A. P. Ragan and Shadrack Grider. It began at the Hardeman County line near Thomas Head's ferry, through the county to the Shelby County line. The second began at the Hardeman line and passed through Somerville, the nearest and best route to the Shelby County line. This was surveyed by Jesse Dupree, Andrew Haynes, H. M. Johnson, H. C. Payne, M. Beauford, J. Hudson and James Douglass. The public schools of Tennessee had their origin in the cession of the territory, now embraced in the State to the United States Government, by an act passed in 1789 which was in accordance with an act of Congress in 1780 (see page 200). A part of the provision of said act was that 100,000 acres of said land should be reserved for colleges, one in East and one in West Tennessee. Also 100,000 acres was reserved for founding academies in the respective counties and one section of each civil township was reserved for common schools. In addition to these conditions certain military grants were reserved for the Continental soldier of North Carolina, as these claims were frequently laid without regard to the points of the compass, congressional lines or anything else other than the peculiar whims of the claimant. These causes led to conflicting claims and innumerable lawsuits. To obviate the difficulty, in 1806 Congress made Tennessee its agent to carry out the letter of the cession act of North Carolina. Various acts were passed by the General Assembly of this State to aid in carrying out the original plan intended by the parent State, North Carolina. These provisions are more fully set forth in the educational chapter of this work. In some counties immediate steps were taken for carrying out the provisions of this act. Some counties were more tardy than others in this work and it was not till the adoption of the constitution of 1834-36 that all took advantage of this law. With the money arising from the sale of these public lands, small levies made by the county court and certain fines and forfeitures the counties were enabled to meet the demand for popular education. These schools were generally named in honor of some distinguished individual or simply named "male academy" or "female academy." The two latter were the names adopted for the schools of Somerville. The first teaching, however, in the place was in the old log courthouse in 1826. This was done by Mrs. Walker, mother of Simon Walker, second register of the county. The first step taken for popularizing education was in building the "male academy" in 1831. This was built under the old seminary law growing out of the old Cession Act. This was a brick building and stood near the site of the present male academy. P. B. Gleen was the first teacher in this school. The male academy was used for church services until 1837, and for schools until 1854 when it was burned. It was rebult in 1855 and is yet a good building but is not now in use. W. G. Gray, B. F. Gray, J. C. Cooper, A. G. Hunter, John Brown, I. C. Hudson, J. B. McClellan, R. A. Parker, B. H. Henderson and W. L. Hannum were the first trustees of the male academy.

In 1831 two acres of ground was deeded by George Brown to B. H. Henderson, Jesse Allen, W. L. Gray, W. Cooper and John Brown, for the female academy. This was erected about 1833, with Mathew Ray as first teacher. This school was in operation till 1853, when it was abandoned for the Somerville Female Institute. This was built on lands purchased of R. L. Ford in July, 1850. A handsome building was erected in 1853, at a cost of about $15,000. Dr. Jurry was the first president of the institute. This building was burned in 1876, and was rebuilt the following year. The present handsome building was erected at a cost of about $10,000. It is owned by twenty-one stockholders, embracing the leading citizens of Somerville. For the last two years the institute has been managed as a consolidated school at which all the pupils of the town attend. The schools are under the management of Prof. R. F. Chew, who is assisted by an excellent corps of teachers. The course embraces all that is taught in schools of its character.

The schools of the county were organized under the present system in 1874, under R. W. Pitman, who served till 1877 when he was superseded by William Maris, who served two terms till 1881. Mrs. Nora Cannon then served one term, when she was succeeded by W. J. Elam, who served two terms. Mrs. Nora Cannon is now the superintendent. The salary of the superintendent was fixed at $600, but was soon changed to $250, and again to $150, but was raised again to $600 in 1876, and in 1877 was changed to $250, and so remained till 1881 when it was raised to $800, and in 1887 it was raised to $350. The following tabular statement will show the progress of the schools since 1883, the first available report:

	White Schools.	Colored Schools.	Scholastic Population.		Enrollment.		Attendance.
			White.	Colored.	White.	Colored.	Days.
1883....	29	37	2,249	5,574	750	1,952	57
1884....	39	55	3,194	7,213	1,165	2,800	66
1885...	44	63	2,931	7,555	941	3,385	62
1886....	55	79	2,981	7,376	1,156	3,821	66

The total cost of these schools for each year, has been as follows: 1883, $11,868.26; 1884, $12,560; 1885, $12,484.61; 1886, $11,361.82. The average daily attendance of white children for 1884 was 702, for 1885, 647, and for 1886 it was 927. The average attendance for colored children for the same years was 2,171, 2,295 and 2,568 respectively. Teachers' salaries have increased from $26.49 to about $30. The whole of the school property belonging to the public schools amounts to about $4,000. There are several incorporated schools in the county. The Walsedge Academy was incorporated in 1885, by G. B. Baskerville, C. A. Jackson, J. S. Rhea and Mat. Rhea. The Rossville School was incorporated in 1886 by A. V. Warr, H. J. Patterson, L. D. Wells, H. B. Stall, J. T. Tombers and R. C. Stone. In addition to these, there are consolidated schools at Somerville, La Grange, Moscow, Macon, Fayette Corner, Center Point and Oakland.

The advent of civilization into this county was followed, or was accompanied by the religion of civilization. The worship of the Christian's God by civilized people soon took the place of the worship of the

Great Spirit by the untutored savage of the virgin forest. With the coming of civilized worship also came church creeds and church dogmas. These are usually looked upon as the great bane of the church. However, may not these be a blessing rather than a curse. Schisms springing from enmity, envy or personal aggrandizement are to be frowned down, but honest difference of opinion can do no one any harm. To quote another, "Where the mind is free, religion never has dangerous enemies. Atheism is the mistake of the metaphysician, not of human nature. Infidelity gains the victory when it wrestles with hypocrisy or superstition, not when its antagonist is reason. When an ecclesiastical establishment requires universal conformity, some consciences must necessarily be wronged and oppressed." Religious denominations differ not so much in the great fundamental truths upon which the church is based, as upon church policy and church polity. The former is divine, the latter is the work of human hands, and is the outgrowth of antecedents, a peculiar mental make up. It would be impossible to chain the fiery impetuous pioneer Methodist of the frontier, to the cool, calculating studious cultivated matter-of-fact Presbyterian. Do this and you would lose both. Neither would it do to bind the Baptist of the new country in church fellowship to the formal Episcopal, whose forms are very foreign to the new country.

Rev. Charles Cumming began preaching Presbyterianism in Tennessee as early as 1772, in the Holston Valley of East Tennessee. Rev. T. B. Craighead and Rev. William McGee preached in the vicinity of Nashville about 1790. The first preaching in the region of Fayette County was done in all probability by Rev. Samuel Hedge and Rev. Alexander Campbell about 1829-30. The church in Somerville was organized in February, 1829, by Rev. Alexander Campbell. The pastors of Somerville have been as follows: Rev. Alexander Campbell, 1829-31; Rev. James Hamilton to July, 1831; Rev. W. S. Lacy, 1837-39: Rev. Samuel Williams, 1839 to his death, July 6, 1846; Rev. H. Chamberlain, 1846-49; Rev. R. E. Sherrel, January, 1851, to February, 1856; James Paine, August, 1856, to April, 1860; Rev. Edwin Cater, 1860-61; Rev. Russell, Rev. R. C. Reed, Rev. F. M. Howell, Rev. W. S. Cochran, to 1882; Rev. B. M. Farris is still the pastor. The first elders were B. H. Henderson, Peter R. Bland and George Williams. The first deacons were A. J. Lensberry and John McIntosh. The present deacons are M. Rhea, James G. Knox and James I. Rhea. The whole number of elders of the church since its organization is twenty eight. The present house of worship was erected in 1840. It is a substantial brick structure and is in a good state of preservation. The present membership of the church is 110.

Rahobeth Church was erected December 8, 1837. The most distinguished ministers at that time were Revs. Henry M. Kerr and William S. Lacy. Among the first members were Abner and James McHenry, Arthur Beatty, Lucilla Beatty, Thomas McFadden, Catharine, Isabell and Frances N. Kerr; Uriah, Mary, Moses, Maggie N., Cyrus and Eliza Alexander; James C., Martha, S. M. and E. C. McFadden; Sarah Whitsett, David and Sarah Crawford; Thomas Patton; E. P. and Mary Cowan; James W., Wilson and Jane A. Alexander; James Wilson, S. Buford, Mary McKnight; E. C. and Mary Brown, Samuel and Malinda Brown, being a total membership at the time of thirty-five. The elders were Thomas Patton, Arthur Beatty, Abner McHenry and D. Crawford. Other distinguished ministers of this church were Rev. S. J. Baird and Samuel Williams. The church house at this place was built about 1840.

The first Presbyterian Church in the vicinity of Hickory Withe, was organized at Prosperity in 1834. This was not far from Oakland. A log building was erected at this place. In 1850 the membership of Prosperity was divided, and one portion went to the organization at Hickory Withe and the other to Moscow. The building at Hickory Withe, erected in 1850 on the ground of Joe Patterson, still stands. To this church belonged the Blands, Kerrs, Youngs, Thompsons, Lynns, Alexanders and others. The most prominent ministers of this church have been Henry Kerr, S. S. McCoy, Metcalf and Rev. Gill for the last twenty-six years, The church at the Withe numbers ninety members, and has four elders and three deacons with Rev. Gill as pastor.

The Moscow Church, as stated above, was organized from a part of the old members of Prosperity in 1850. Rev. R. S. Gill is also pastor of this church. The church numbers fifty-three members and has four elders and two deacons. The house was erected in 1853.

The Presbyterian synodical school was established at La Grange. This was a flourishing institution in 1858. Its greatest prosperity was when under the management of Rev. Sloan. "Grim visaged war" came and not only was the school broken up but the building itself was destroyed. The membership of the church at this place now is only about fourteen.

The Episcopal Church was organized at Somerville about 1853, and an elegant church house was erected in 1858. The membership of this church is not great and for some time there has been no rector employed. This influential body also has an organization and house of worship at La Grange.

Methodism was introduced into this country about 1774. Its growth and influence has been wonderful. From 799 members in Tennessee in 1802 the number had increased in the Memphis Conference alone in 1885, to 127 traveling preachers, 233 local preachers, 28,584 white members, 21,884 Sunday-school scholars, and collections for foreign missions, $6,757.62; domestic missions, 1,032.41. The eccentric Lorenzo Dow and Peter Cartwright were largely instrumental in establishing Methodism in Middle Tennessee whence it moved west. The first Methodist Church was erected in this county in 1837, and enlarged in 1867. There is now an elegant brick house of worship. The membership at this place numbers about eighty. The Methodists also have churches at La Grange, Moscow, Bellmont, Braden, Williston, Macon, Haffords Chapel, Asbury, Oak Grove, Shiloh, Liberty and Union.

The first Baptist Church built in Somerville was in 1840. This church was burned and a new one erected in 1884. The membership of this is small and regular services are not maintained. There is quite a number of other Baptist Churches in the county.

The military history of this county properly begins with the Mexican war. Under call of the President of the United States for 50,000 volunteers, the apportionment for Tennessee was finally settled at 2,400; of these 800 were for the cavalry service. A company for this regiment was raised in Fayette County, mainly in the region of Hickory Withe, by Capt. Joseph Lenow, now of Memphis. The cavalry regiment rendezvoused at Camp Carroll near the Big Spring, ten miles east of Memphis. The Eagle Guard, of Memphis, and the Fayette cavalry were the only companies from West Tennessee belonging to the cavalry service. The remainder of the regiment was from Middle and East Tennessee. Each company numbered about ninety-seven men. The regimental officers were J. E. Thomas, colonel; R. D. Allison, lieutenant-colonel, and Richard Waterhouse, major. The regiment left Memphis Monday, July 27, 1846, and moved overland by way of Little Rock, Fulton, Robbin's Ferry and San Antonio, and joined Gen. Taylor's forces at Matamoras. The work of the regiment was mainly scouting and doing guard duty. After a year's service the regiment returned with little loss. Capt. Lenow, and possible two or three others, are the only ones of that body of men now living.

The first organized body of men from Fayette County for the Confederate service in the late war was Company A of the Sixth Regiment. These men were called the Somerville Avengers. The company organized at Somerville in April, 1861, by electing W. M. R. Johns captain, J. W. Burton first lieutenant, R. C. Williams second lieutenant, A. N. Thomas third lieutenant. The company was ordered to Camp Beauregard, where they were organized, with troops from Haywood and Madison Counties, into the Sixth Regiment. The men were mustered into the service on May 15. The regimental and field officers chosen were W. H. Stephens, colonel; T. P. Jones, lieutenant-colonel; G. C. Porter, major; R. R. Dashiell, surgeon; J. S. Fenner, assistant surgeon. The men of the regiment were all comparatively young. The company numbered 108 men and the regiment 1,200. The regiment left Jackson on May 26 for Union City, where it was subjected to severe camp discipline, and soon after was engaged with the enemy. At the reorganization at Corinth after the battle of Shiloh, A. C. Williamson became captain, J. B. Stanley first lieutenant, James Seabrook second lieutenant, and — Day third lieutenant. Maj. G. C. Porter passed through the grades of major, lieutenant-colonel and colonel. The regiment was engaged on April 6 and 7 at Shiloh, Company A losing E. J. Chillers, R. A. Jones, J. H. McCalpin, E. J. Melane, Jason Purios, R. E. Peebles, G. H. Tomlinson and J. E. Thomas. At Perryville, October 8, it lost C. W. Ross, A. D. Ganell, C. R. Palmer, N. O. Richmond, J. D. Shaw, T. E. Estes, M. P. Estes, W. J. Voss, J. T. A. Rayner and L. C. Harris. After the Kentucky campaign, and before the battle of Murfreesboro, the Sixth was consolidated with the Ninth.

The Ninth Regiment also organized at Camp Beauregard, near Jackson, on May 22, 1861. The officers chosen were H. L. Douglass, colonel; C. S. Hurt, lieutenant-colonel; G. H. White, major; W. E. Rogers, surgeon; J. Brown, adjutant. A portion of Company A which was organized at Dancyville, Hardeman County, was made up from Fayette County. Company D was organized at Fayette Corner. This company was composed of single men, except H. H. Mitchell, Joe Somers and J. Williams—the latter being in every battle that his regiment engaged in. The officers of this company were C. S. Hust, captain, who was chosen officer at the organization of the regiment; S. G. Carnes, first lieutenant; J. M. Mathews, second lieutenant; H. C. Irby, third lieutenant; W. D. Irby, orderly sergeant. H. C. Irby became captain and W. D. Irby second lieutenant. The Ninth followed about the same course as the Sixth. Conpany D, from first to last, lost nineteen killed, fifteen by wounds and ten by disease. The loss in A was seventeen killed and wounded.

Company L was organized in April, 1862, at Dancyville. It was composed largely of conscripts. Its first officers were W. J. Lyle, captain; G. R. Prewitt, first lieutenant; Milton Ragland, second lieutenant; T. W. Nail, third lieutenant. In August, 1862, Company L was consolidated with D, with which the remainder of that company served. After the Kentucky campaign the Ninth and Sixth were consolidated at Murfreesboro. (A fuller sketch of these two regiments may be seen on pages 567, 569 and 570 of the State history of this volume.)

The Thirteenth was mustered into the Confederate service at Jackson, June 3, 1862. The Fayette County troops were Company A, Fayette Rifles, captain, W. C. Burton, and Company E from Moscow. The officers of E were A. J. Vaughan, captain; Beverly L. Dyer, first lieutenant; T. D. Allen, second lieutenant; Clifton Craddock, third lieutenant. On the organization of the regiment Vaughan became lieutenant-colonel; Dyer was elected captain, Allen first lieutenant, Craddock second lieutenant, and Richard M. Harwell third lieutenant. At the reorganization at Corinth, Dyer was elected captain, J. A. Woods first lieutenant, Dyer second lieutenant, and Allen third lieutenant, who was in a short time succeeded by W. J. Rodgers. Company G, the Gaines Guards, captain, W. E. Wingfield, was from La Grange. Company H, Yancy Rifles, R. W. Pitman, was from Hickory Withe, and Company L, Zollicoffer Avengers, captain, C. P. Jones. At the organization J. V. Wright became colonel, A. J. Vaughan lieutenant-colonel, and W. E. Wingfield, major. The losses by companies were A, 33 men; E, —; G, 17 men; H, 31 men; L, 24 men. (A regimental history is given on page 572 of this work.)

Company K of the Thirty-eighth Regiment was organized at Moscow in March, 1862, and joined the regiment at Eastport in the following April. The officers of the company were B. H. Holland, captain; J. I. Crossett, first lieutenant; Columbus Gwynn, second lieutenant; T. A. J. Brownell, third lieutenant. After the battle of Corinth, at the reorganization, B. H. Holland was again chosen captain, Calvin Miller first lieutenant, M. Oliphant second lieutenant, Thomas Babbitt third lieutenant. The first colonel of this regiment was Robt. F. Looney of Memphis. (See page 585 for a sketch of this regiment.)

The nucleus of the Seventh Cavalry was Logwood's battalion, which was organized at Memphis in the fall of 1861. The first officers of the battalion were T. H. Logwood, lieutenant-colonel; C. H. Hall, major; J. H. Somerville, adjutant. This battalion saw service at New Madrid and Hickman and other points, and on June 10, 1862, it was reorganized. Company B was from Hardeman, Fayette and Tipton Counties. The officers of this company were J. P. Russell, captain; H. T. Sale, first lieutenant; I. N. Slinser, second lieutenant; Robt. J. Black, third lieutenant. Company K was from Shelby and Fayette. The officers were J. A. Anderson, J. S. Hiller, J. Trent and E. R. Scruggs.

Forrest's old regiment was made up mainly from north Mississippi and the border counties. Company K was enlisted mainly under Capt. W. A. Bell at Somerville. This regiment followed the various fortunes of its indomitable leader through Tennessee, Mississippi and elsewhere.

The Fourteenth Cavalry was raised mainly on the line of the Memphis & Charleston Railroad. Many of the men were old, furloughed and discharged soldiers. These were recruited within the Federal lines. Fayette furnished companies B, D and H. The officers of Company B were J. Deberry, N. A. Senter and J. B. Holt. Those of company D were L. A. Thomas, J. W. Rich and James Drake. The commissioned officers of company H were James Gwynn, J. ——, B. F. Tatum and D. L. Hill.

The regimental and field officers were J. J. Neely, colonel; R. H. White, lieutenant-colonel; Gwynn Thurmond, major; J. H. Turner, surgeon; A. F. Topp, quartermaster, and S. Hannum, adjutant. The regiment was organized at New Albany on the Tallahatchie River and at Pikeville the men were armed with Enfield rifles and were assigned to Richardson's brigade. These men did effective service in Tennessee, Alabama and Mississippi. They fought several small engagements near Somerville, at Collierville, was in the raid through West Tennessee and assisted in the capture of Fort Pillow and other important places. The regiment lost heavily at Yazoo City, and with Gen. Hood in his raid through Tennessee. The regiment surrendered at Gainesville, Ala., in April, 1865.

Eldridge's battery was made up in Fayette and adjoining counties. About twenty men were from Fayette. The battery was organized at Nashville in 1861, with J. W. Eldridge, captain; Eldridge Wright, Thomas Jones, J. W. Mebane, S. H. Wadkins, lieutenants. The last three named were from Fayette County. On December 6, 1862, the battery was reorganized and Eldridge Wright was made captain, J. W. Mebane, J. W. Phillips and J. C. Grant (of Fayette) lieutenants in the order named. Captain Wright was killed at Murfreesboro and was succeeded by Lieut. Mebane. Capt. Mebane was killed at Lost Mountain and Lieut. Phillips became captain. The other officers in order were J. C. Grant and L. L. Wright. The battery participated in all the important battles in Tennessee and Georgia and surrendered in Mississippi in 1865 with only eleven men. From April, 1862, to the close of the war Fayette County was frequently the scene of deadly encounter by small bodies of troops. Moscow, La Grange and other points were the rendezvous of large bodies of Federal troops. Grant, Sherman, Logan and Hurlbut were encamped along the line of the Memphis & Louisville Railroad with their hosts of Federal soldiers.

HARDEMAN COUNTY.

THE county lies in the upper plateaus of West Tennessee near the head waters of the Big Hatchie. The surface is broken in the northern part, hilly in the eastern and irregular in the southern part but generally level in the center and western part. The soil is generally of a gray or dark color, a large portions of it having a reddish sandy subsoil. A large portion of the county is of alluvial formation and all of it of the more recent formation. The Orange sand, La Grange sands, the Ripley group of the crustaceous series are the prevailing formations. The crustacean groups are found mainly in the eastern part of the county; these yield beds of limestone and layers of clay and sand. Indications of iron ore are seen in some sections, limestone in others and sandstone in various places. The sand is usually highly colored with iron oxides. This ferruginous character of the formation naturally gives outlet to Chalybeate Springs. In 1882 W. H. Moore and others formed a corporation to open up a health resort at Dunlap chalybeate springs about two and a half miles south of Bolivar. The Big Hatchie is the principal drainage of the county. Its tributaries are Little Hatchie, Wade Creek, Piney Creek, Gray Creek, Mill Creek, Clever Creek, Hickory Creek, Clear Creek, Pleasant Run, Spring Creek, Cub Creek, Porter Creek, Muddy Creek and numerous smaller streams. The water in these streams is comparatively clear. Numerous springs are found in the county and good drinking water is easily found by digging or boring. The soil is well adapted for the growth of cotton and the cereals. Garden products are extensively grown. The most of the cereals grown are corn, wheat, oats and rye. The garden products are mainly potatoes, beans and peas. The dairy products are also valuable. An increase in pasture lands and a more extensive growth of grasses would doubtless bring about very profitable stock raising. The Illinois Central and the Memphis & Charleston Railroads afford ample facilities for market while the Hatchie and its tributaries afford good facilities for mills, gins and other machinery. Some very valuable timbers are found in Hardeman County. The most valuable are the oak (*Quercus*) with several varieties (*nigra, obtusiloba, rubra*), and hickory (*Carza*), gum (*Tupelo*), poplar (*Lyriodendron tulipifera*), pine (*Pinus*) and many other kinds.

The treaty which opened West Tennessee for settlement by the whites was signed on October 19, 1818, by Isaac Shelby and Andrew Jackson for the President of the United States, Mr. Monroe, and the chiefs and head men for the Chickasaw Indians. This territory was allowed to the Indians as hunting-ground for two years longer, so that it was not till about 1820 that the whites were given an opportunity to settle within the territory. The rapid progress of settlement is seen from the fact that the courts were organized in the fall of 1823, and the first census, 1830, shows a population of 11,655, one-half of that of 1880. This rapid settlement came in from North and South Carolina, Virginia, north Alabama and largely from Middle Tennessee. The characteristics of those old States are quite prominent in the population of Hardeman County. The first to enter this county for permanent residence came in 1819 and 1820. Col. Thomas J. Hardeman, the first county clerk and for whom the county was named; Col. Ezekiel Polk; his son, William Polk, and son-in-law, Thomas McNeal. William Polk was the first chairman of the county court, and was a man of good sense but eccentric. Thomas McNeal was the father of the prominent McNeal family of Bolivar. It was at McNeal's house that the first courts were held. Jacob Pirtle or Purtle, one of the first justices, raised a crop of corn near Thomas McNeal's in 1821. Joseph Warner settled at Fowler's Ferry on the Hatchie about 1821-22. His place was known as Warnersville. In the vicinity of Bolivar such men as the Polks, Bills, McNeals, Woods, Fentresses, Millers and Hardemans will always be known. In the neighborhood of William Shinault were the Bonars, Hutleys, Whitakers and others. In the Cokeram settlement were William Love, W. E. Norment and others. Abner Pillow owned a large plantation near old Mt. Hope Church. Elisha Boyd and William Rossen settled southeast of Bolivar near Piney; Benjamin near Middleburg. Other settlers followed fast.

Aside from the hand-mills, mortars and tub-mills, the first mill built in the county was by Samuel Polk on Pleasant Run, a short distance from Bolivar, about 1823; a second one was built about six miles from Bolivar by John Golden for Col. John Murray, on Mud Creek; another was built in 1824 by David Jarnigan. Butler's Ferry and Fowler's Ferry were established on the Hatchie about 1822. The rates of ferriage then, as now, were fixed by law, varying from one cent to fifty cents. Roads were cut out from the different neighborhoods to the county seat, and usually in the direction of the county seats of the surrounding counties.

Hardeman County is one of the middle tier of counties of West Tennessee. It is bounded on the north by Haywood and Madison; on the east by Chester and McNairy Counties; on the south by the State of Mississippi, and on the west by Fayette and Haywood Counties. The most of the county is embraced in the Tenth Surveyor's District, a portion, however, is contained in the Ninth. The county originally contained 621 square miles, the dimensions being twenty-three miles from east to west and twenty-seven miles from north to south. A failure to correctly locate the 35° parallel led to an additional amount of territory for Hardeman County and the other counties of the southern boundary of West Tennessee. The establishment of the 35° parallel as a southern boundary began in 1735, and was extended in 1764, again in 1818 by Gen. Coffee, and lastly by Gen. Winchester in 1819. A line was run for the State of Mississippi by John Thompson which differed materially from Winchester's line. The matter was finally settled by joint commissioners of the two States, and ratified by Tennessee November 9, 1839, and by Mississippi February 8, 1838. The new line differed from the Thompson line about three-fourths of a mile at the Tennessee River and only ten links at the Mississippi. The establishment of the true parallel added a strip about three and a half miles wide to the southern part of Hardeman County. This body of land was a V shaped piece, and gradually widened from the Tennessee to the Mississippi River. The commissioners on the part of Tennessee for settling the boundary were John D. Graham, of Shelby County and Austin Miller, of Hardeman. The formation of Chester County in 1882 took off a considerable portion of the northeast corner of the county. The county was erected by an act passed at Murfreesboro, October 16, 1823, but was not organized under a regular government of its own till November 17 of the same year. The territory was cut off of Hardin County, which like most of the western counties, was under the jurisdiction of Stewart County originally. The county seat was established by the county court at Hatchie Town, about one mile north of Bolivar on the Hatchie River, in 1823. Twenty-six acres of land were deeded to the town commissioners by William Ramsey on condition that he was to have one choice lot. This place did not suit the fancy of Commissioners James Fentress, William Martin, Benjamin Reynolds and Robert Jetton, who had been appointed by the Legislature to select county seats for the counties in West Tennessee. The present site of Bolivar was chosen by them. About fifty acres of land were donated by William Ramsey and Ezekiel Polk, each of whom received one choice lot. This was on April 22, 1824. After fixing on the site the business was turned over to the town commissioners, who had been selected to sell the town lots and erect public buildings. These commissioners were West Harris, T. J. Hardeman, John Y. Cockeram, Nathan Steele and John H. Bills. The new county seat was named Bolivar in honor of the great South American liberator, Simon Bolivar, and the county was named Hardeman in honor of Col. Thomas Jones Hardeman, a pioneer settler of the county.

The courts met at the house of Thomas McNeal until the selection of the permanent county seat. A temporary log house was then erected for the accommodation of the courts in the court square. Soon after a good brick building was erected, which then had ample accommodations for the courts and room for the officers. Neither the date nor the cost of this building is a matter of record. This house stood till May 4, 1864, when it was consumed in a general conflagration which destroyed most of the business part of the town and many of the county records. The fire was caused by the Federal soldiers. In 1827 the citizens expressed great dissatisfaction with the appearance of the public square. They opposed the erection of business houses on the same, and thought they "detracted from the beauty of the same," and a committee of C. C. Collier, Pitser Miller, Austin Miller, West Harris, J. Pitchford and N. Steele were appointed to raise subscriptions to purchase the property of their owners. It seems no good came of this, as private parties owned lots on the north and the south side of the square until preparations were made for the erection of the present building.

In 1830 an order was passed to build a brick wall around the public square, but this proved a very unprofitable investment, and in 1839 J. H. Bills, F. Shoemake and Allen Hill were ordered to sell the brick and erect a wooden fence in its stead. Improvements were made on the courthouse from time to time, in 1845, again in 1856, as necessity required, until its final destruction in 1864. Steps were begun for the erection of a new courthouse in 1866. It was ascertained from the property owners on the square—Porter, Bills, McNeal, Taylor and Goodall—that $2,175 would buy their interests. This was reduced $730 by individual subscriptions. A committee of E. P. McNeal, P. T. Jones and E. G. Coleman finally purchased the entire amount for $1,675. The county now owns the entire square. By an act of the Legislature passed in March, 1868, the county was allowed to sell $25,000 worth of bonds to build the new courthouse. This was soon completed, and Joseph Miller invited the court to occupy one room of the house in December, 1868. The county now owns a splendid brick courthouse, with good offices, with several fire and burglar proof safes and vaults. In the town is a bell and town clock.

Following civilization comes crime; crime, courts; courts, jails; and jails, penitentiaries. In the fall of 1824 Thomas McNeal and Wm. Ramsey were ordered to build a jail as "they think best, near the permanent courthouse." The cost was not to exceed $40. The second jail stood where Mr. J. A. Wilson's residence now stands. This was built about 1830. The principal part of the material was furnished by James

Tunage and Pitser Miller. In 1843 J. H. Bells, Pitser Miller, Austin Miller and Eli Crisp were selected to draw up plans for a new jail. The lot purchased was known as the Fentress lot, which cost $245. The contract was let to L. Burt and Thomas M. Bennett. Part of the work was done by Carter & Grace, and a part by Ed. Oswald. This jail was completed in 1844, and stood nearly in front of the present jail, where it remained till 1874, when it was destroyed by fire. The present elegant jail and sheriff's residence was erected in 1875, for the erection of which the Legislature in March, 1875, gave the county permission to sell $20,000 of 8 per cent bonds.

The first official reference to the poor is the setting apart one year's provisions for Jane Reagan, widow of Crawford Reagan, in November, 1824. The poor were kept by individuals in different parts of the county, and allowance made by the county court till 1843, when a poorhouse and poor farm were purchased. This was begun in 1840, but it was not ready for use till 1844. It was opened by Thomas Robley. This was managed by a superintendent and three commissioners of the poor. During the existence of the poorhouse all paupers were kept there. The poorhouse was sold afterward, and since that time the keeping of the paupers is let out by private contract with individuals made by the commissioners of the poor. The expenses for the poor have been kept well within bounds. The rate for 1887 is $100 per head per annum.

About the time of the organization of the county, stage routes were opened through Bolivar by way of Somerville to Memphis, Savannah, Waynesboro and Lawrenceburg, to Nashville and several other routes. The Hatchie River was also considered an important public thoroughfare for commercial purposes. Large appropriations were made each year for its improvement; vast sums have been spent on it and other unnavigable streams, often to assist some needy congressman. By a recent "fiat" of the Legislature, contrary to the "fiat" of nature, the Hatchie is still a navigable stream to Brownsville. The steamboat "Black Rover" from Pittsburgh, was the first boat to reach the town of Hatchie in 1828. Notwithstanding the poor navigation of Hatchie, vast quantities of produce have been taken out of it in keelboats and other small boats.

The first railroad in the county was the Memphis & Charleston. This was chartered February 4, 1846, with a capital stock of $800,000. Gen. James C. Jones, Col. Sam Tate, Capt. Joseph Lenow and Minor Meriwether aided largely in the completion of the road. This road purchased the franchise and the road-bed of the Memphis & La Grange Road, which had been chartered in 1835 and partially completed in 1842. For the first of these roads the State gave $217,000, and for the latter $1,700,000. This road was completed in 1857. The following taken from the coroner's inquest as found in the minutes of the county court indicates the completion of the road at that time: "Inquest.—W. C. Adams fell from the mail train on the Memphis & Charleston Railroad, in a state of intoxication, and was killed October 7, 1858." This road extends through the southern part of the county. The next road was the Mississippi Central. The northern terminus of this road was at Jackson. The road was chartered in 1853-54, and was completed to that point in 1858. In 1877 it was consolidated with the Great Northern Connection, thus making a system of 1,700 miles of road. It is now called the Illinois Central. To aid the Mississippi Central the State of Tennessee issued bonds to the amount of $1,124,000. Other roads are in contemplation.

Steps were taken by the General Assembly of 1884-85, for the erection of the third asylum for the unfortunate of the State, and $85,000 was appropriated as a nucleus of the amount of the new institution. In the summer of 1886 a site was selected lying two and one-half miles west of Bolivar for the asylum. One hundred acres out of a 738-acre tract was purchased by the commissioners, Dr. W. P. Jones, Dr. J. H. Callender and Hon. John M. East, from Paul T. Jones *et al.* for $8,000, with the refusal of any or all the remainder at $20 per acre. For a description of the building see page 294, and for full page engraving see page 140.

Sheriffs: J. C. N. Robertson, 1823-36; Wm. Stockton, 1836-38; J. C. N. Robertson, 1838-40; J. R. Harris, 1840-46; C. P. Polk, 1846-52; A. G. Shaw, 1852-56; W. T. Jones, October, 1856; J. W. Deming, 1856-62; J. B. Franklin, 1865-67; * * * * J. J. Neely, 1870-76; W. W. Farley, 1876-82; A. F. Yopp, 1882—.

County clerks: T. J. Hardeman, 1823-36; R. P. Neely, 1836-40; Samuel McDowell, 1840-44; R. D. Casey, 1844-48; R. P. Neely, 1848-62; W. C. Dorion, 1870-82; W. W. Farley, 1882—.

Circuit clerks: J. H. Bills, 1823-36; E. C. Crisp, 1836-62; T. B. McDowell, 1865-70; J. M. Richardson, 1870-78; Bradford, 1878-82; G. G. Adams, 1882-86; T. M. Newsom, 1887.

Registers: Elisha Boyd, 1823-36; Samuel McDowell, 1836-48; A. J. Campbell, 1848-62; W. C. Fleming, 1865-66; B. H. Anderson, 1866-67; C. H. Anderson, 1867-74; R. F. Amons, 1874-86;—Day 1886, incumbent.

Chairmen: Wm. Polk, 1823-27; James Ruffin, 1827-32; Wm. Polk, 1832-34; Allen Hill, 1834-35; E. D. Tarver, 1835-36; E. C. Crisp, 1836-37; E. R. Belcher, 1837-39; E. C. Crisp, 1839-40; C. P. Polk, 1840-41; Wm. Moore, 1841-42; W. O. Ferguson, 1842-45; T. M. Bennett, 1845;

W. O. Ferguson, 1845-52; E. R. Newsom, 1853-54; W. O. Ferguson, 1854-56; J. J. Neely, 1856-58; William Fort, 1858-60; C. H. Anderson, 1860-62; Wm. Fort and John H. Bills, 1865-70; J. B. Harris, 1870-76; C. H. Anderson, 1876 to the present.

Judges: Joshua Haskell, W. B. Turley, W. C. Dunlap, V. D. Barry, John Read, J. C. Humphrey, Geo. W. Reeves, T. J. Flippen.

Chancellors: Calvin Jones, 1852-54; I. B. Williams, 1854-62; John W. Harris, 1861-70; James Fentress, 1870-73; H. J. Lumpton, 1873-86; A. G. Hawkins, 1886.

Clerk-master; E. C. Crisp, 1852-62; Francis Fentress, 1866-70; I. B. McDowell, 1870-74; M. H. Pirtle, 1874-76; James Fentress, Jr., 1876-82; W. C. Dorion, 1882-87; G. G. Adams, 1887.

Solicitors: V. D. Barry, 1824-34; Roger Barton, 1834-42; E. W. M. King, 1842-58; W. P. Finney, 1858-62; W. F. Tally, 1865-72; J. J. Dupuy, 1872-86; S. L. Cockroft, 1887.

As elsewhere stated the first county court was organized November 17, 1823, at the house of Thomas McNeal, where it continued to meet till November, 1825, when it first met at Bolivar. The justices presenting themselves were Elisha Boyd, John Reagan, John Rosson, Robt. Box, William Polk, Stephen Bennett, John Y. Cockeram, A. J. Taylor and Jacob Pirtle. These met and were qualified by John Thomas, "acting justice of the peace in and for Madison County." On the next day John H. Bills exhibited his commission and was qualified. Wm. Polk was chosen chairman; Julius Cæsar Napoleon Robertson was chosen sheriff and tax collector; Elisha Boyd, register; Andrew Taylor, ranger; Caleb Brock, trustee; John Reagan, coroner. The constables chosen were J. H. Arnold, Elijah Gossett, Wm. Pirtle, Andrew Jones and Joseph Haynes. Elections were ordered at Fowler's Ferry—Walter Robertson and Wm. Shinaults for field officers. The first *venire* for the county court consisted of John Wilson, David Gossett, John Allison, Jacob Edwards, Robt. Boydstun, Barnabas Chambers, Wm. Riggs, S. Tisdal, Isaac Melroy, Asa Robertson, Moses Henley, Sam Montgomery, Nathaniel Steele, Sam Harper, Wm. Mayfield, Jas. Tippett, Peter Minor, S. Duncan, Wm. Simpson, John May, James Lane, Ed. Burleson, Wm. Ramsey, R. Crawford, N. Reagan and Thomas Dare. The tax levy for 1824 was $18\frac{3}{4}$ cents on each 100 acres of land, the same amount for each town lot, $12\frac{1}{2}$ cents for each white poll and 25 cents for each black poll. The attorneys admitted in February, 1824, were Alex. B. Bradford, J. H. Talbot, Austin Miller and R. C. Allen. A singular feature of this is, they all became very distinguished men.

The "listers" for the year 1824 were E. W. Boyd, John Rosson, Wm.

Polk, Andrew Taylor, Jacob Pirtle, Robt. Box and John Reagan. Each had a division with natural boundaries. Valentine D. Barry was the first solicitor-general. He received $50 for *ex officio* services for 1824. Each of the other officers received about $40 for his services. The first case of slander was the suit of Green B. Chambers against Elias Fort. This was in August, 1824. The costs of the suit were paid by the plaintiff. Allowances were made to Wm. Ramsey and Ezekiel ——— for wolf scalps. In 1826 Wm. Groomes was tried for petit larceny, and a jury of Benjamin Tilghman, David Amons, J. Elkins, B. Chambers, J. M. Whitthorn, T. B. Peyton, Wm. Chapman, John Campbell, Michael McKinnie, A. M. Ramsey, Wm. McMillan and Jas. Martin decided him guilty and ordered that he should receive twenty-five "lashes upon the bare back at the public whipping post in the public square within one hour after the adjournment of court." James L. White for a similar offense received ten lashes and a fine of 25 cents and three months in the county jail. The first general elections were held at Bolivar, Warnersville, Shinault's, Cockeram's and Robertson's. The judges at the first were A. Kilpatrick, Charles Stewart and Thomas McNeal; the second, W. B. Robinson, Arthur Tilghman and Amos Warner; the third, Joe Hatley, W. Whitaker and Ben Bowers; the fourth, Wm. Love, Peter ——— and W. E. Norment; the fifth, Jas. Chisam, Jas. Tippett and Jas. Scott. At the January term, 1828, the court passed several rules pertaining to the business of the court, and among others was this: "No spirituous liquors shall be sold in the courthouse during business hours." David Fentress was fined $15 for contempt for rising in the bar immediately after the court had rendered its opinion and saying: "I do not care what the court says, the jury are men of sense and are judges of the law and the facts." In 1829 Peter, a man of color, sued John Sanders for trespass and by a jury was awarded $7.75 damages. The first inquest in the county was held by John Reagan, coroner, on February 23, 1825, on the body of an Indian who had been murdered. By order of the court, July 6, 1829, V. D. Barry was allowed an upper room in the courthouse for an office. D. H. Coe was admitted to the bar, April 8, 1830. On July 7, 1834, Pitser Miller was allowed $67.47 for the bell for the courthouse. Edwin Polk was admitted to the bar as practitioner May 6, 1839, and W. B. Johnson, January 6, 1840; R. Alexander Clement, December 6, 1841, and John Robertson, January 1, 1843. In December, 1841, the county court memorialized the General Assembly to extend the privileges of the Insane Asylum. Inquests were held on the body of J. D. W. Tate on July 3, 1848, and Gilbert L. Crisp on April 1, 1852, who shot himself with a pistol at the southeast corner of the square in trying to hit Thomas Shaw with it. The coroner was called upon to investigate the cause of the death of J. J. Lanier in April, 1855, when it was found that he came to his death by Aaron Whitly with a shot gun, "with force and arms, maliciously and willfully." Thomas Webb fell into Spring Creek in a fit and was drowned, June 6, 1855. H. G. Newland was killed by Thomas L. Duncan with a pistol "willfully, maliciously," in November, 1855. J. G. White came to his death by "visitation of God," on April 7, 1856. J. H. Alexander was killed at Wayland Spring by the falling of a tree while encamped in his wagon, September 5, 1858. James Clark was killed by J. J. Thomas in the "heat of blood," July 5, 1854. F. M. Thomas was killed December 26, 1857, by James Vaughan "with a heavy weight." Hannah, slave of James Avant, was killed by a blow by Richard Croft, October 10, 1857; Peter, Wilson, Alfred and Archie, slaves, were killed by accident or otherwise in 1858. In 1859 inquests were held on the bodies of M. W. Harvey, Elias Farson, Wm. S. Hughes, John Mills and Daniel Sheets. A coincident is connected with the case of "Charlie" who "wickedly, unlawfully and wilfully" hung himself in jail June 30, 1854. He had before this killed a fellow slave of Joel Ferguson and had been tried and convicted of murder, but cheated the gallows. The circuit court of Hardeman County was organized in 1824 with Joshua Haskell as judge and V. D. Barry as solicitor. The first case to the penitentiary from this county was Truman Burns for an assault and battery with intent to commit murder. His term was three years from December 4, 1834. A loss of records renders it impossible to follow the circuit court proceedings. Bolivar not being a great commercial center it has not been the center of great cases of litigation; however, some very eminent men have been connected with the Bolivar bar. Among them may be mentioned V. D. Barry, Austin Miller, David Fentress, Henry Barry, John Fentress, Alex. Robertson, Roger Barton, Granville Searcy, W. C. Dunlap and E. W. M. King. Judge James Fentress of more recent date is now principal attorney for the Illinois Central Railroad. The bar is now represented by R. H. Wood, Frances Fentress, A. T. McNeal, Jesse Norment, A. J. Coates, Chas. A. Miller and Austin Miller. The chancery court for this division was not organized till October 25, 1852. Calvin Jones was the first chancellor.

The selection of Bolivar as the seat of justice for the county was made by James Fentress, Wm. Martin, Benjamin Reynolds and Robert Jetton, who had been chosen by the Legislature of the State for that purpose. Hatchie, Bolivar and Hainline's Ford were the places under advisement. For the town site William Ramsey and Ezekiel Polk each gave within a fraction of twenty-five acres of ground, each being allowed to reserve one choice lot. The deeds of transfer were made December 29, 1824. On the selection of the site and the confirmation of the deeds the auction of the lots and management of the business was turned over to the town commissioners which consisted of West Harris, T. J. Hardeman, John G. Cockeram, Nathaniel Steele and John H. Bills. The first purchases of lots were made by Nathan Avery, Thomas J. Hardeman, Robert Price, Alex Kirkpatrick, David Laird, T. N. Giles, W. D. McKay, A. J. Willis, Littleton Henderson, Needham Stevens, Joe and William Atwood, Robert Rosser, David Fentress, Samuel Polk, M. Randolph, Charles Stewart, James L. McDonald, D. W. Wood, D. F. Brown, Allen Hill, James Hedges, Francis Shoemake, Chancey Davenport, John Knuckolls (Nuckolls), R. P. T. Stone, D. Mims, J. T. Cockeram, William Ramsey and Ezekiel Polk. As stated elsewhere the courts did not meet in Bolivar till the fall of 1824.

The first business at the county seat was done at Hatchie by J. W. Wood & Co., Joe and John McCain and Armour & Lake. The former had also a house in Memphis and the latter a house in Jackson. A vast amount of business was done at the river long after the town was moved to Bolivar. Large cotton sheds stood at the river where cotton was stored for shipment down the river before the building of the railroad. Business houses were built in Bolivar in 1825 by Joe and John McCain, D. W. Wood and Reynolds. These were log houses and stood on the west side near the center of the block. Soon after houses were opened by William H. Henderson, David Shoemake, Leech & Bro., Pitser Miller and Bills & McNeal. Stores were then all general stores and a large part of the trade was with the Indians. Their trade was in peltries obtained in hunting and money obtained from their annual allowance made by the General Government. The general management of public affairs of the town was by the town commissioners, which body was made perpetual by elections held by the commissioners themselves. This form of government continued till November 29, 1847, when an act passed the General Assembly " to incorporate the town of Bolivar in the county of Hardeman." The corporation was given the usual power of such bodies. Enlargements were made to the place in January, 1856, and in February, 1860. Amendments were made to the charter in 1869 and again in 1873. The present officers of the board are Charles Wellens, mayor; A. J. Coates, recorder, with five aldermen.

The principal business of Bolivar is done by the following firms: General stores—Kahn Bros., D. E. Durrett, J. A. Wilson & Son, Barrett & Bro.; groceries—G. T. Ferguson, Joseph Tate, W. A. Mercer, Jones

Bros., W. H. Reynolds and W. J. Redd; drug stores—Emerson & Savage and B. V. Hudson; liverymen—Emerson & Savage, Noah Nuckolls and Nooner & Newbern.

The hotels are the Houston House and Acton House.

The first newspaper published in the place was the Bolivar *Palladium*, published some time before 1830. Then followed the Bolivar *Herald*, and then the Bolivar *Democrat*, which was founded about 1845, by J. J. Neeley, and continued to the war. The Bolivar *Bulletin* was founded in 1866 by M. R. Parrish, who continued its publication till 1874; it was then published about one year by H. M. and M. T. Polk; this was followed by Hardin, Clark & Macon, who continued about one year. J. M. Hubbard then managed the paper till 1877, when it passed into the hands of G. W. Armistead, who controlled the paper till November, 1883. The Weatherby Bros. then took charge and ran the paper till March, 1866. The paper then passed into the hands of Hon. Jesse Norment, who still has charge of it. The *Bulletin* is a progressive Democratic paper. Its columns are full of good reading matter and it is a paper living for the future and not in the past.

Bolivar has been singularly unfortunate in fires within the last two or more decades. The first great fire occurred May 4, 1864, when the courthouse and the greater part of the houses of the town were burned. In 1876 the west side and southwest was swept away. In 1878 and again in 1885 the east side was burned. These have all been replaced by good brick business houses. The first fire company was organized in 1832, with forty-seven members.

The bank at Bolivar, the first in the history of the town, was chartered in September, 1886, by W. C. Dorion, G. T. Ingram, Isaac Kahn, C. A. Miller, W. A. Mercer, W. T. Anderson, A. T. McNeal, D. E. Durrett, J. Norment, R. M. Wright, J. C. Savage and W. Durden. The capital stock is $30,000. The officers are A. T. McNeal, president; and W. C. Dorion, cashier. The directors are A. T. McNeal, D. E. Durrett, W. A. Mercer, W. C. Dorion, Sam'l Kahn, Austin Miller and G. T. Ingram.

The old cemetery lying in the eastern part of the town was purchased by the town commissioner in July, 1826. This was the common burying-ground till 1860, when the Union Cemetery was purchased from Pitser Miller, by J. H. Bills and J. J. Neely, the Masonic Lodge, No. 54 (Clinton) and the Odd Fellows Lodge, No. 27. This is now the general burying-ground. The Polk Cemetery was deeded by Edwin Polk to James K. Polk, Jr., A. T. McNeal, Wm. Neely, W. T. Bills, W. C. Collier and Wm. Nelson, on October 23, 1845, to be forever a family burying-ground. Col. Ezekiel Polk was the first buried here. In 1821 he wrote his own epitaph, beginning with the lines,

> Here lies the dust of old E. P.
> One instance of morality.
> Pennsylvania born, Carolina bred,
> In Tennessee died upon his bed.

He died in 1824.

Bolivar is well supplied with lodges. Clinton Lodge No. 54, F. & A. M. was granted a dispensation by the Most Worshipful Master of the State on October 7, 1824. The dispensation was granted to Carter C. Collier, John H. Bills and Thomas J. Hardeman to "open a lodge of the Ancient York Masons at the Hardeman Court House." The lodge met at the house of Thomas McNeal, on October 28, 1824. The following temporary organization was effected: C. C. Collier, W. M.; J. H. Bills, S. W.; T. J. Hardeman, J. W.; E. Kirkpatrick, S. D.; C. Brock, J. D.; V. D. Barry, Treas., R. Biddle, C. and H. Cockburn Tyler. A petition was received from Wm. Polk for membership. The second meeting was held at Mrs. Polk's. There were present the visiting brethren Wm. Arnold, W. R. Hess, Wm. Stoddert, Wm. Polk and J. F. Theobald. There were admitted in the year 1824 C. Beech, J. Haynes, S. B. Harper J. L. Sanders, Wm. Ramsey, A. Taylor, Dan Cuthbert, J. M. McKean, J. C. N. Robertson, D. F. Brown and E. R. Anderson.

Chapter No. 34 was granted a dispensation on November 5, 1850. The following were the officers *pro tem.;* W. Wright, P. G. H. P.; Jas. G. Bell, King; D. J. Allen, Scribe; Samuel Dennis, Chaplain of Post; Wm. Shore, Principal Sojourner; W. O. Ferguson, R. A. C.; Thompson Allen, Master of 3d Veil; E. C. Crisp, 2d Veil; A. G. Nelson, 1st Veil; W. W. Farley, P. S., and Timothy Fox, Guard. The by-laws of Lafayette Chapter were adopted for temporary use. The first members received were P. D. J. Wells, Vincent Allen, J. B. McDowell, J. H. Bills, W. C. Harkins, W. H. Fenel and C. G. Joy.

Bolivar Council, No. 16, was chartered October 15, 1851, and it began work November 5, 1851. The following were the organizations: Thrice Illustrious Grand Master, D. J. Wells; Deputy Illustrious Grand Master, G. B. Peters; Principal Conductor, Isaac N. Bills; Wm. Nuckolls, Grand Treasurer; J. B. McDowell, Grand Recorder; C. G. Joy, Grand Captain of the Guard; Daniel B. Cheairs, G. C. C.; Timothy Fox, Grand Marshal and Sloan Warren, Grand Steward. The rules of Brownsville Council, No. 10, were adopted for temporary use.

Bolivar Lodge, No. 27, I. O. O. F. was chartered in 1851, and in connection with the Presbyterian Church in 1853 they erected their hall. The charter was granted to Howell A. Tatum, Wm. H. Poindexter, Robt.

D. McRae, G. C. Gray and Richard S. Parham. The membership of the lodge now is about seventy-five.

Lodge No. 499, K. of H., was chartered October 15, 1877, to the following: L. B. Adams, R. A. Tate, A. J. Swineboard and J. M. Richardson, Dictators; W. H. Reynolds, Guard; J. H. Pope, Reporter; Leonidas Bills, Financial Reporter; J. W. Tate, Treas.; C. M. Wellens, Guardian; L. M. Crawford and C. E. Derrett, members.

The K. & L. of H. was organized September 30, 1880, by J. W. Smith of Grand Junction. The charter members were Mrs. S. F. McKinnie, L. M. Carrington, M. M. Bailey, Kate Richardson and Miss Maggie Dorion, Mr. J. A. McKinnie, C. G. Joy, J. A. Wilson, R. L. Napier, A. F. Bailey, A. M. Lambeth, A. J. Swineboard, C. A. Miller, W. C. Dorion, G. G. Adams, J. M. Swineboard, L. L. Miller, P. E. Yopp, A. M. Armistead and Miss Laura Carrington. The present membership is twenty-two.

The first settler at Grand Junction was D. R. Bryant. The place was founded about 1854 at the crossing or junction of the Memphis & Charleston, and the Illinois Central Railroad, hence the name. It contains about 600 inhabitants. It was occupied by the Federals as an important post during the last three years of the war. It contains three general stores: Hatton & Hancock, Arnett & Prewitt, and Wellens & Co. Two important hotels are there; the one at the Junction is kept by Wellens & Hawkins, and the other by J. N. Middleton. There are also two large marble establishments: Stinson & Son and C. J. Rodgers. The principal articles of produce handled are cotton and fruits.

Saulsbury lies east of Grand Junction on the Memphis & Charleston railroad. It was founded about 1854, and named in honor of Dr. Saul. The town was incorporated in 1856 with fifty-six voters. The business of the place is done by J. D. Saul & Son, W. H. R. Elliott, Wright & Dunden, and one or two others. The place has excellent school and church privileges. The non-euphonious name of U Bet marks a station on the Memphis & Charleston Railroad sixty-four miles east of Memphis and is known in railway parlance as "64." It contains one business house.

Middleton was named in honor of the family of that name. It lies east of the last named place on the same road. It has five or six business houses and contains altogether sixty-one lots.

Pocahontas is in District No. 19, near the southeast corner of the county. It was named in honor of Pocahontas of Capt. John Smith fame. The village is laid off into about fifty town lots and has about a half dozen stores and good church and school facilities.

Middlebury sprang up on the Illinois Central soon after its completion. It is about midway between Grand Junction and Bolivar.

Hickory Valley is a few miles south of Middlebury, on the Illinois Central. The place was chartered in May, 1884. It then contained thirty-four voters and 159 inhabitants. It contains an excellent school and has good church facilities.

The villge of Toone is situated in District No. 15, on the Illinois Central Railroad. It had its origin about the time of the railroad, and its name is from a family of that county. The place contains four or five business houses, churches and an excellent school.

Whiteville is in District No. 22, in the western part of the county. It is surrounded by some of the best farming land in the county. This is among the earliest settled communities of Hardeman County. Among the earlier inhabitants of the place were T. B. Norment, C. W. Henry, J. S. Buford, G. Davis, B. A. Henry, D. Caldwell, J. S. Osborne, J. C. Parner, Orin Harris, W. W. Farley, B. A. Harris, John Warner, J. S. Bayley, F. N. Brown, C. H. Williams, G. A. Sanders, J. C. Green, J. S. Norment and others. The place was incorporated in October, 1854. Business houses are also found at Cedar Chapel, Naylors, Crainesville, New Castle, and Clover Port.

Aside from militia service and the service rendered by individuals before they became inhabitants of Hardeman County, the military career of the county begins with 1836. The assassination of Gen. Thompson on December 23, 1835, and the massacre of Maj. Dade in the Wahoo Swamp, with a whole company of men on the same day, led to a call by the General Government and the State of Tennessee for troops to avenge the insult of Osceola and the Seminoles. On the call for 2,000 men over fifty companies tendered their services. The overplus had to remain at home, and among those was the company from Hardeman County. The services of this company were again tendered for the defense of the Sabine, near which Gen. Houston was struggling with the Mexicans under Santa Anna, which brought about a threatened invasion of American territory. Again these over anxious men met with disappointment. They were again denied the privilege of measuring arms with their enemies. In 1838 one company, the "Hardeman Guards," was accepted to assist Scott in the removal of the Indians to their new reservation according to the stipulations of the treaty. The following is the muster roll of Capt. (Gen.) R. P. Neely's company, as far as is remembered: R. P. Neely, L. D. Casey, John Hindman, J. W. Pitkin, J. B. Teague, Robt. Walton, I. M. Macon, Wm. F. Roberts, R. A. Westbrook, William Pugh, Jas. Mills, W. F. Tipler, Wm. Porter, J. S. Thompson, J. S.

Raines, H. B. Brown, Tilghman C. Fort, —— Wiggins, Allen Wells, Jas. Raines, John C. Chamless, J. S. Chamless, W. C. Dunlap, Nathan Chaffin, Jesse Chaffin, Zadoc Casey, Wm. Chandler, N. Melton, J. C. H. Fowler, M. Rodgers, Nelson Wiley, Peter P. Stone, Lemuel Sills, Joel P. Pugh, W. C. Pugh, W. Pitkin, John Maxwell, L. Grantham, Wm. Kearly, J. H. McElroy, H. H. Hawkins, J. Grantham, W. C. May, Robt. Campbell, L. Armstrong, Wm. Tune, Wm. Hickman, Wiley Dean, John P. Smith, J. J. Bailey, West Kearly, Wm. Roark, David Benton, R. Forsyth, W. Sanders, Willis Taylor, Wm. Alexander, W. J. Smith, David Goodnight, —— Floyd (wagoner), West Welkins, James Crow, James Oliver, John Covington, L. Phillips, Wm. Lakey, Thomas Timmons, J. H. Hindman, Joshua Grantham, J. Clift, James Dawson, H. Ross and Hugh Shaw. Of the 104 men who were enlisted nine are yet living. A reunion of the survivors is held each May at Bolivar. In the Mexican war a whole company of volunteers was again offered, but they again met with disappointment, as only a few individuals got into the service and they went into companies from other counties; but in the late war the military spirit of all was fully satisfied. The first troops for the Confederate service from Hardeman County were the "Pillow Guards." These were placed in the Fourth Tennessee (Confederate), and were organized at Germantown May 18, 1861. The officers of the company were R. P. Neely, captain; L. M. Brown, W. C. Dorion and A. T. McNeal, lieutenants. On the organization of the regiment R. P. Neely was elected colonel, (See page 566 for sketch of regiment.)

The Ninth Regiment was organized May 22, 1862, at Camp Beauregard, Jackson, Tenn. H. L. Douglass was elected colonel of this regiment. Company F, Middleton Tigers, was from the vicinity of Middleton. The officers of this company were S. H. White, captain; J. S. Neely, J. M. Mason and J. H. Jones, lieutenants. This company was composed almost entirely of farmers. A regimental sketch is given page 569–70 of the State history.

Two companies were furnished during the war by Hardeman County for the Twenty-second Regiment. The Hatchie Hunters: captain, R. H. Wood, and lieutenants, J. M. Richardson, Wm. Parkinson and —— Shoffler. The commissioned officers of the other company were J. M. Richardson, captain, and lieutenants, Gynn Thurmond, J. McKinnie and —— Cargill. For a regimental history see pages 577 and 571–72.

About fifteen or twenty men from Hardeman were in Company B of the Thirty-third Regiment. The commissioned officers of this company were Thomas Lacey, captain; W. B. Manly, Thomas Bond and L.

M. Johnson, lieutenants. Gen. A. W. Campbell was elected colonel. A sketch of the regiment may also be found in this volume.

The One Hundred and Fifty-fourth was one of the first to enter the service. It was originally a militia regiment that was organized under the militia law of the State in 1860. It was organized at Memphis, and early in 1861 its services were tendered the State. Thomas Hancock raised a company for this regiment at Saulsbury. Preston Smith was elected its first colonel. The history of this company is given with that regiment.

What became Company E of the Seventh Cavalry was raised in Hardeman County. The officers were J. J. Neely, captain; Leonidas Bills, W. W. McCarley and J. G. Patrick, lieutenants. These men were originally assigned to what has become known in history as Logwood's Battalion. The officers of the battalion were I. H. Logwood, lieutenant-colonel; C. H. Hull, major and J. H. Somerville, adjutant. This battalion was organized in the fall of 1861 and first saw service about New Madrid. On June 10, 1862, the battalion was reorganized. There being a disagreement among the men in regard to the election of officers, the Hardeman boys withdrew and were attached to the Seventh. Their services are marked by the numerous battles of Forrest's command. Company K was a part of Forrest's scouts and was enlisted in Hardeman County. J. C. Savage became captain of this company. The commissioned officers as mustered were Wiley Higgs, captain; W. P. Johnson-J. C. Savage and John Ramsey, lieutenants. The services of this company were in the various scouts, skirmishes and battles in Tennessee, south Mississippi and Alabama.

The Fourteenth Cavalry was recruited inside the Federal lines north of the Memphis & Charleston Railroad by J. J. Neely. The regimental and field officers were J. J. Neely, colonel; R. H. White, lieutenant-colonel; Gynn Thurmond, major; J. H. Turner, surgeon, A. F. Topp, quartermaster, and S. Hannum, adjutant. The men were taken out in squads or companies between the Federal posts at La Grange, Grand Junction, Middleton and elsewhere. They were organized at New Albany on the Tallahatchie and those who had not received arms were armed with Enfield rifles at Pikeville. The Fourteenth was attached to Richardson's brigade which was composed of the Twelfth, Thirteenth, Fourteenth and Fifteenth Regiments of Tennessee Cavalry. This brigade, called Richardson's, was commanded most of the time by J. J. Neely. Those belonging to the Fourteenth from this county were companies A, R. R. White, captain; S. J. Cox, N. Callahan and J. B. Harris, lieutenants; E, W. W. Hall, captain; James Moore, Jasper Smith and M. Hall, lieutenants; F, Gynn Thurmond, captain; J. Robertson and Wm. Pirtle, lieutenants. A severe skirmish and running fight occurred between portions of this brigade and Hurst's Sixth Federal Regiment beginning near where the asylum now is and extending to Whiteville. The battle resulted in considerable loss to the Federals. One company was raised in the county for the artillery service, Polk's battery, by M. T. Polk, who was elected captain; T. R. Smith and Wm. Caruthers were lieutenants.

In August, 1861, the militia of the different districts of the county was organized into companies or parts of companies for drill and other service. The county court by that time had spent $726 on families of volunteers who were in the service. In addition to the company organizations J. R. Robertson was made general commander for the county and E. C. Crisp was agent for the ordnance department of the State. Guards were allowed 50 cents per day or night for guard duty. All guns suitable for service were ordered turned over to the ordnance department to be paid for at a fixed price. In August $857 was spent for arms and in October $1,500 for indigent families and in December $2,600 was spent. Like sums followed other months but no figures can be found. Suffice it to say that no soldier's family suffered for the necessities of life when a neighbor had the means of relieving their wants.

Although the bodies of Confederate soldiers are buried from the Mississippi to the Potomac and from the Gulf to the Ohio, a fine marble monument was erected in the courthouse yard at the close of the war, as a memorial to the volunteers of Hardeman County. This was a volunteer offering by the comrades and friends of the fallen and was one of the first if not the first in the State.

Schools were established west of the Alleghany Mountains by the General Assembly for North Carolina in 1785. The territorial legislature in 1786 also passed laws for the encouragement of schools. In 1806 began the general founding of academies. Modifications, changes, and the passage of general laws pertaining to schools have taken place almost every year of the State's existence. In 1851 a law passed empowering commissioners to employ female teachers in any school and to pay them in the same manner as was provided for male teachers. Edwin Crawford is said to have been the first school-teacher in the county. His school was in the Shinault neighborhood in 1823-24. The first public school buildings in the county were the male and female academies. The first was built in 1830 and the latter in 1832. These buildings continued in use to within recent date. The old male academy is now used as a private residence and the latter is now used for the public schools of

Bolivar. Some eminent men and educators have been connected with the academy of Bolivar. The public schools were put into operation in 1874. The last report of the county superintendent shows that there are now two brick, sixty frame and thirty-three log schoolhouses in the county. Of the scholastic population 4,595 are white and 3,968 are colored. Eighty-two white teachers are employed and forty-six colored. The amount paid in salaries is $15,109.23. The county superintendent receives $200 per annum. The average length of school term is but sixty-one days. Besides the ordinary common school, schools of a higher grade are taught at the principal towns in the county. The school at Hickory Valley, called Home Valley School, is under the charge of Edmond Fusch; the Bolivar High School is under the charge of Prof. H. J. Fusch with two assistants. The Grand Junction Male and Female Institute is presided over by W. A. H. McDaniel. The Toone Institute is superintended by T. S. Minter. The Woodland Academy of Saulsbury has Ferd M. Malone for its principal. The Clover Point Academy is in charge of M. Rose. These are properly consolidated schools and have a school term of about ten months. Middleton, Pocahontas, Crainesville, Whiteville and New Castle usually have good schools of high order.

The first Cumberland Presbyterian Church in the county if not the first church of any denomination was the society at New Hope which was constituted in March, 1825, by Rev. James Guthrie, an itinerant preacher. No record of membership was kept or has been preserved earlier than October, 1839. On the 6th and 7th of October, 1839, a record of membership was prepared by the clerk of the session and it shows a membership of seventy-six. The pastor at that time was Rev. Israel Pickens, and the elders were Hugh Caruthers, Henry T. Rucker and Stephen Jerman. On October 20, 1839, the session adopted strong resolutions on the question of temperance. It was of the opinion that "ardent spirits is a moral crime of great turpitude," and it resolved to use all proper effort to induce members to refrain from a practice so iniquitous on penalty of expulsion, and it resolved further not to ordain a man to preach the Gospel, or a ruling elder who used vinous or spirituous liquor as a beverage or trafficked in the same for gain. It resolved further that a man is not qualified for the sacrament of the supper who is indirectly engaged in throwing firebrands into the community, spreading poverty, wretchedness, crime and death amongst his fellow beings. Those were unanimously adopted and ordered furnished to the clerk of each session. The Caruthers, Wilks, Jerman, Rucker, Steele, Dodson, Harris, Gray, Murray, Pirtle and other families were members at this time. There were also about thirty-five blacks, members at this time. To 1860, New Hope had received 242 communicants besides eighty-five blacks. Death and removals have always kept the membership far below that number at any one time. By the clerk's report the membership now is forty-four.

The register's office shows that there was both a church house and camp-ground at Mount Comfort in 1827. This was built on a lot deeded by William Barrett to Peter G. Reeves, Chas. Stewart, Samuel Lambert and Hardy Scott. There was also a camp-ground at New Hope at a very early date. The fervor of the worship at these camp-meetings equaled that of apostolic times. The churches above mentioned were two of the pioneers of the county. Mount Comfort now has thirty-eight communicants.

The lot for the Cumberland Presbyterian Church of Bolivar was purchased of Austin and Lorenzo Goodlett in 1868 by L. B. Adams, James Toone and G. W. Swineboard as elders. This congregation now shows a membership of twenty-eight. There is a congregation at Bethel with twenty-one members, one at Canaan also with twenty-one, a congregation at Hickory Valley with twenty-six, one at Saulsbury with forty-two, one at Toone with sixty-five, and one at Whiteville with thirty members.

The date of the organization of the Methodist Episcopal Church in Hardeman County is not exactly known, but it is almost contemporaneous with the county. The organization at Bolivar was some time near 1830, but the loss of the first church register renders it impossible to tell who all the first members were or by whom the church was organized. The first church stood not far below the southwest corner of the public square on Market Street. This house was erected sometime between 1834 and 1839. Worship was continued at the place till 1873–74, when steps were taken to erect the present building. The latter, which is scarcely completed, was built in 1874–75 at a cost of about $6,000. The church membership is about eighty. The church maintains an excellent Sabbath-school, which has been under the charge of Dr. Newbern for the last quarter of a century. Besides the church at Bolivar there is one at Mount Vernon built about 1853. Pleasant Grove, Toone, Concord, Wiley, Hickory Grove, Whiteville, New Castle, Cawley, Saulsbury, Middleton (built in 1869 by the Methodist Episcopal Church and Masonic Lodge, No. 264), Big Springs, and Rehobeth (built in 1853 on land of Wm. R. Jacobs). The trustees at this time were Wm. Jacobs, Asa Brown, Geo. Thompson and Abe Sellars. Walnut Grove was built about the same time as Rehobeth. Bethlehem was built in 1854. The trustees were Duke W. Hulum, J. S. Clanch, William Person, S. G. Pegram, P. F.

Pruet, John Hunt and Anson Heartfield. The church at Middlebury was built in 1859; the trustees at that time were M. J. Harner, D. J. Newbern, W. D. Cheshire, S. M. Williams and L. M. Williams. There are churches at Grand Junction, Brick Church, Crainesville, Beech Church and Porter Creek. The latter was built in 1853, then possibly a few other churches in the county. The Methodists are the most numerous of any denomination in the county.

The second church in the county in membership is the Missionary Baptist Church. Doubtless the first of the kind organized in the county was the church at Clover Creek, which according to the official report was organized in 1826. A church deed was made by John Teague to J. B. Truscott, trustee of the Baptist Church, on October 25, 1849. This is now the strongest church within the bounds of the association, having 173 members. The church at Bolivar was organized not far from 1830, and a brick church erected on the spot where the church now stands soon after. This was destroyed by fire during the war, and with it the church records. A new frame building was erected on the old site after the close of the war. This church now has a membership of fifty-four. Walnut Grove is the second church in size in the association, having a membership of 168. The church was built on a five-acre tract, deeded to the trustees by Joseph Vandergriff. The church was organized in 1850. The church at Mt. Pleasant was erected on a lot obtained from Jacob Bartholomew in 1846. The membership now is not large. The church at Saulsbury was constituted in 1866. There is a good house of worship and a membership of eighty-six by the last report. The church at Crainesville was organized in 1880, and now has a membership of fifty-one. The church house was erected in 1882. The Middleton Church reports a membership of thirteen; some time since the old church was sold to the colored Baptists. Palestine was constituted in 1869, and now has a strength of fifty-nine, and Pleasant Grove with the same membership was constituted in 1844. Piney Grove was constituted in 1836, and has a membership of 166, while Porter Creek, with a membership of sixty-seven, was constituted in 1855. There are also strong churches at Pocahontas, Rocky Springs, Rock Springs, Saulsbury and Toone.

The first Presbyterian Church organized in Hardeman County was at Mt. Bethany, on March 14, 1830, by Revs. Samuel Hedge and Alex. Campbell. The first pastor for this church was Rev. James Hamilton. The members consisted of Mr. and Mrs. M. A. Lewis, A. R. Alexander and wife, Eli Kilpatrick and wife, Jesse D. Hall and wife, J. J. Hall, S. McCurley, W. McCurley, Ann Alexander, Mary Alexander, John Mathews and wife, Mr. Limerick, D. Alexander, J. W. Mathews and Miss Isabell

Mathews; James, Steve, George and Aggie (colored). The elders were A. R. Campbell and John Mathews. The membership at one time numbered 146. The membership afterward went to other congregations. In 1851 twenty-four acres of land at Mt. Bethany was transferred by deed by the trustees, George Wood, R. H. D. Ewell and J. W. Mathews, to E. P. McNeal, for the Methodist Church. The Presbyterian Church at Bolivar was organized on November 12, 1852, at the Methodist Church in Bolivar, by Revs. P. R. Bland and G. W. Coons. It consisted of the following members: Mrs. Lucy A. Bills, Mrs. Matilda Fentress, Mrs. Catharine Coleman, Mrs. May Wood, Mrs. Louisa Collier, Thomas B. Adams, Mrs. Mary Adams, Mrs. Mary Macon, Miss Ella David, George Wood, Mrs. Elizabeth Neely, Mrs. Maria ————, Clara Bills, John R. Wood, James Fentress, Wm. Coleman, Alfred Coleman, Miss May B. Neely, Miss Louisa Neely and Mrs. Isabella McDowell. Dr. George Wood, formerly elder of Mt. Bethany, was chosen elder of this church. Miss Laurel Hall was the first additional member admitted. The deed to the church lot was made on September 1, 1853, by Thomas E. Morse to the elders of the Presbyterian Church, and Bolivar Lodge, No. 27, I. O. O. F. The house was soon completed at a cost of $2,115. The congregations of Bolivar and Mt. Bethany on August 23, 1853, extended a call to the Rev. Mr. Buell of the Nashville Presbytery. This was accepted at a salary of $723 per annum, and he arrived November 23, 1853, and delivered his first sermon in Bolivar, December 4, 1853. The following is a list of pastors of this church, with their time of service: William P. Buell, Nov., 1853, to July, 1854; W. H. Thompson, August, 1853, to September 14, 1867; H. C. Brown, November 27, 1870, to December, 1872; George Summey, October 14, 1873, to May 9, 1875; W. R. Smith, June 10, 1876, to April 3, 1879; John S. Park, April 20, 1879, to July 5, 1881; William G. Keady, August 7, 1881, to January 14, 1886. S. R. Hope is pastor elect.

The following are the elders, with time of service: George Wood, November 12, 1852, to July 20, 1870; Paul T. Jones, June 9, 1858; R. S. Hardy, May 6, 1865, to June 12, 1882; Thomas C. Jones, April 13, 1867 to September 7, 1873; James Fentress, April 26, 1868, to 1881; Robert L. Walker, October 23, 1870; Francis Fentress, June 26, 1881. The church also has five deacons and about fifty communicants. Since its organization the church has received about 200 members. This church also has a congregation of thirty-five members at Hickory Valley. This was organized in 1877 by Revs. A. Johnson and N. K. Smith, with seventeen members. A house of worship was erected here in 1882. Rev. Johnson organized a church at Grand Junction the same year with thirteen members. The membership here now is but nominal. There is a congregation of about twenty-five members at Saulsbury. They also have a house of worship. This congregation formerly worshiped at Berlin, where it had been since about 1847.

Services were first held in Bolivar for the Episcopal Church at St. James Parish in the beginning of 1834 by Dr. Daniel Stephens. It was a mission until April 17, 1834, when the parish was organized by Right Rev. Bishop James H. Otey. The articles of association were signed by Calvin Jones, May C. White, Margeret Stephens, F. B. W. J. Jones, Sarah H. Stephens, Thos. C. Jones, Courtney Pickett, Ann E. Fitzhugh, May R. Blanks, May Hardeman, Prudence Bills, M. E. Stephens, Rosanna T. A. Robinson, B. Polk, Emily Todd, Sophia Polk, E. McNeal, Wm. Todd, Sophia Polk, W. H. Wood, W. H. Stephens, Clarissa McNeal, W. C. White, Samuel N. Stephens, Eugenia Wilson, A. G. Wilson, E. C. Crisp, A. T. McNeal, T. M. Hardeman, J. J. Williams, W. B. Turley, J. H. Bills, T. J. Hardeman, H. Goodrich, R. Neely, Allen Hill, D. F. Brown, W. W. Bomar and a few others. Rev. Daniel Stephens was chosen rector, Calvin Jones was chosen senior warden and T. C. Jones, junior warden. Services were held in the courthouse until 1840, when McNeal, Polk and Goodrich were appointed a building committee with full power to select the site, raise funds and build the house. On July 15, 1840, a deed was made by E. R. Belcher to Calvin Jones, Pitser Miller and the remaining vestry-men for the lot at the corner of Washington and Lafayette Streets for the sum of $175. A contract was made July 27 between the building committee and John Shepherd. The house was to be of brick 32x44 feet. On May 2, 1842, the thanks of the vestry were tendered to Wade T. Smith, John Welch, Sr., and others of Philadelphia, for their liberality in presenting the church a bell and a pair of astral lamps. In May, 1869, E. P. McNeal, Leonidas Bills and A. T. McNeal were appointed a building committee for the vestry and congregation for St. James Church for the erection of a new church and Sunday-school building. Additional grounds were purchased and a contract entered into with Willis & Sloan for the erection of the splendid edifice now owned by this church. The whole cost $11,500, with certain conditions. The building is of brick of the Gothic style of architecture and is 43x70 feet. The building was to be completed by August 1, 1870. The schoolroom adjoins the church and is a frame structure; some of the furniture of the old church was used in furnishing the schoolroom. Near the church and school lot is the rectory and rectory grounds containing nearly five acres. The rectors of the church have been Dr. Stephens, 1840–46; Lewis Jansen, 1853; J. G. Jacobs, 1855; J. T. Pickett, 1858–60; W. C. Gray, 1860–81; W. G. Davenport, 1881–85. At present the church is without a rector. The number of communicants is about sixty.

In May, 1872, E. A. McNeal, L. Bills, R. L. Lightfoot and A. T. McNeal were appointed a permanent committee to contract for grounds and to erect a school building for St. James Hall Female School as contemplated by the vestry; the school to be owned by the Episcopal Church but under the immediate control of the vestry of the church at Bolivar. A subscription paper was started and amounts ranging from $25 to $1 were subscribed. About $10,000 was thus secured in a short time. A very beautiful site containing between fifteen and twenty acres was secured and the work of erection begun without delay. The specifications of the building were furnished by the architect, James B. Crook of Memphis. By a report of the building, executive and financial committee in August, 1875, it appears the work was entirely completed and the building free from debt. The school opened in 1873. Right Rev. C. T. Quintard, D. D., LL. D., bishop of Tennessee, is patron and visitor. The school has been in annual session since its opening and is well patronized. The buildings are well furnished and are most delightfully situated. The school work is under control of Miss H. L. Totten.

FAYETTE COUNTY.

Maj. Samuel J. Alexander, an influential farmer and merchant of Macon, Fayette Co., Tenn., was born in Henderson County December 1, 1833, and is the son of John M. and Cynthia (Williamson) Alexander, both natives of Mecklenberg County, N. C. The father was of Scotch-Irish descent, the mother was of German. The father was born December 16, 1810, and died at our subject's home May 10, 1877. The mother was born December 20, 1815, and died June 26, 1856. They married in North Carolina May 5, 1831. In early life they moved to Henderson County, Tenn., but not being satisfied there, they moved to Fayette County two years later, and settled eleven miles west of Somerville, where the father engaged in farming; he was a consistent member of the Cumberland Presbyterian Church up to the time his wife died, when for convenience he joined the Methodist Church. Our subject was the oldest of six children. He was educated at Macon Masonic College, and after leaving college was salesman for the firm of Dougan & White, at Macon, for two years, then bought Mr. White's interest, and from then until now has continued the business, excepting the years he was in the war. Mr. Alexander began life without means, but by his energy and business tact has acquired a comfortable estate, owning in addition to a half interest in the $4,000 stock of goods, over 4,000 acres of land in Fayette County and $2,000 worth of stock in the Vanderbilt Insurance Company of Memphis, and $550 in the Memphis & Charleston Railroad Company. Mr. Alexander has recently erected an elegant residence in Macon; it is the best finished house in the county. October 20, 1858, he married Miss Mollie W. Towles, who was born in Virginia, June 12, 1841. They have no children except an adopted daughter, who is a granddaughter of the Rev. T. L. Boswell, D. D., of the Memphis Conference. In the summer of 1862 he went into the Confederate Army as private, but was soon promoted to major and commissary of subsistence, and served in this capacity until the war closed. He is a sound Democrat, and a very prominent member of the Methodist Episcopal Church South, and contributes very liberally to its support. Mrs. Alexander is a member of the Missionary Baptist Church, and is a woman of deep piety. Mr. Alexander is regarded as one of the most useful citizens of Fayette County.

Moses L. Anderson, a well known and enterprising citizen of La Grange, Fayette Co., Tenn., was born in this county, July 29, 1838, and is a son of Joel and Lena G. (Roberts) Anderson. The father was born in Halifax County, Va., in 1793, and died in Fayette County, July, 1841. The mother was born in Chesterfield County, Va., in 1804, and died near La Grange in 1871. They were married in Fayette County, Tenn., July 29, 1837. The father in 1835 established a foundry at La Grange, but the last years of his life were spent in farming. Politically he was a Whig and a consistent member of the Methodist Church; the mother was Missionary Baptist. Our subject was an only child by his father's second marriage; he had fine educational advantages, and attended school one year at the University of Virginia, and at the time the La Grange College was established, he spent two years in it, and after completing his education, he turned his attention to agricultural pursuits. In 1860 he bought a farm three miles northwest of La Grange, where he lived until 1878, when he moved to La Grange, but has never sold any of his land. For twenty-five years Mr. Anderson has been one of the leading citizens of Fayette County and owns 2,000 acres of land in Fayette County and in Denton County, Miss., and an extensive foundry at La Grange with a large manufacturing department attached, of cast plows, and in connection with the foundry building a steam cotton-gin and a grist-mill valued at $5,000. March 31, 1870, Mr. Anderson married Miss Maria B.

Smith, who was born in Marshall County, Miss., July 15, 1849, and to this union one son and four daughters have been born. Mr. and Mrs. Anderson are worthy members of the Missionary Baptist Church and contribute liberally to its support. He is a Democrat and a man who does a great deal to advance the interests of his country.

Dr. Benjamin F. Baird, a physician of Fayette County, was born in the county April 27, 1836, and is a son of Capt. Charles and Nancy (Robards) Baird, both natives of Robertson County, Tenn., and of Scotch-Irish descent coming from the house of Stuarts. The father was born in 1796 and died in Fayette County in 1871. The mother was born in 1814 and died in 1867. The parents married in Robertson County. In 1832 they moved to Fayette County and settled in the Fifteenth District, twelve miles south of Somerville, where they spent the rest of their lives. The father engaged in agricultural pursuits all of his life. For a number of years he was captain of the State militia. He was a cultivated man and taught school for seven years when first grown; he was a kind, upright man, a loyal Democrat and with his wife a member of the Primitive Baptist Church. Dr. B. F. Baird was the fourth of eight children; after receiving a good education in the fall of 1854 he took his first course of lectures at the Memphis Medical College, then returned home and practiced a year, and then returned to the college and graduated in the spring of 1856, and located in Fayette County near his old home, where he soon built up a large practice and was regarded as one of the leading physicians of the county. In 1859 he went to Arkansas and located in Dallas County near Tulip where he practiced medicine for three years, then moved his family back to Fayette County and he entered the Confederate Army as surgeon of the Fifteenth Tennessee Regiment of Cavalry in Forrest's command and served until the war closed. In 1865 he resumed his practice in Fayette County. In October, 1878, he moved to Hickory Valley, a little town in Hardeman County, and continued the practice of medicine until 1885, when he retured to the Fifteenth District in Fayette County where he now lives. Dr. Baird is a successful and eminent physician; he owns 350 acres of land in Fayette and Hardeman Counties. Dr. Baird has been married twice, first to Julia Mitchell, born in North Carolina in 1840 and died in Fayette County September 25, 1876; they were married November 27, 1859, and January 10, 1877, he married Julia Eubank, born in Hardeman County November 13, 1860. Eight sons were born to the first marriage—three are dead—and two sons and a daughter were born to the second marriage; the two sons died. Dr. Baird is a Democrat, and with his wife holds membership with the Medodist Episcopal

Church South; the first wife also belonged to that church. He ranks as one of the substantial, influential citizens of Fayette County.

James W. Bass, citizen and farmer of Hardeman County, was born in Rutherford County, Tenn., July 4, 1848, and is a son of Thomas W. and Nannie P. (Avent) Bass. The father was born in 1822, and is now living in Rutherford County near Murfreesboro. The mother is several years younger than her husband, and is still living. In 1852, they moved to West Tennessee and lived until the war, dividing the time in Madison, Gibson and Hardeman Counties. The father entered the Confederate Army in 1862, in the Twelfth Tennessee Regiment of Cavalry, and was quartermaster or foragemaster of the regiment until the war closed; was captured and kept for several months a prisoner at Alton, Ill. Two years after the war he moved his family back to Rutherford County, where he has since lived and farmed. With his wife he belongs to the Methodist Episcopal Church South. Our subject is the second of ten children; he had a good education, and when eight years old moved with his parents to Hardeman County and has since made it his home. After finishing school he sold goods for various parties in New Castle for eight years, and in 1875 he established, with Thomas Polk, a store in New Castle and was in the mercantile business for two years. In 1876 he purchased the farm where he now lives, and moved to it in 1879. Mr. Bass owns now over 1,600 acres of land in Hardeman County and in Arkansas. December 20, 1874, he married Miss Olivia B. Kent, born in Lee County, Ark., November 26, 1856. They have one daughter born December 7, 1879. Our subject is a Democrat, and in August, 1882, was elected magistrate and still holds the office; he is not a church member; his wife is a Roman Catholic. He is an honest man and a kind neighbor, and exerts an influence for good in his county.

George W. Bowling, one of the prominent planters of Marshall County, Miss., was born in Madison County, Ala., near Hazel Green, March 21, 1818. He is a son of Alexander and Elizabeth (Worthy) Bowling. The father was born in Virginia in 1790 and died in Lawrence County, Ala., January 1, 1843. The mother was born in 1790, in Chester County, S. C., and died in Lawrence County, Ala., in 1880. They moved to Alabama in 1816. The father and mother were both members of the Missionary Baptist Church, and he was a most successful farmer. Our subject was the sixth child of eleven children. After finishing his education he commenced farming. In 1849 he moved to Marshall County, Miss., bought land there and has since made it his home, and before the war was one of the most extensive cotton planters in the county, owning a great many slaves;

his losses by the war were enormous, his slaves being freed, and the Federal soldiers burned a large quantity of cotton for him, but since then he has acquired a large estate by his energy and perseverance and owns in Fayette County and in Marshall County, Miss., over 1,600 acres of land. Mr. Bowling has been married three times, first to Miss Elizabeth Walton, and by this marriage had five children; the mother died in 1856; he then married Mrs. Felicia O. Key whose maiden name was Bowers; they had three children, and she died November 3, 1869, and our subject married Miss Laura Brooks who died July 6, 1880, and two children were born to this marriage. Of the ten children to the three marriages five are living. Mr. Bowling is a Democrat. He is not a church member but is in sympathy with the Missionary Baptist Church and a man of fine moral character. He is a resident of Marshall County, Miss.

Wilson L. Burnett, an active farmer of Fayette County, Tenn., was born in Iredell County, N. C., September 27, 1832, and is a son of Jeremiah and Mary F. (Ellis) Burnett. The father was a native of Spartanburg County, S. C., and the mother of Iredell County, N. C., both of Scotch-Irish descent. The father was born September 18, 1807, and is now a resident of Fayette County. The mother was born January 20, 1810; they were married in 1831 in North Carolina, and moved to Tennessee in 1849, settling nine miles south of Somerville. The father was a successful farmer, and with his wife a consistent member of the Methodist Episcopal Church South. Our subject is the oldest of ten children. He was quite young when he moved to Fayette County with his parents, and has since then made it his home. In 1857 his father gave him the farm where he now lives, and he has since added to it, owning now over 800 acres of good land in Fayette County and 960 acres in Pontotoc County, Miss. December 22, 1852, he married Miss Ellen J. Tomlinson, born in Iredell County, N. C., in 1834. Fourteen children were born to this marriage—seven sons and seven daughters—one son and four daughters are dead. Mr. Burnett has always been a true Democrat, and with his wife and five children belongs to the Methodist Church and freely responds to all calls for money for the church or for charity. In August, 1862, he entered the Confederate Army; was first in Outlaw's battalion, but soon joined Gen. Forrest's forces in the Fourteenth Tennessee Regiment of Cavalry, the colonel being Col. Jack Neely. Mr. Burnett remained until the battle of Franklin, Tenn., and was in many battles. In 1864, after an absence of over two years, he was paroled at Memphis and took the oath of allegiance, then returned home and resumed farming. He is a good neighbor, an upright man, liked and trusted by all.

Joshua E. Burnett, farmer and stock raiser of Fayette County, was borne in Iredell County, N. C., August 17, 1834, and is a son of Jeremiah and Mary (Ellis) Burnett. The father was born in South Carolina, September 18, 1807, and is now a resident of Fayette County, aged seventy-nine years. The mother was born in North Carolina January 20, 1810, and is now seventy-six years old. They moved to Tennessee in 1849 and settled twelve miles south of Somerville; two years later they moved three miles further north where they have since lived. The father has always been a farmer; he is a Democrat, and both parents are members of the Methodist Episcopal Church South. December 22, 1886, this aged couple celebrated their golden wedding, and over 500 relatives and friends were present. Our subject is the second born of ten children; after finishing his education he commenced farming. In the spring of 1861 he entered the Confederate Army, and enlisted in Company B, Thirteenth Tennessee Regiment, known as the "Macon Grays." Joseph Granbery was captain and John V. Wright, first colonel. Our subject was changed into Cheatham's division and remained in service until the end, though a year before the war closed he was changed to Forrest's cavalry; he was in several hard-fought battles: Belmont Mo., Shiloh, Richmond and Perryville, Ky., Murfreesboro, Chickamauga and Missionary Ridge; he was surrendered at Memphis in the spring of 1865 and returned home after an absence of four years and resumed farming. March 22, 1865, he married Miss Adelia Garvin, born in Fayette County, June 5, 1841. Five sons and four daughters have been born to them; two sons are dead. In 1866 with the assistance of his father he bought the farm where he now lives, but has greatly increased it, now owning over 1,100 acres of good land in Fayette County. Mr. Burnett is a Democrat, and with his wife and three children belongs to the Methodist Episcopal Church South. He is a generous man and one of strict integrity.

Dr. William J. Cannon, one of the pioneer practicing physicians of Fayette County, and one of its most influential and enterprising citizens, was born August 7, 1827, in Raleigh, N. C., and is of a family of three sons and three daughters, born to Robert and Ann T. (Hill) Cannon, who were natives of Pitt and Franklin Counties, N. C. Our subject and two sisters alone surviving. The parents moved to Raleigh, N. C., soon after their marriage in Franklin County, and the father was a most successful merchant there until his death in 1883. The mother afterward married Col. Samuel B. Sprouell; to this union one daughter was born, who died. The mother died in 1844. In 1842 Dr. Cannon entered

Chapel Hill College, in North Carolina, and remained there until after his mother's death, then moved to Fayette County, Tenn., and in 1847 began the study of medicine in Somerville. In 1849 he entered the Medical University of Pennsylvania, and attended three full courses of lectures, then commenced the practice of medicine at Jacksonport, Jackson Co., Ark., where he remained until 1884, when he married Catharine Wirt, of Fayette County, and soon after located in Fayette County, at his present residence, which consists of 1,800 acres of fine land nine miles north of the county seat. Dr. Cannon has splendidly improved the place, which is under a fine state of cultivation. He has surrounded his family with the numerous comforts that wealth affords and a cultivated taste suggests, having been very successful professionally and financially. He is extensively known and highly esteemed in Fayette and adjoining counties. By his marriage he had two sons and four daughters; only two daughters are living. Politically Dr. Cannon is a Democrat, he is also a member of the I. O. O. F., and with his family belongs to the Episcopal Church.

Stephen G. Carnes, a farmer of Fayette County, was born in Hardeman County, Tenn., August 3, 1829, and with two sisters constitutes the surviving members of a family of two sons and four daughters, born to David B. and Mary (Gracy) Carnes, natives of North Carolina; both came to Tennessee when young and married in Hardeman County, where they farmed until the father died in 1842; the mother died in the same county in 1875. The father, previous to this marriage, had married in North Carolina a Miss Scott, and to them three sons and three daughters were born, two daughters living. This wife died in 1827. Our subject's mother had also been married before her marriage to Mr. Carnes, to Samuel Steel, by whom she had one son and two daughters, one of each living. Our subject remained at home until the war, but had purchased a farm which he managed in addition to assisting at the home place. He entered the Ninth Tennessee Infantry of the Confederate Army, where he was first lieutenant a year, then returned home a year and joined Henderson's scouts until the war closed, when he returned to the old home place, and in 1869 married Miss Bettie Cooper, and they have had two sons, Henry C. and John B. In 1872 he moved near Somerville, and in 1880 to his present farm consisting of 300 acres, well improved and located. He also owns in Fayette County another tract of 160 acres. Mr. Carnes is a Cumberland Presbyterian; Mrs. Carnes, an Episcopalian. He is also a member of the F. & A. M., the K. of H. and K. & L. of H. and an ardent Democrat. Mr. Carnes is a man of fine social standing, and possesses many sterling qualities that are justly appreciated by the community in which he lives.

Marcus L. Chambers, farmer and merchant of Chambersville, Fayette County, was born in Robertson County, Tenn., February 28, 1833, and is a son of Dr. Gools B. and Rebecca (Gordon) Chambers, natives of Halifax County, Va., and Robertson County, Tenn. The father was born in 1802 and died in Fayette County in 1881. The mother was born in 1805 and died in Fayette County in 1878. They were married in Robertson County, Tenn., in 1823, and in 1836 moved to Fayette County and settled in the Fifteenth District nine miles north of Somerville, where they lived until they died. In early life the father was engaged in agricultural pursuits. In 1844 he entered the Botanical Medical College at Memphis Tenn., and after receiving his diploma returned home and was a successful practicing physician for seventeen years in Fayette County. In 1862 he retired from practice and resumed farming. Both parents were members of the Primitive Baptist Church. Our subject was the fifth of fourteen children. He received a good education, then gave his time exclusively to farming until 1884, when he established a store at Chambersville, and is now in the mercantile business in connection with farming, and besides a $4,000 stock of goods he owns 800 acres of land in Fayette County and is now erecting a handsome and unique residence in Chambersville. Mr. Chambers has been married twice; first, October 25, 1859, to Miss Fannie E. Wade, who was born in Virginia in 1840 and died in January, 1864. Three children were born to them, one dead. He married again the same year Miss Mary E. Curls, born in Mississippi in 1848, and by this marriage had eleven children—five sons and six daughters; one son and two daughters are dead. Politically Mr. Chambers is a Democrat. He does not belong to any church; his first wife was a Methodist. He is an enterprising business man and in every respect a valuable citizen.

Elder Daniel G. Chambers, a well known minister of the Primitive Baptist Church, engaged in farming in Fayette County, was born in Robertson County, Tenn., January 5, 1835, and is a son of Gools B. and Rebecca (Gordon) Chambers. The father was born in Halifax County, Va., August 11, 1802, being of English descent, and died in Fayette County, Tenn., June 21, 1881. The mother was born in Robertson County, Tenn., April 13, 1805, and was of Scotch-Irish descent and died in Fayette County March 26, 1878. They married in Robertson County in 1823. In 1836 they moved to Fayette County and settled in the Fifteenth District, nine miles east of Somerville. In early life the father gave his time to farming. In 1844 he attended the Botanical Medical College at Memphis, Tenn., and after receiving his diploma he returned to Fayette County and practiced medicine there for seventeen years. In

1862 he retired from the practice and again gave his time to farming. They were both Primitive Baptists. Our subject was the seventh of thirteen children; he had the advantage of a good education; he was still an infant when his parents moved to Fayette County and has always made it his home. In 1860 Mr. Chambers purchased a farm and has been a most enterprising farmer, now owning more than 500 acres of land in Fayette County. October 3, 1859, he married Miss Mary F. Taylor, a cultured lady, born in Fayette County. One son and three daughters were born to them: Martha F., born May 1, 1860; Magaret L., born October 5, 1862; Thomas G., born August 1, 1865, and Amanda C., born May 27, 1867. In early life Mr. Chambers professed religion and for seven or eight years past has been a popular preacher in the Primitive Baptist Church. He is a good man and a most valuable citizen.

Robert N. Christian was born in Mississippi August 31, 1842, and is the son of Robert N. and Caroline (Suther) Christian, natives of North Carolina. Our subject received a fair education and was engaged in steamboating until the breaking out of the war. At that time he entered the Confederate service as a private in the One Hundred and Fifty-fourth Tennessee Regiment and was afterward transferred to the Thirty-fourth Mississippi Regiment, where he remained till the close of the war. He participated in all of the principal battles and was wounded five different times. At the close of the war he came to Somerville and devoted his time and attention to mercantile pursuits, being engaged in that capacity ever since. He started in life with a fair education, a pair of stout arms and a willing heart. He is now considered one of the substantial men of Somerville. August 1, 1866, he married Valeria F. Shaw, daughter of A. M. and Ann L. Shaw of Somerville. To this union were born nine children—five sons and four daughters: Annie L., Alsey B., Eddie L., Louis, Robert W., Mary E., Carrie V., Mary W. and Joe D. Mr. Christian is a Democrat in politics.

James A. Clay, a farmer of Fayette County, was born in Gibson County, Tenn., January 12, 1837 and is a son of John W. and Sarah M. (McCree) Clay. The father was born in Halifax County, Va., October 24, 1813, and died in Fayette County June 9, 1859. The mother was born in Iredell County, N. C., June 5, 1816, and died in Fayette County July 29, 1866. They married January 26, 1836, in Rutherford County, Tenn., and moved from Middle Tennessee to Gibson County, but two years later moved to Fayette County and settled at La Grange, where they lived until they died. They were both strict members of the Methodist Church. Our subject was the oldest of ten children; he was educated at

La Grange College. His parents moved to the county when he was a child and he has since lived in it. He began farming quite young. November 20, 1867, he married Miss Anna J. Cartwright, a native of Fayette County, born February 11, 1844. They have had three children: Maggie L., born June 11, 1869; Annie O., born March 12, 1871, and James N., born January 7, 1874. December, 1869, he purchased the farm where he now lives, fifteen miles southwest of Somerville, and now owns 800 acres of land in Fayette County clear of all incumbrances. Politically Mr. Clay is an Independent, but is usually in sympathy with the Democratic party. He does not belong to any church but is by preference a Methodist. Mrs. Clay and all of the children belong to the Methodist Church. Mr. Clay holds the respect and confidence of the community and is a man of unblemished integrity.

Samuel I. Crawford, a prominent farmer of Fayette County, is a native of the county, born July 4, 1852, and is the son of William M. and Rachel (Walker) Crawford, both natives of North Carolina. The father was born September 27, 1808, and died in Fayette County, September 15, 1878; the mother was born November 20, 1818, and is still living. They were married in 1838 in North Carolina, and in 1849 moved to Fayette County, Tenn., four miles southwest of Somerville and remained a year, then moved to the Eighth District seven miles southwest of Somerville, and lived there seventeen years. In 1868 they moved to Williston, where the father died of yellow fever in 1878; he was an exemplary member of the Methodist Episcopal Church South, as the mother is also. Our subject is the youngest of four children; he was chiefly educated at the Bingham Military School in Orange County, N. C. After completing his education he kept books for ten years for W. H. Crawford & Co. at Williston. In 1877 he purchased a farm near Williston and has since given his time to farming, meeting with marked success. February 3, 1875, he married Miss Josie Phillips, a native of Fayette County and a niece of the well known Dr. J. W. Phillips of Williston. She was born May 18, 1855, and by this marriage they have had five children, all boys. Mr. Crawford is a Democrat and manifests a deep interest in the party. He is a member of the Methodist Episcopal Church South, and Mrs. Crawford, who is a woman of deep piety, is a worthy member of the Missionary Baptist Church. Mr. Crawford is an honest man of sound judgment and kind heart.

J. H. Cocke, a merchant at Lambert, was born in January, 1845, in Fayette County, being one of two sons born to Thomas R. and Mary J. (Jones) Cocke, the brother residing at Somerville. The father was born in Virginia and the mother in Alabama; they married in Fayette County and he practiced law at La Grange, where the mother died in

October, 1845, and in the fall of same year he married Laura J. Winston, who was also a native of Alabama. They had two sons and nine daughters, eight daughters living. The father resided at La Grange until 1848, then moved to Somerville, and retired from the practice of law, and died in 1883. He was chairman of the county court from 1865 until his death. J. H. Cocke remained at home until 1864, then went into the Confederate Army, in the Fourteenth Tennessee Cavalry under Forrest, and served until the war closed, when he accepted a clerkship at Memphis, then returned to Somerville and farmed until 1883, when he commenced merchandising at Lambert, his stock of goods being valued at $2,500. May, 1870, he married Mary G. Cocke, of Fayette County, and has had four sons and four daughters, three sons and two daughters living. Mr. Cocke is a Democrat. In 1876 he was elected justice of the peace and still holds the office. He is regarded as a man of strict integrity and good business capacity.

John S. R. Cowan, a merchant of Moscow, Tenn., was born in Fayette County, October 16, 1846, and is a son of Alexander F. and Rebecca (Bull) Cowan. The father was a native of Rowan County, N. C., born in 1822 and died in Marshall County, Miss., January 25, 1855. The mother was born in Dickson County, Tenn., in 1829, and died in Marshall County, Miss., in July, 1862. They married in Fayette County in 1845, and soon after settled in District No. 2, eight miles northeast of Somerville, where they lived five years, then moved to Byhalia, Marshall Co., Miss., and spent four years, when they moved to Early Grove, in the same county, and spent the rest of their lives. The father was a successful carriage-maker by trade, and a Democrat in politics and a consistent member of the Episcopal Church, and the mother also belonged to that church. Our subject was the oldest of six children, and is now the only one living. He secured a good education at Wilson Hall Academy, in Marshall County, Miss., then engaged in the printing business at Holly Springs, Miss., in the office of the *Southern Herald*, conducted by Col. Thomas A. Falconer, and was associated in business with the late distinguished Col. Kimlock Falconer, a son of Thomas A. Falconer. Mr. Cowan spent three years in this business. In the spring of 1862 he entered the Confederate Army, and although so young remained until the war closed. His company was known as Goodman's Guards and formed a part of Samuel Benton's Thirty-fourth Mississippi Regiment. Thomas A. Falconer was captain of the regiment; Mr. Cowan participated in the battles of Farmington, Miss., Perryville, Ky., Chickamauga, and Lookout Mountain. The latter is known as the "battle of the clouds," and our subject was captured in the Walthall's brigade, and was immediately sent to Rock Island, Ill., via Nashville, Tenn., and was at the Maxwell House when the catastrophe of the stairway occurred, but sustained no serious damage. He was held a prisoner at Rock Island until the summer of 1865, then returned to Fayette County after an absence of three years. In 1866-67 he engaged in farming; in 1868 he established a store at Moscow, commencing with very little money but by good management, he now owns a stock valued at $7,000 several town lots at Moscow, and 500 acres of land in Arkansas. February 10, 1869, he married Miss Elizabeth A. C. Thompson, who was born in Fayette County in 1850. Six children were born to this marriage—five sons and a daughter—four are dead. Walter B., aged fifteen, and Lulie, aged seven, are living. Mr. Cowan is a Democrat, and while he is not connected with any church, is a strictly moral man. His wife died about three years ago. September, 1886, he was the Democratic nominee to represent Fayette County in the Legislature but was defeated by the Republican candidate by 150 votes, the county having a Republican majority of 1,500 votes, and to reduce the majority so much speaks well for the esteem and popularity of Mr. Cowan, and his standing in the county.

William P. Cowan, an enterprising merchant of La Grange, Fayette Co., Tenn., was born February 3, 1852, in Marshall County, Miss., and is a son of David P. and Lugenia (Bull) Cowan. The father was born in North Carolina in 1811 and died in Marshall County, Miss., in 1854. The mother was born in Middle Tennessee about 1834, and is still living with our subject, who was the only child. William P. Cowan, by his own efforts, secured a good education; then spent twelve years in farming, and then went into partnership with his cousin, John S. R. Cowan, of Moscow, in Fayette County, in the grocery business at La Grange, and continued for nine years. In 1882 he commenced the dry goods business in partnership with his brother-in-law, J. B. Sims, and since then has been a leading merchant of the place. They carry a stock valued at $3,000, and he owns a valuable farm of 450 acres in Fayette County. December 20, 1876, he was married to Miss Onora Sims, a native of South Carolina, born October 15, 1853, and they have had three children; one son died, two daughters are living. Mr. Cowan has never united with any church, though a firm believer in the Christian religion and a man of good morals and strict integrity.

Joseph I. Crossett, a valuable farmer and citizen of Fayette County, Tenn., was born in Chester County, S. C., August 26, 1824, and is a son of Joseph and Mary (Wilson) Crossett, both natives of South Carolina. The father was of Irish descent and born in 1793, and died at Moscow, in Fayette County, April 17, 1837. The mother was born in 1799 and died September 15, 1850, in Fayette County. They married in South Carolina about 1819, and in 1826 moved to Carroll County, Tenn., where they lived seven years. In 1833 they moved to Fayette County and settled in Moscow, where they lived until they died. The father was a successful mechanic, and both parents were worthy members of the Old School Presbyterian Church. Our subject is the third of seven children. By his own efforts he secured a good practical education in his youth. His father died when he was but thirteen years old, and the care of his mother and four sisters devolved upon him. He was but a child when his parents moved to Fayette County, and has always made it his home. He and a younger brother cared for their mother until her death. Mr. Crossett commenced life without any money, and had a hard struggle but, owing to temperate habits and industry, met eventually with flattering success. In the spring of 1850 he bought a farm of 120 acres in the Twelfth District, two miles northwest of Moscow, joining the place where he now lives. In 1866 he was elected magistrate in this district, and held the office for twelve years. Mr. Crossett is a man honored for his integrity and kindness, possessing many noble traits of character. He has never used liquor or tobacco in any form, and has never been at law with his neighbors. He now owns over 700 acres of good land in Fayette County, a cotton-gin, etc. January 14, 1847, he married Miss Arrozene Goodwin, who was born near Huntsville, Ala., May 18, 1821. Four sons and two daughters were born to this union; two sons are dead. Mr. Crossett is a sound Democrat and an influential and worthy member of the Methodist Episcopal Church South. Mrs. Crossett is a Cumberland Presbyterian and three of the children belong to the Methodist Church. In the spring of 1862 Mr. Crossett entered the Confederate Army, in Company H, Thirty-eighth Tennessee Regiment of Infantry, commanded by Col. R. F. Looney. He was made first lieutenant. The regiment was organized at Corinth, Miss., and was engaged in the battle of Shiloh. Soon after this battle Mr. Crossett was taken sick and returned home, receiving a discharge in July, but in November, 1863, he returned to the service, joining Forrest's cavalry, enlisting in Col. Rufus Neely's regiment, where he remained until the war closed. He was made forage-master during Hood's raid at Corinth, and served in this capacity until the close of the war; then returned home and resumed farming.

William I. Davis was born in Montgomery County, N. C., July 3, 1821, and is a son of Young and Sarah (Gatley) Davis. The father was born in North Carolina, October 18, 1800, and the mother in Virginia in the same year. The father died in South Carolina in 1864, the mother in

1866. They married in North Carolina in 1819; in 1849 they moved to South Carolina, where they lived until they died. The father followed the blacksmith's trade in connection with farming. Our subject is the oldest of seven children; by his own efforts he secured a good education. In 1847 he moved to Tennessee and settled in Hardeman County; two years later he moved to Fayette County, and settled ten miles southeast of Somerville, where he lived about twenty-eight years and in 1878 moved to his present farm. Mr. Davis now owns over 900 acres of valuable land in Fayette County. He was married the first time November 29, 1844, to Miss Patience Harris, who died November 20, 1864, leaving eight children. December, 1865, he married Mrs. Pamelia C. (Morris) Snow; no children have been born to this last union. Mr. Davis, his wife and all of the children are members of the Methodist Church. He is a Democrat, and is a man of fine character and unusual energy.

Josiah H. Dortch, attorney at law at Somerville, Tenn., was born in Somerville February 15, 1858, and is the son of Hon. William B. and Lucy W. (Higgason) Dortch, who were natives of North Carolina and Tennessee, and were married May 4, 1856, our subject being the only issue of their marriage. The father was a distinguished lawyer at Somerville and died March 10, 1882. The mother is still living. Josiah H. Dortch attended the Southwestern Presbyterian University at Clarksville, Tenn., and then attended the Vanderbilt University at Nashville and graduated there in 1878. He then practiced law awhile, and afterward became the editor of the Somerville *Falcon*, and was connected with that paper until 1882, when he resumed the practice of law, and since then has been one of the most prominent members of the Somerville bar. In February, 1886, he was appointed circuit court clerk of Fayette County, and filled that office until the expiration of the term September 1, 1886. Mr. Dortch has made a fine reputation as a lawyer of ability, and is unusually well read in his profession for a man of his age. He is a Democrat and takes an active part in politics, being at present chairman of the Democratic Executive Committee of Fayette County. December 3, 1884, he married Lula B., daughter of W. A. and Mary E. Harris of Somerville. Mr. Dortch is a member of the F. &. A. M. and has been secretary of Lodge No. 73, at Somerville for the past seven years, and is one of Somerville's leading citizens.

John A. Farley, citizen and farmer of Fayette County, Tenn., was born in Laurens Co., S. C., August 8, 1808, and was a son of Thompson and Frances (Whitlow) Farley, who were natives of Virginia of English descent. The father was born in 1765 and died in 1850, in Shelby County, Tenn. The mother was born in 1777 and died in South Carolina, February 3, 1826. They had married in South Carolina, in 1804. The father came to Tennessee in 1835 and spent the rest of his life with his two daughters, who were living in the State. He was a successful farmer. Our subject was the third of six children; he received a good education and quite early commenced farming. In the winter of 1844-45 he came to Tennessee and settled in Fayette County, twenty-six miles west of Somerville, and purchased a section of land, and has since resided in the county, and by his own efforts has made a handsome estate, now owning 1,000 acres of land in Fayette and Shelby Counties, and in Marshall County, Miss. March 14, 1837, he married Susan Davis, who was born in Laurens County, S. C., April 26, 1819, and they have six children—two sons and four daughters; one of each is dead. Mr. Farley is a Democrat and a worthy member of the Christian Church as his wife is also. He contributes liberally to the church and all charitable enterprises, and has been a very useful citizen.

J. H. Garnett, a farmer and merchant residing in Fayette County, was born April 12, 1834, in Franklin County, Tenn., and is one of three sons and two daughters born to Eli and Sallie (Robinson) Garnett, our subject and a brother being the only ones living. The father was a native of Virginia, and came to Franklin County, Tenn., when young and married there, the mother being a native of that county. He was in the shoe trade and made that county his home, with the exception of a few years' residence in Missouri, until his death in 1855. The mother died in 1835. When our subject was sixteen years old he was employed by a merchant at Lockensville, Ala., for two years; he then returned to Franklin County, but in a few years moved to Hardeman County, Tenn., and made it his home until the war, when he enlisted in Gen. Forrest's calvary, but owing to bad health was discharged after the battle of Shiloh. After the war Mr. Garnett was for a while employed by a merchant at La Grange. Tenn., and afterward by a Memphis firm. In December, 1869, he married Miss Frances Rutledge of Fayette County, and turned his attention to agricultural pursuits, locating on his present farm of 1,500 acres, on hwich he established a general merchandise store in 1879, chiefly for the convenience of his own plantation, and where the postoffice has recently been established that is called Yum Yum. One son and five daughters were born to his marriage; one daughter died in infancy. Those living are named Minnie, Mamie, Mattie, John H. and Elmer. Mr. Garnett is an F. & A. M. He is a Democrat, and with his family belongs to the Methodist Church. He is one of the prosperous and substantial citizens of Fayette County.

Rev. S. S. Gill, pastor of the Presbyterian Church under the Memphis Presbytery, was born December 5, 1829, in Haywood County, Tenn., and is of a family of seven sons and one daughter born to David and Maria (Scott) Gill. The father was a native of North Carolina and the mother of South Carolina. They came to Tennessee in childhood and were married in Giles County, Tenn., and located at Brownsville, where the father was a house carpenter for seven years; they then moved to Chulohoma, Marshall Co., Miss., where he worked at his trade two years, then located on a farm in same county, where he remained twelve years, and in 1851 located on a farm near Horne Lake, DeSoto Co., Miss., where the mother died, and in a few years after the father moved to Graves County, Ky., where he died in 1879. Our subject graduated at the University of Mississippi in 1854, after completing the preparatory course under John A. Rousseau, near Horne Lake. He then spent three years in the theological seminary at Danville, Ky., and was licensed to preach in the presbytery of northern Mississippi in 1857, and labored in that field until 1860, having been ordained in 1859. In 1860 he moved to Fayette County, taking charge of Hickory Withe and Macon Churches, which he has retained ever since with the exception of an interval of ten years, during which he had other work in place of Macon Church. December 22, 1864, he married James Anna Webb, a native of Somerville, Fayette County, who is a devout member of the Presbyterian Church. In 1878 Mr. Gill located at his present home, consisting of 108 acres one mile north of Hickory Withe. He is a Democrat in politics, and as a minister has greatly endeared himself to the members of his church. Mr. Gill has been an earnest worker in the church and has done a great deal for the town and county, and is a cultured man and a true Christian.

Fred Goosmann, a citizen of Somerville, Tenn., engaged in the jewelry business, was born in Lingen, Germany, July 5, 1852, and is the son of Fred and Mary J. Goosmann, both natives of Germany, but now residents of Cincinnati, Ohio. Our subject was educated in Germany, and has been in the jewelry business from boyhood. In 1866 he immigrated to America and located at Cincinnati, Ohio, remaining there until 1870, when he moved south and settled at Somerville, Tenn., and engaged in his present business. Mr. Goosmann is carrying a large stock of jewelry, clocks, watches, etc., and ranks as one of the correct and substantial business men of Fayette County. December 7, 1875, he was married to Mattie F. Simmons of Somerville, and they have had six children: George F., Jennie C., William H. M., Willie M., Lillie B. and Emma L. Mr. and Mrs. Goosmann are Presbyterians; he is a member of the K. of H., and in politics is a Republican. He is a man of good moral character, and of a kind, generous disposition, and successful as a business man.

James H. Granbery, of Fayette County, was born in Bertie County, N. C., June 6, 1827, and is a son of John and Jane (Frasier) Granbery, both natives of North Carolina. The father's ancestors came from England, and the mother was of Scotch descent. The father was born in 1800 and died in Fayette County in 1873. The mother was born in 1802 and died in the same county in 1846. They married in North Carolina in 1819, and in 1835 moved to Fayette County and settled where Macon now stands, twelve miles southwest of Somerville. They are buried side by side in the family graveyard at Macon. The father was a farmer, and in politics a Whig. Our subject was the fifth of nine children. He secured a good education, then gave his attention to farming. April 19, 1866, he was married to Miss Lou Brown, who was born in Memphis, Tenn., December 4, 1842. She was a niece of the distinguished Dr. R. A. Brown, who was one of the first settlers of Macon and a first cousin to Senator Isham G. Harris, and third cousin to Gen. E. Kirby Smith. Three sons born to this marriage are living: John W. Granbery, born July 8, 1870; Robert D., born November 28, 1873, and Langly, born November 23, 1882. In 1863 Mr. Granbery went into the Confederate service, enlisting in Company B., Twelfth Tennessee Cavalry, and joined Forrest. He was in the battles of Yazoo and Harrisburg, Miss., and Athens and Trussville, Ala. On account of ill health he returned home in the winter of 1865 and did not again join the army. In early life his father gave him a few hundred acres of land. He has increased it to 1,100 acres, and it is part of the most productive land in the county, and is cultivated by tenants, this bringing him a handsome income annually. Mr. Granbery is a true Democrat. He does not belong to any church, but prefers the Presbyterian Church. He is one of the leading citizens of the county, and active in every measure that will advance its interests.

William B. Granbery, M. D., a retired physician residing at Somerville, Tenn., was born in Hertford County, N. C., November 23, 1835, and is the son of John and Jane (Frasier) Granbery, both natives of North Carolina. They moved to Fayette County with our subject in 1835. Dr. Granbery was raised on a farm, and educated chiefly at Macon Masonic College, in Fayette County. In 1855 he commenced the study of medicine under Dr. R. A. Donoho, of Fayette County, and in the fall of 1856 he entered the Medical University at New Orleans, La., and attended one course of lectures, and in 1857 he entered the University of Pennsylvania, at Philadelphia, and graduated from that institution in the spring of 1858. He then commenced the practice of medicine in Fayette County, being constantly engaged with professional duties until 1882, when he retired and moved to Somerville, where he has since been speculating and loaning money, also giving some time to farming. He owns 1,100 acres of valuable and well improved land in Fayette County. Dr. Granbery was very successful as a physician, and has been so in business matters. October 16, 1858, he married Emma J., daughter of Thomas G. and Ann L. Neal, of Fayette County, and they have six children: Anna Cossie, Kate O., Thomas N., William R., Ruby E. and Roy. Mrs. Emma J. Granbery died December 21, 1884, and December 22, 1886, Dr. Granbery married Love O., daughter of N. R. and Elizabeth J. Cartwright, of Fayette County. He is a member of the F. & A. M. and K. of H. In politics he is a Democrat. He is one of the influential and leading citizens of Fayette County.

W. F. Hancock, a merchant of Grand Junction, and citizen of La Grange, Fayette County, was born November 19, 1829, in Hardeman County, Tenn., and is one of eight children born to Robert and Mary K. (Jones) Hancock, our subject; a brother and a sister are still living. The parents were natives of North Carolina, where they married, and in 1820 moved to Fayette County, Tenn., locating twelve miles northeast of La Grange, but in a few years moved to Hardeman County where they lived until they died, with the exception of two years spent in Mississippi. At the time of the father's death in 1841 he was proprietor of a hotel in Bolivar. The mother died in 1865. Our subject remained at home until his father's death, then filled various clerkships, including eight years in Memphis, when the war commenced, and he enlisted as first lieutenant in Forrest's command, but owing to ill health was soon discharged. In 1855 he married Kate M. Mask, a native of Hardeman County, and they had three daughters, all living: Martha C., Sarah L. and Mary B. Their mother died in 1865, and in 1878 Mr. Hancock married Mollie F. Jones; they have four children: William F., Wiley J., Irene and Ida Lee. In January, 1885, he engaged in the mercantile business at Grand Junction under the firm name of Hancock & Hatton; they carry a stock of general merchandise valued at $5,000. Mr. Hancock is a K. of H. and an enthusiastic Democrat. Mrs. Hancock and family are members of the Methodist Church.

James C. Harrell was born in Fayette County, Tenn., October 5, 1839, and is the son of William and Temperance (Barnes) Harrell, both natives of Nash County, N. C. The father was born in 1802 and died in Fayette County, October 20, 1856. The mother was born in 1814 and died in the same county October, 1878. They were both of Irish descent and in early life moved to Fayette County. Our subject was educated at La Grange College, Tennessee, and Broaddus College, Mississippi; then commenced farming which he has continued ever since, except during his service in the Confederate Army. In 1867 he established a store at Rossville, but moved the business to Elba in 1870 and still lives at the old homestead and cultivates the old plantation. March 17, 1859, he married Miss Fannie Mitchell, born April 20, 1843, and they have had eleven children, ten of them living. Mr. Harrell has always been a Democrat, and for several terms has held the office of magistrate. In 1884 he was elected to the Legislature, and was placed on the committees of public schools, railroads, penitentiary, agriculture and public roads. He was a thorough business member and was never absent from his desk. Mr. Harrell is a Royal Arch Mason, a Knight of Honor and a member of the A. O. U. W. He was originally a Baptist, but since 1874 he has been a member of the Christian Church. In 1862 he enlisted as first lieutenant in Company C in Ballentine's regiment, and served with it in Mississippi, Alabama, Georgia and Tennessee, participating under Van Dorn in the battles of Holly Springs, Jackson, Murfreesboro and the Georgia campaign from Dalton to Atlanta, and with Hood from the evacuation at Lovejoy through the battles at Franklin and Nashville and was surrendered at Selma, Ala., under Gen. Frank Armstrong in April, 1865. Mr. Harrell is a quiet, pleasant gentleman of marked force of character, exerting a wide influence in his county and esteemed by all.

Hudson Harris, a well known farmer of Fayette County, Tenn., was born in Anson County, N. C., March 1, 1828, and is the son of Turner and Jane (Webb) Harris, both natives of North Carolina, and of English descent. The father was born in 1807, and died in Fayette County in 1865. The mother was a few years younger and died in the same county in 1846. They married in North Carolina in 1825, and in 1834 settled in Hardeman County, Tenn., and two years later moved to Fayette County and settled sixteen miles southwest of Somerville, where they died. They were both Missionary Baptists, and the father was a farmer all of his life and a Democrat. Our subject was the second of eight children. He was but six years old when his parents moved to Tennessee; he was well educated, and commenced farming at an early age. In 1853 he purchased a farm in Fayette County, and the next year moved to it and has since then been actively engaged in farming and now owns over 400 acres in Fayette County, and a large watermill on the North Fork of Wolf River, a cotton-gin, etc. August 6, 1850, Mr. Harris was married to Jane Williams, who was born in Fayette County, Tenn., January 4, 1833, and they have had five sons and three daughters; one of each has died. Mr. and Mrs. Harris are worthy members of the Missionary Baptist Church. They are useful members of society and stand well in their community.

Charles H. Havens, a prosperous and energetic citizen of Hickory Withe, was born October 22, 1844, in Germany, and is a son of Henry D. Havens, and is one of two sons, both living. The parents were both born and married in Germany. Our subject's mother died when he was an infant. The father afterward married Dora Copeman, and in 1849 came to America and settled in Saline County, Mo., where he remained until he died in 1878. By his last marriage two sons and two daughters were born, all living, and their mother is living in Kansas. Our subject remained at home until sixteen years old, then went to Vernon County, Mo., and in 1860 went to Texas, and at the commencement of the war enlisted in the Seventh Missouri Infantry (Confederate Army) at Little Rock, Ark. He was taken prisoner in 1864 at Waverly, Mo., and held as a prisoner until the spring of 1865, when he was exchanged at Richmond, Va., and at the close of the war located in Shelby County, Tenn., where he engaged in farming and milling in connection with cotton-ginning until 1880, then moved to his present location at Hickory Withe, where he started a grist and cotton-mill, and soon added a saw-mill and planing-mill and has done a large and prosperous business with all. In 1868 Mr. Havens married Matilda Ophelia Teal, a native of Shelby County, Tenn. They have had three sons and five daughters. One son and one daughter died. In politics he is a Democrat. Mr. Havens and family stand well in the community and are greatly esteemed for their good qualities.

Newton A. Holman, of Fayette County, was born in Davie County, N. C., March 2, 1836, and is a son of Wilson and Elizabeth (Turner) Holman, both natives of North Carolina. The father was born in Iredell County February 17, 1810, and died in Itawamba County, Miss., August 17, 1847. The mother was born in Rowan County April 8, 1810, and died in Itawamba County, Miss., March 7, 1846. They married October 25, 1832, in North Carolina, and in 1845 went to Mississippi and settled in Itawamba County. The father was a farmer; he belonged to the Baptist Church, and the mother was an Episcopalian. Our subject was the third of seven children. He was educated at the Olin High School in Iredell County, N. C., then engaged in the mercantile business four years, two years at Salisbury, N. C., and two at Turnersburg, N. C. In 1866 he moved and settled in Fayette County, fourteen miles south of Somerville, and has farmed ever since. Mr. Holman began life in very limited circumstances, but now owns 270 acres of good land in Fayette County. December 22, 1859, he married Miss Sallie E. (Turner), who was born in Iredell County, N. C., August, 1840, and they have had three children—two sons and a daughter. Elizabeth O., born October 8, 1862; Wilfred L., born February 28, 1865, and Luther A., born December 29, 1866. Mr. and Mrs. Holman and their son, Luther A., are consistent members of the Missionary Baptist Church. Mr. Holman is a Democrat, deeply interested in the party. He is a man quiet and unassuming but a true gentleman, holding the confidence of all who know him.

John H. Hook was born in Wayne County, N. C., October 21, 1829, and is a son of Lovard and Sarah (Applewhite) Hook, both natives of North Carolina. The father was born in 1795 and died in Fayette County December, 1844. The mother was born in 1809 and died in 1883. They married in North Carolina in 1827; in 1833 they immigrated to Alabama and three years later moved to Fayette County, sixteen miles southwest of Somerville, where they died. The father was a farmer. Our subject was the oldest of nine children; he was but seven years old when his parents moved to Fayette County and, omitting the years from 1853 to 1857 which he spent in Texas and Kansas, he has since made it his home. After completing his education he commenced farming. In 1867 he came into possession of the old homestead; the original tract contained 300 acres, but by his industry he has increased it to over 800 acres. January 5, 1868, Mr. Hook married Miss Mildred Compton, born in North Carolina May 13, 1845, and died March 6, 1878. One son and three daughters were born to this marriage, one of each dead. They were Lovard E., born August 8, 1869; Ella A., born January 22, 1872; Florence M., born March 7, 1874, and Jessie H., February 16, 1876. Lovard E. died February 24, 1871, and Ella A., August 26, 1872. January 15, 1880, Mr. Hook married Miss Sophia M. Oursler, born in Fayette County February 27, 1851. They have no children. The first wife was a member of the Missionary Baptist Church; our subject and present wife are influential members of the Methodist Church and are of fine social standing.

Uriah A. Irwin, a prosperous merchant at Oakland, Fayette Co., Tenn., was born in that county September 10, 1848, and is the son of William and Nancy (Alexander) Irwin, who were both natives of North Carolina, Mecklenburg County. The father was born in 1812 and died in Fayette County in 1845. The mother was born in 1814 and died in Fayette County in 1876. In 1832 the parents moved to Hardin County, near Savannah, Tenn., but not being satisfied, a year later they moved to Fayette County and settled seven miles southwest of Somerville. The father was always a farmer, in politics a Whig and with his wife belonged to the Associate Reformed Presbyterian Church. Our subject was the youngest of four children and had a good education, being educated at the Macon Masonic College; he then spent a year farming, then in 1868 went to Hickory Withe and for fourteen months engaged in the mercantile business there, when he returned to his farm and gave his time to it for four years, when he accepted a clerkship in the house of Alexander & Bro. for a year, then again commenced farming which he continued until 1875, when he moved to Oakland and went into the mercantile business with his brother, the firm being T. L. Irwin & Bro. Mr. Irwin has been married twice; first to Miss Ida Cleere, a native of Fayette County, born in 1856; this excellent wife died August 16, 1882, leaving a son and a daughter. February 4, 1885, he married Miss Annie A. Anderson, who was born in Virginia in 1859. They have one son. Mr. Irwin is liberal in his political views but gives his support to the Democratic party; he is a consistent member of the Presbyterian Church. He is a correct and enterprising business man and is greatly esteemed for his many good qualities.

A. J. Ivy, a citizen and ex-merchant, of Hickory Withe, Fayette County, was born September 6, 1837, in Halifax County, N. C., and has one brother and three sisters living. The parents were both natives of North Carolina; the father was born in Halifax County, and the mother in Franklin County; they married in Halifax County, and farmed in Franklin County until the year of our subject's birth when they moved to Fayette County, Tenn., locating near Hickory Withe, where they farmed until the father's death in June, 1854. The mother died in February, 1879. In 1861 our subject enlisted in the Confederate Army, in the Seventh Tennessee Cavalry. He was soon promoted to orderly sergeant and served until the war closed. He was in the Georgia campaign, and in the battles of Belmont, Corinth, Nashville and Franklin and many others. After the war he returned home and resumed farming until 1873, when he commenced merchandising at Hickory Withe holding an interest in a stock of goods with A. Weber, successor to Weber & Wilson. In 1885 he sold his interest to R. H. Bone and retired. January, 1867, he married Nancy J. Thompson, and three children have been born: Pearla T., Eliza L. and Charles P. Their mother died June 29, 1877. Mr. Ivy owns two tracts of land, in one 101 acres, and in the other 142 acres. He is a Cumberland Presbyterian and an F. & A. M., and his support is always to the Democratic party.

George W. S. Johnson was born in Iredell County, N. C., November 7, 1822, and is a son of Curtis and Mary (Sharpe) Johnson, both natives of Iredell County, N. C. Our subject is of Scotch-Irish descent. The father was born in 1795 and died in Fayette County in 1858. The mother was born in 1793 and died in same county in 1881; they married in 1817, and in 1835 they moved to Missouri, and in 1837 to Fayette County and settled eight miles southeast of Somerville and lived twelve or fourteen years; then moved seven miles south of Somerville, where they died. Both parents were consistent members of the Methodist Church. Our subject was the third of four children, and after finishing his education commenced farming. In 1845 his wife's father gave him a good farm containing 115 acres; in 1859 he sold it and bought another farm, and now owns 390 acres of the best land in Fayette County. January 9, 1845, he married Miss Mary Stidham, born in Fayette County, March 3, 1825; her father was one of the pioneers of Fayette County. They have no children. Mr. Johnson is not a member of any church, but accepts the Christian faith, and is in every respect a strictly moral man and contributes liberally to the Methodists, his wife being an earnest and influential member of that church, and it being his church by preference. He is a sound Democrat and a man possessing many noble traits of character.

William Johnson was born in Louisa County, Va., June 22, 1824, and is a son of Thomas I. and Martha H. (Cocke) Johnson, both natives of Virginia. The father was born in March, 1800, and died in Fayette County in 1870. The mother was born in May, 1806, and died in 1868. They married in Virginia in 1823; the father was of Scotch descent, the mother, it is thought, of English. In 1838 they moved to Fayette County, locating nineteen miles southwest of Somerville, on Wolf River, in the Eleventh District. The father was always a farmer; both parents were members of the Christian Church. Our subject is the oldest of ten children. He had fine educational advantages, having graduated at the University of Virginia, and after completing his literary studies there, entered the law department and attended one term; then returned home and two years later married Miss Margaret V. Tate, born in Alabama in 1832. Six sons and three daughters were born to them; one son and two daughters are dead. They married May 30, 1848. Mr. Johnson has resided in Fayette County since he was fourteen years of age, with the exception of the time passed in college in Virginia. In 1848 he came into possession of a farm and turned his attention to farming. In 1871 he moved to Macon, on account of the high school for his children, and lived there five years, but running his farm also. In 1876 he moved back to his farm. He now owns over 700 acres of valuable land in Fayette County. In 1858 he was elected magistrate, and has filled the office ever since, except during the war. July 18, 1873, his wife died;

she was a devout member of the Christian Church, though was formerly a Methodist. April 13, 1875, Mr. Johnson married Miss Sarah E. Blain of Fayette County; no children have been born to this marriage. They are both worthy members of the Missionary Baptist Church. Mr. Johnson is a Democrat.

Judge Calvin Jones, an old and prominent citizen of Fayette County, was born in Person County, N. C., July 8, 1810, and is the son of Wilson and Rebecca (McKissack) Jones. He graduated from the University of North Carolina, and in 1831 was elected assistant professor of ancient languages at the University of Alabama and remained there until 1833, when he commenced the study of law, reading under Gov. Aaron V. Brown, of Pulaski, Tenn., and was admitted to the bar in 1835. In 1837 Judge Jones moved to Somerville and practiced law until 1847 when he was elected chancellor of the western division of Tennessee by the Legislature, and filled this office until 1854, when he resigned and resumed the practice of law at Somerville. Judge Jones has been one of the most popular lawyers of Fayette County; he possesses the happy faculty of making friends under all circumstances, and as chancellor was liked by every one. October 15, 1835, he married Mildred, daughter of James and Susan Williamson of North Carolina, and had three sons: Thomas W., Alexander W. and James M. Mr. and Mrs. Jones are members of the Presbyterian Church and he contributes freely of his money to the church and to all charitable objects. He is a member of the F. &. A. M., and politically is a Democrat.

Wiley B. Jones was born in Buckingham County, Va., September 25, 1813, and is a son of Author and Sarah (Baker) Jones, natives of Virginia. The father was of Welsh descent and the mother of Irish. The father was born October 24, 1769, and died near Tuscumbia, Ala., October 24, 1836. The mother was born January 4, 1779, and died in Alabama September 4, 1828. They moved to Alabama in 1817 and settled in Madison County, and in 1836 moved near Tuscumbia where they spent the remainder of their days. They were both devout members of the Baptist Church and the father a most successful farmer, and a Democrat. Wiley B. Jones was the youngest of nine children and the only one living. He was chiefly educated at Tuscumbia, Ala., and at La Grange College in Alabama, when that institution was under the supervision of Bishop Robert Paine of the Methodist Episcopal Church South. After leaving college he farmed during 1832–34, in northern Alabama, and in 1835 moved to Tennessee and settled in Fayette County twelve miles southeast of Somerville, where he lived for thirty-five years, and in 1880 moved to La Grange, but continued to look after his farming interests a few years; at different times in his life he engaged in the mercantile business, but has made farming his chief occupation, and by judicious management now owns over 4,000 acres of land in Tennessee and Arkansas. July 17, 1832, he married Miss Mary O. Bass, born in Rutherford County, Tenn., February 7, 1816. Mrs. Jones and four children are members of the Methodist Church. Mr. Jones is not a church member but accepts the Christian faith. He gives his earnest support to the Democratic party. He is a man of fine social position and esteemed by all.

William Ketchum, farmer and merchant of Oakland, Tenn., was born in Fayette County July 18, 1849, and was the son of Levi and Georgie (Walker) Ketchum. The father was born in Kentucky in 1801, and died in Memphis while under treatment for gout, his home being five miles west of Somerville. He was a most successful farmer. Before the war he was a Whig; he opposed the war but was in sympathy with the South, and he was a consistent member of the Missionary Baptist Church. The mother was born in Fayette County in 1820, and is still living. Our subject is the second of five children, he received a good education and commenced farming at an early age. In 1880 he went into the mercantile business at Somerville, in partnership with a younger brother, and two years later located at Oakland and continued the business in connection with farming. He was united in marriage with Miss Ella Cartwright, born in Fayette County, February 16, 1853, and they have had three sons and a daughter; the latter died April 7, 1873. The others were born as follows: Lucile W., October 25, 1872; Morgan C., February 2, 1874; Adrian W., December 3, 1877, and Leon N., April 22, 1883. Mr. Ketchum is a Democrat and manifests a deep interest in the success of his party. Mr. and Mrs. Ketchum are both prominent members of the Methodist Church, and of the social circle of Oakland.

William A. Koonce, sheriff of Fayette County, was born in Somerville, Fayette Co., Tenn., May 12, 1840, and is the son of J. and Mary (Crook) Koonce, natives of Alabama and South Carolina respectively. The father was one of the first settlers of Somerville, and about 1832 he was elected county court clerk of Fayette County, Tenn., and served until 1858. He then moved with his family to St. Francis County, Ark., where he died in 1867. His wife died in 1876. Our subject was educated at Somerville, and in 1858 moved to Arkansas and engaged in agricultural pursuits until the breaking out of the war. He then enlisted as a private in the Third Confederate Cavalry, Col. J. H. McGehee commanding, and in 1863 was made quartermaster of the regiment and served as such until the surrender. After the war he engaged in agricultural pursuits in Arkansas, and was thus engaged until 1868, when he came back to Tennessee and entered into the mercantile business at Stanton in Haywood County, remaining there until 1879, when he moved to Somerville and was engaged in no permanent business until 1886, when he was elected sheriff of Fayette County. December 1, 1860, he married Laura R. Glasscock, daughter of Katherine (Gregory) Glasscock, of Arkansas. To this union was born one son December 1, 1861, and died in January of the next year. Mr. Koonce is a Democrat in politics, a Mason, a K. of H. and he and Mrs. Koonce are members of the Baptist Church.

L. B. Lamb, a farmer residing near Lambert, Fayette Co., Tenn., was born in July, 1839, in Shelby County, Tenn., and is one of two sons and a daughter born to Paschal and Sarah (Osborn) Lamb, and is the only one now living. The father was a native of Alabama and came to Shelby County, Tenn., when young, and married there, his wife being a native of South Carolina. The father farmed in Shelby County until his death in 1840. The mother afterward married Jesse Henson and lived in Arkansas until his death, when she returned to Fayette County, where she died in 1877. By her marriage to Mr. Henson she had seven children, two living. L. B. Lamb remained at home until seventeen years old, then worked for a relation in Arkansas two years, receiving for his services a bridle, saddle and horse; he was then in the mercantile business for a year at Jonesboro, Ark., and then returned to Fayette County, and in 1861 he went into the Confederate Army in the Fifty-First Tennessee Infantry, and was taken prisoner at Fort Donelson and held five months, when he escaped and walked home. In 1865 he married Martha V. Douglass, a native of Fayette County, and they farmed in Shelby County until her death in 1867. Two children were born to them, but they died in infancy. Mr. Lamb after this located at Lambert, and was a merchant there until 1881, when he moved to a farm near Galway, where he remained until 1886, then located at his present home, a tract of 800 acres, where in 1885 he had erected a saw-mill and cotton-gin. October 25, 1875, he married Mrs. A. E. Cocke, who has a son, Allen, living. To this union four sons have been born, all living: Levy Leroy, Robt. P., Lowell and Cleveland. Mr. and Mrs. Lamb and family are all Cumberland Presbyterians. In politics he is a Democrat. He is a man of energy and force of character.

Hon. Abner D. Lewis, register of Fayette County, was born in Charlotte County, Va., March 1, 1831, and is the son of Corbin and Nancy (Dobbs) Lewis, natives of Virginia. Our subject was brought to Madison

County, Ala., by his parents when quite small and was raised on the farm. He secured his education at Huntsville, Ala. In 1851 he commenced the study of medicine with Dr. D. Wharton, of Madison County, Ala., and in the same year entered the medical college at Richmond, Va. He attended one course of lectures at that place, and in 1854 graduated from the Richmond Virginia College, an excellent institution. He then commenced practicing his profession at Richmond, Va., and remained there until 1856, when he moved to Tennessee and located at La Grange Fayette County. He remained there practicing his profession until 1858, when he went to Arkansas and engaged in agricultural pursuits and speculating in lands in both Tennessee and Arkansas until 1865, when he turned his attention to mercantile pursuits. In 1876 he was elected to the State Legislature from Fayette County, and held that office three terms (until 1882). He was then elected postmaster at La Grange, and held this office until 1884. He was a partner of the firm of J. W. Dyer & Co. during this time, and during the same year turned his attention to the mercantile business again. He followed this occupation till 1886, when he was elected register of Fayette County. May 5, 1857, he was married to Sarah E. A. Parham, daughter of William S. and Sarah Rives, natives of Virginia. She died November 3, 1874, leaving a family of four children: E. E., Sarah E., Richard H. and Charley. In 1881 Mr. Lewis married Mattie C. McNamee, daughter of C. and Emily McNamee, of Fayette County. They have two children by this union, Kathleen and Elton. Mr. Lewis is a Republican in politics; a member of the Masonic fraternity, also of the I. O. O. F., and he and Mrs. Lewis are members of the Methodist Episcopal Church.

Thomas G. McClellan, trustee of Fayette County, is of Scotch-Irish descent, and was born in Jonesboro, Tenn., March 13, 1825, and is the son of Isaac B. and Margaret R. (Grier) McClellan, natives of Virginia and Pennsylvania. Our subject came with his parents to Somerville in 1826, and was raised and educated at this place. From 1840 to 1865 he was in the mercantile business, but was then appointed clerk and master of the chancery court at Somerville, and retained the office until 1870. Mr. McClellan then engaged in the mercantile business for six years, when he was elected tax collector of Fayette County; and when the offices of tax collector and trustee were consolidated in August, 1876, he was elected trustee, and still holds the office, having been re-elected seven times, having given satisfaction as an officer and being highly esteemed as a man. He has been quite successful in all of his business enterprises. In 1837 he joined the Methodist Episcopal Church, and is a strictly moral man. August 28, 1848, Mr. McClellan married Fannie E., daughter of Charles B. and Martha (Old) Porter, and they have four children: Mattie B., Fannie M., Mollie L. and Thomas G. Politically Mr. McClellan is a Democrat, and he is a member of the F. & A. M.

S. A. Miller, a farmer and old resident of the Third District of Fayette County, was born in 1823 in Virginia, and was one of eight children, six of whom are living. The parents were Simon and Martha (Rivers) Miller, both natives of Virginia. The father was born in 1790, and moved to Fayette County in 1833, being among the early and prominent citizens of the county, a farmer by occupation, and died in April, 1865. The mother was a few years younger than her husband and died in 1837. S. A. Miller was raised and educated at home. In 1849 he married Miss Lucinda S., daughter of Mathew and Mary (Looney) Rhea, both natives of East Tennessee and early settlers of Fayette County. Prof. Rhea, Mrs. Miller's father, was a teacher in the academy at Somerville for many years, and one of the leading citizens of the county; her mother was a sister of Col. Robert Looney, of Memphis. Mrs. Miller was born in Maury County in 1826. Mr. Miller resides upon the same tract of land that his father settled upon when he moved to Fayette County, and he is one of the most successful farmers in the county, being greatly esteemed by all who know him. In politics is a Democrat, and is a moral, industrious citizen.

Hiram C. Moorman, attorney at law at Somerville, Tenn., was born in Hardeman County, Tenn., January 31, 1842, and is the son of Robert and Martha E. (Morgan) Moorman, who were natives of Virginia and Tennessee. Our subject was raised on a farm. In 1858 he entered Bethel College at McLemoresville, Tenn., where he graduated in 1860 and then commenced the study of law, attending the Cumberland Law School at Lebanon, Tenn., until the war commenced, when he went into the Confederate service as a private in the Thirteenth Tennessee Regiment, and was afterward promoted to first lieutenant, then to captain, and afterward to adjutant-general, and at the close of the war was acting as inspector-general, of Cheatham's division. After the war Mr. Moorman taught school a short time, then resumed the study of law, and was admitted to the bar in 1867, and in 1868 he located at Somerville, Tenn., and is now one of the most popular lawyers in Fayette County, having attained an eminent position in the legal profession. January 19, 1870, Mr. Moorman married Nettie, daughter of Thomas L. and Frances Armstrong of Fayette County, and has had six children, one daughter and five sons: Thomas A., Robert M., Hiram C., Marion R., Annie E. and Frances B. Mr. Moorman is a sound Democrat and a member of the K. of H. He is one of the leading citizens and able lawyers of Somerville.

William D. Munroe, a farmer of Hickory Withe, was born June 18, 1831, in Cumberland County, Va., and is one of three sons and three daughters born to David W. and Mahala C. (Dowdy) Munroe. Our subject, two brothers and a sister are the surviving members of this family. The father was born in Marlboro, Mass., March 22, 1798, and the mother in Cumberland County, Va., May 22, 1806, where they married and followed the tailor's trade until December, 1836, when they came to Fayette County, located on the farm where our subject now resides and owns, and followed farming in connection with their trade, until the father died April 5, 1865. The mother is living with our subject. William D. Munroe remained at home until 1849, then went to Memphis and clerked for a year, then spent four years clerking near Somerville, and in the spring of 1850 bought a half interest in a stock of merchandise at Desha County, Ark., and when the war commenced moved the stock to Brownsville, Ark.; but his father's death caused him to move to Tennessee to be with his mother. In 1862 Mr. Munroe entered the Confederate service, joining the Twelfth Tennessee Cavalry, and a year later was taken prisoner and held several months, was then released and returned home, where he has since remained, excepting three years spent in merchandising in Marshall County, Miss., and two years at Lone Oak, Ark. He owns thirty acres in the home tract, and 180 in another tract in Fayette County. Mr. Munroe has never married; his mother and sister live with him, and they all belong to the Cumberland Presbyterian Church. Politically he is a Democrat, and is an industrious, upright man.

Dr. Robert G. Patterson, a well known physician and influential citizen of Fayette County, was born in Maury County, Tenn., December 22, 1817, and is the son of John T. and Charity (Thornton) Patterson. The father was a native of Kentucky and the mother of Georgia; they married in Maury County, then moved to Fayette County where they died. The father built the first house in Fayette County. In 1819 he visited the county on an exploring tour and in 1820 moved his family and settled nine miles east of where Somerville now stands, and for three or four years he had no neighbors but the Indians, but in a few years he had a good home. He was a blacksmith, and followed his trade in connection with farming. He died July, 1842, and the mother in 1872. Dr. Patterson was the second of five children; he was carefully trained and well educated in the common schools of the county; he was a child when his father moved to Fayette County and has made it since then his home. In 1846 he attended his first course of lectures at the Memphis Medical College, and in 1847 he went to the Botanical Medical College at Cincinnati, Ohio, where he received his diploma in the spring of 1848, then returned to Fayette County and commenced the practice of medicine and in a short time was one of the leading physicians of the county, carrying an extensive practice. For eight years past he has in a great measure retired from the active and laborious practice. Except in his own neighborhood Dr. Patterson has been successful as a business man as well as a physician; he now owns over 4,000 acres of land in Fayette County and 1,000 in Arkansas. He has been married twice, first April 15, 1852, to Miss Cynthia A. Low of Hardeman County. This wife lived twenty-five years and in 1878 he married her younger sister, Mary E. Low, who is still living. They have one daughter, Mary C., born September 7, 1880. Dr. Patterson is a loyal Democrat. He is not connected with any church, but is a temperate, moral man, firmly believing in the Christian religion, and has, as a physician and a kindhearted man, greatly endeared himself to the citizens of his county.

A. L. Pearson, a well known farmer of Fayette County, Tenn., was born in Christian County, Ky., near Hopkinsville, October 24, 1812, and is the son of Samuel and Rebecca (Reader) Pearson, both natives of South Carolina. The father was of English descent, born May 5, 1771, and died in Fayette County, Tenn., September 20, 1856, at the advanced age of eighty-six. The mother was supposed to be of English descent also, and was a few years younger than her husband and died in Christian County, Ky., May 9, 1818. They married in South Carolina December 10, 1797, and moved to Kentucky in 1803. Two years after our subject's mother died, the father married Mrs. Elizabeth (Stanley) Pipkins, and for seventeen years after this marriage remained a citizen of Kentucky. The second wife died July 29, 1833, and three years later the father moved to Fayette County, Tenn., settling twenty miles south of Somerville, where he died. He was by trade a blacksmith, which he followed in connection with farming. He was a Whig in politics, and with our subject's mother belonged to the Primitive Baptist Church. Our subject is the ninth of eleven children. He was still young when his father moved to Fayette County and settled in the Tenth District where he has since resided. He received a good education. In 1839 he purchased a farm of 160 acres, and in 1842 with the assistance of an older brother he added 200 more acres to this, and March 10, 1842, he married Miss Martha L. Rodgers, who was born in Maury County, Tenn., in 1826, and they had eleven children—six sons and five daughters—two sons and four daughters are dead. Mr. Pearson has been an energetic man all of his life, and though he began poor he now owns 680 acres of good land in Fayette County, a cotton-gin, etc. He is a Democrat, and with his wife and two of the children belongs to the Cumberland Presbyterian Church. He has many warm friends and is an upright, generous man.

Edwin D. Peebles, confectioner at Somerville, was born in Fayette County, Tenn., near Somerville, July 14, 1860, and is the son of Edwin D. and Nannie (Whitaker) Peebles, natives respectively of North Carolina and Tennessee. Our subject was reared on the farm and received a fair education in the common schools. In 1879 he moved with his parents to Arkansas and followed farming principally, but devoted some attention to mercantile pursuits. In 1884 he left Arkansas and moved back to Somerville, Tenn., where he devoted his time and attention to agricultural pursuits. He continued in this until September 1, 1886, when he engaged in his present business. He started in life a poor boy; but by industry and perseverance has accumulated considerable property. He is now carrying a fine stock of goods in his line and is considered a wide-awake, industrious young man. January 14, 1886, he married Mary White, of Fayette County. He is a Democrat in politics and a member of the Methodist Episcopal Church.

Dr. Joseph W. Phillips, a widely known and skillful physician of Williston, Fayette County, was born in the county July 31, 1836, and is a son of Pettus and Dorcas (Pettus) Phillips, who were both natives of Mecklenburg County, Va. The father was born June 2, 1794, and died in Fayette County September 18, 1867. The mother was born September 11, 1795, and died in Fayette County May 14, 1861. They married June 2, 1814, in their native State, and in 1831 moved to Tennessee and settled first in Haywood County, eight miles north of Brownsville, but three years later moved to Fayette County and settled near Somerville, but at the end of the year moved to the Fourteenth District, seven miles south of Somerville, where they remained until they died. The father was a very successful farmer; both parents were consistent members of the Missionary Baptist Church and were highly esteemed in the community. Dr. Joseph Phillips was the youngest of twenty-one children. He had good educational advantages and after finishing his literary course, commenced the study of medicine and in the fall of 1855 entered the Memphis Botanical Medical College, where he received his diploma in the spring of 1857 and after graduating was, for a term of four months' demonstrator of anatomy in the college. He then returned to Fayette County and commenced the practice of medicine, and has been a most successful practitioner ever since, excepting the years he served in the Confederate Army. In 1878 he was with the yellow fever sufferers at Williston, and by his skill and courage greatly endeared himself to the people, and the next year he moved to Williston and still resides there.

Dr. Phillips has, from the first, been extremely popular as a physician. In 1861 he entered, as private, the Confederate service, in what was known as Johnson's Light Artillery, and was soon promoted to orderly sergeant, second lieutenant and first lieutenant, and during the last eighteen months was captain of Johnson's Light Artillery, and surrendered at Meridian, Miss., in the spring of 1865. After an absence of nearly four years he returned home and resumed his profession. The war swept away all of his property and left him without means, but his ability as a physician soon enabled him to build up an extensive practice and he now owns 650 acres of land in Fayette County, besides other property. January 22, 1868, he married Miss Catharine Holden, who was born in Fayette County, October 25, 1844, and they have had three sons and three daughters; one daughter died. Mrs. Phillips is a prominent member of the Episcopal Church. Dr. Phillips does not belong to any church, but is a sincere believer in the Christian faith, and a true and liberal friend of the church. He is a gentleman of ability and culture and has hosts of friends in West Tennessee.

William C. Pierce, of Fayette County, Tenn., was born in York District, S. C., September 23, 1834, and is a son of Cordelia N. and Mary (Gabbie) Pierce. The father was born in North Carolina, February 14, 1792, and died in Fayette County in 1856. The mother was born in South Carolina, August 29, 1796, and is still living at the advanced age of ninety years. They married in 1824, and in 1837 moved to Fayette County, Tenn., and settled seven miles west of Somerville. The father was engaged in agricultural pursuits all of his life; he was a sound Democrat and with his wife belonged to the Presbyterian Church. Our subject was the sixth of seven children; he was but an infant when his parents moved to Fayette County, and has since made it his home. In 1865 he bought a farm nine miles west of Somerville and moved to it the same year. Fifteen years later he exchanged this farm for one six miles west of Somerville, where he now resides. Mr. Pierce began life rather poor, but is now, as a result of his own efforts, in comfortable circumstances, owning 400 acres of land, a fine cotton-gin, etc. January 3, 1861, he married Miss Sallie Castleton, born in Alabama, June 24, 1837; four sons and five daughters have been born to them; one of each is dead. In 1862 Mr. Pierce entered the Confederate service, enlisting in Company B, Twelfth Tennessee Cavalry and joined Forrest's command, where he remained until a few months before the close of the war, and was in all of the engagements his regiment was in; but he was taken sick in the winter of 1865 and unable to again enter the service. Politically he is a Democrat, and with his wife and one of his daughters belongs to the

Presbyterian Church. Mr. Pierce contributes freely of his means to the Church. He is a successful farmer and a worthy member of society.

James Price was born in Fayette County, Tenn., May 22, 1839, and is a son of Henry M. and Mahala (Norman) Price. The father was a native of South Carolina, born July 4, 1804, and died in Fayette County, June 19, 1880. The mother was born in Rutherford County, Tenn., in 1799 and died in Fayette County in February, 1886. Our subject is of German-Irish descent. The parents were married in Mississippi in 1827, and spent two years in that State. In 1829 they settled in Fayette County, seven miles south from Somerville, where they lived until they died. The father was always a farmer, and both parents were consistent members of the Primitive Baptist Church, the father having served as deacon for thirty years. Our subject was the seventh of ten children; after finishing his education he turned his attention to farming, and in 1868 came into possession of a farm in the Eleventh District and moved to it in 1870; eight years later he moved to the place where he now lives, which he purchased in 1880. He now owns 420 acres of good land in Fayette County, which he has secured through his own energy and good management. December 16, 1868, he married Miss Sarah F. Stidham, born in Fayette County October 2, 1843. She is a lady of marked intelligence and culture. Three daughters were born to this marriage, two dead; they were as follows: Zula C., born October 14, 1871, and died February 19, 1872; Lela V., born July 12, 1875, and Lula O., born October 13, 1879, and died June 15, 1880. Mr. Price is a Democrat; he is by preference a Primitive Baptist, though he has never united with any church. He farms with system and judgment, and is regarded as one of the reliable, progressive citizens of the county.

William C. Reeves, a well known farmer of Fayette County, was born in Winchester, Franklin Co., Tenn., November 15, 1815, being the son of Abner and Elizabeth (Russey) Reeves. It was thought that the father was born about 1780, in North Carolina or Virginia. He died in Winchester, Tenn., in 1821. The mother was born in North Carolina, March 20, 1788, and died in Somerville, Tenn., April 23, 1873. The father was a blacksmith and very successful. The mother remained in Franklin County several years after his death. In 1832 she moved, with our subject and her brother, to Fayette County, where she resided until her death. Our subject was the second of four children. He received a good education, chiefly at Winchester. At sixteen he moved to West Tennessee, and after spending a year in Hardeman County moved to Fayette County, but in 1837 he purchased a farm in Hardeman County, and after living there two years moved again to Fayette County, which he has since made his home, being one of the most substantial citizens of the county, and owning over 400 acres of valuable land. Mr. Reeves has had the unusual misfortune of losing six wives. He was first married to Miss Sallie Farris, April 18, 1835. She died March 20, 1837; second, to Miss Lucy Farris, a sister of his first wife, December 19, 1839—she died June 26, 1852; third, to Miss Mary McCarley, December 25, 1852—she died October 14, 1857; fourth, to Miss Mary A. Reeves, May 6, 1858—she died January 28, 1860; fifth, to Mrs. Elizabeth (Walsh) Holt, November 12, 1861—she died February 6, 1874; and sixth, to Mrs. Ann J. (Tyler) Todd, who died October 13, 1884. Our subject is a Democrat and a member of the Methodist Episcopal Church South. Mr. Reeves is a man of fine character and industrious habits.

John C. Reeves, county court clerk of Fayette County, was born in Orange County, N. C., May 17, 1812, and is the son of Rev. Willis and Mary (Hill nee Clayton) Reeves, natives of North Carolina and Virginia. Our subject was raised and educated on a farm. In early life he learned the printer's trade with Lawrence & Lemay, editors of the Raleigh Star, at Raleigh, N. C. In the fall of 1835 he came to Fayette County, and in January, 1836, went to Memphis and worked as a printer for some nine months, and then returned to Fayette County and spent a portion of his time at his father's, near Somerville, and in Somerville, and in December, 1837, he bought the Somerville Reporter, and was editor and proprietor of that paper until March, 1844, when he formed a partnership with Robert J. Yancey, and they continued the publication up to March, 1848, when he sold out to Mr. Yancey, and was in no permanent business until April, 1859, when he established the Somerville Times, but discontinued its publication when the war commenced. In October, 1865, Mr. Reeves was county court clerk of Fayette County, being appointed by Gov. W. G. Brownlow, and held the office until September, 1874, when he turned his attention to farming, and in 1886 he was again elected county court clerk of Fayette County. In politics he is a Republican, and is an upright, substantial citizen, and stands well in the community.

G. A. Reichardt, farmer and stock raiser, residing in Fayette County, Tenn., was born in Prussia, August 20, 1847, and is the only one living of two sons and two daughters, born to August and Willimine (Brauer) Reichardt, who were natives of Prussia, and married there and farmed until 1854, when they moved with their four children to America, and located in Fayette County, where the father farmed until his death, April 24, 1882, seventy-two years old. The mother is still living. Our subject's brother never married and died in 1882; the sisters were married, and they died in 1878. Mr. Reichardt married in 1871 Julia Whitaker, daughter of Isaac W. Whitaker, one of the pioneer settlers of West Tennessee. Mrs. Reichardt's paternal grandfather was a leading spirit in the Revolutionary war. Mr. Reichardt remained at home until 1880, then located on his present farm of 600 acres four miles northwest of Somerville; he also owns 280 acres in another tract of land in Fayette County, besides a dwelling house and part interest in a business house in Somerville. By his marriage he had four children, all living, Edna Willimine, Carl August, William Edward and Frederick Earl. He is a member of the K. of H. and an F. & A. M. and a worthy member of the Presbyterian Church, Mrs. Reichardt being a Baptist. Mr. Reichardt has been a successful business man; he is strictly honest in all of his transactions and has the respect and confidence of all who know him.

Albert H. Rhodes was born in Fayette County, Tenn., August 20, 1848, and is of a family of twelve children born to William and Elizabeth (Moore) Rhodes, our subject, one brother and a sister being the surviving members. The parents were natives of North Carolina and were married there, and in 1836 moved to Fayette County, Tenn., locating near the present Fayette Corners, where they resided until they died. The father when young received good educational advantages, having graduated at Chapel Hill College, North Carolina, and afterward received his medical diploma at Madison Medical College, at Philadelphia. He practiced his profession for many years in Fayette County, then retired and gave his time to agricultural pursuits until his death in January, 1871. The mother died November, 1870. Albert H. Rhodes remained at home until his parents died, then in 1872 attended the Baptist University at Murfreesboro, Tenn., then returned to Fayette County, making his home with a relative until October 27, 1880, when he married Mary Lou Johnson, a native of Hardeman County. Three sons have been born to them, all living: William Albert, Thomas Whitson and Gaston Hervey. Mr. Rhodes has the old home tract of 227 acres, and also owns two other tracts in Fayette County, one of fifty acres and one of 212. He is a member of the Baptist Church and Mrs. Rhodes of the Methodist. His political support is given to the Democratic party. Two of Mr. Rhodes' brothers, Jno. M. and Benjamin Rhodes, were in the Confederate Army, and died of exposure, John M. at Lauderdale Springs, Miss., and Benjamin at New Madrid. Mr. Rhodes is an industrious, upright man, of good social standing, and a prominent church member.

Thomas K. Riddick, attorney at law at Somerville, Tenn., was born in Fayette County, July 9, 1851, and is the son of Dr. E. G. and Harriet A. (Mayo) Riddick, natives of North Carolina. Our subject was raised on a farm and educated at Macon Masonic College, at Macon, Fayette Co., Tenn., where he graduated in 1868 and taught school until 1870, when he commenced the study of law and graduated in his profession at the Cumberland University, at Lebanon, Tenn., and was licensed to practice in 1872. Mr. Riddick then went to Augusta, Ark., and practiced law until 1873, when he returned to Tennessee and located at Somerville where he has since been most successfully engaged in his profession. October 24, 1882, he married Amelia, daughter of Joel L. and Bettie (Perry) Pulliam, of Fayette County, and they have had three children: Lucy T., Joel P. and Harriet M.; Joel P. died December 26, 1884. Mr. and Mrs. Riddick are members of the Methodist Church, and in politics he is a Democrat. He is a self-made man, having commenced with no other capital than a fine education and marked ability.

Dr. John D. Sale, a prominent physician of Moscow, Fayette Co., Tenn., was born in Madison County, Ala., March 10, 1819, and is a son of Dudley and Mancy (Hatcher) Sale. The father was born in Amherst County, Va., in 1780, and died in Madison County, Ala., in 1886. The mother was a native of Elbert County, Ga., born in 1787 and died in Madison County, Ala., in 1843. Our subject was the sixth of twelve children, was educated at La Grange College, Ala., and at the University at Nashville, Tenn., then commenced the study of medicine, and after reading two years under Dr. George Wharton of Meridianville, Ala., he went in the fall of 1839 to the Cincinnati Medical College, and took his first course of lectures. In 1840 he entered the Louisville Medical College, where he received his diploma in 1841. After graduating he remained in the hospital at Louisville during the summer of 1841, and the next winter located at Moscow, Fayette County, and commenced the practice of medicine; two and a half years later he moved to Mount Pleasant, Marshall Co., Miss., where he was the leading physician of the county for twenty-five years, carrying a larger practice than any other physician in the county. In the winter of 1869-70 he moved back to Fayette County, and still continues his practice. For sixteen years, in connection with his professional duties, he has been successfully engaged in farming—he owns 360 acres of land in Fayette County and several lots in Memphis. Dr. Sale has been married twice, first to Miss Susana M. Martin, born in Louisville, Ky., in 1821. (A son and a daughter were born to them; the son died.) She died in Mississippi in 1867. They were married in 1842. June, 1869, he married Mrs. L. M. (Meux) Street, who was born in Haywood County, Tenn., in 1835 and by this marriage Dr. Sale has three daughters. He is a Democrat and with his wife and three children belongs to the Methodist Church. His first wife was also a devout Methodist.

Sydner B. Salmon, farmer and miller of Fayette County, Tenn., was born in Halifax County, Va., April 5, 1830, and is a son of Basdell and Bashaba (Ricketts) Salmon, who were also natives of Halifax County, Va. The father was a tailor by trade and died in Virginia in 1835. In 1840 our subject moved with his mother to Tennessee and located in Fayette County seven miles northwest of Somerville. He was the third of five children and after finishing his education commenced farming. In 1857 he purchased a farm in Fayette County and has been one of the most enterprising and prosperous farmers of the county; besides a large water-mill on the Loosahatchie River he owns 600 acres of good land. October 25, 1855, he was married to Miss Fannie Burtis, a native of New York, born November 24, 1833; two sons and two daughters have been born to them; one of each is dead. Mr. Salmon is a Democrat, and while he has never united with any church he is a strictly moral man, and exceedingly generous in his contributions to the church and charitable objects. Mrs. Salmon is a devout member of the Missionary Baptist Church, and is a woman of great piety.

Calvin A. S. Shaw, circuit court clerk of Somerville, was born in Fayette County, August 26, 1842, and is the son of John T. and Fannie (Pate) Shaw, who were natives of North Carolina. They were married in that State in 1834 and had three sons and two daughters: Eva S., Urcillia P., Henry C., Thomas I. W. and Calvin A. S. The father died in 1846 and the mother in 1844. Our subject was the youngest child; he was raised on a farm in Fayette County by his uncle, Maj. Alsey M. Shaw, and was educated at Somerville. In 1858 he went to Memphis and was engaged in clerking and bookkeeping until the war, when he entered the Confederate service in the One Hundred and Fifty-fourth Tennessee Regiment as a private, his company being known as the Southern Guards; was detached from the One Hundred and Fifty-fourth Regiment and placed in the artillery until 1862, and was then transferred to the Sixth Tennessee Infantry, Company D, under Col. W. H. Stevens and Capt. William M. R. Johns, and this company was known as the "Avengers." Mr. Shaw participated in the battle of Shiloh, where he was wounded and afterward taken home and was then captured by the Federals and was sent to Memphis and was exchanged in 1863. He then joined the calvary service in Gen. Forrest's command and was made first lieutenant and afterward was promoted to the rank of major by Gen. Forrest. After this Gen. Forrest's command was consolidated at West

Point, Miss., and he was thrown out; he then joined Company H, of the Fourteenth Tennessee Cavalry, commanded by J. J. Neely and was soon made captain of the company, which he commanded until the close of the war; he then returned to Somerville and engaged in the mercantile business until 1866, when he commenced farming in Fayette County and continued until 1878, when he moved to Somerville and went into the hotel business which he still continues, being now the proprietor of the Eagle Hotel. August 5, 1866, Mr. Shaw was elected circuit court clerk. April 25, 1886, he married Sallie N. Dickinson, a daughter of Edwin and Cornelia Dickinson of Fayette County. They had three children: Cornelia, Edwin D. and Neal S.; the last two are dead, and Mrs. Shaw died July 25, 1876, and September 4, 1877, he married Eva A. Dickinson, a sister of his first wife, and by this marriage has had five children: Fannie F., Sallie N., Mary M., John T. and Isaiah W.; the latter is dead. Mr. Shaw is of Scotch-Irish descent, he is a Democrat and since 1882 has been mayor of Somerville. He is a good business man and a most useful citizen.

John W. Shaw, engaged in farming and stock raising and residing at Somerville; was born in Fayette County, Tenn., January 22, 1848, and is the son of Josiah Q. and Pheraby M. (Williams) Shaw, natives of North Carolina and Tennessee. Our subject was raised on a farm and educated at Somerville. In 1864 he went into the Confederate Army as a private in the Fourteenth Tennessee Cavalry in Forrest's command, served until the close of the war and was paroled at Gainsville, Ala., May 11, 1865. He then returned to Somerville, Tenn., and engaged in merchandising until 1867, when he turned his attention to farming and has continued it; he owns 200 acres of valuable land near Somerville and a great deal of real estate in the town, including two of the leading business blocks of the town. March 3, 1870, Mr. Shaw married Lizzie H., daughter of the late Dr. Josiah and Amy E. (Cocke) Higgason of Somerville. They have three children: Pheraby M., Lizzie H. and John W., Jr. Mr. and Mrs. Shaw are members of the Presbyterian Church. He is a member of the I. O. O. F. and a Democrat. He is one of the progressive farmers and substantial citizens of Fayette County.

William D. Shelton, farmer and citizen of Fayette County, was born in Shelby County, Tenn., October 27, 1861. Our subject and a sister, Bittie Winston, who died in infancy, were the only children born to the marriage of Jno. W. and Mattie A. (Cross) Shelton, who were both natives of North Carolina but moved to Tennessee when young and were married in Fayette County. The father then taught school in Fayette and Shelby Counties for a few years and was then admitted to the Memphis Conference of the Methodist Church, and a few years later was transferred to the Louisville Conference where he was pastor in many different circuits, until he was placed on the superannuated list and moved to Nashville, Tenn. Our subject entered Vanderbilt University at the age of sixteen and remained until his father's death in 1880, and then followed various occupations in Nashville for a year, including piano tuning and traveling salesman for a few months for a wholesale music firm; then moved with his mother, who still lives with him, and commenced farming in Fayette County, which he still continues in connection with piano tuning. March 12, 1885, he married Miss Ridley Shelton of Fayette County. They have one daughter, Mattie Lee. Mr. Shelton and his mother are members of the Methodist Church, and in politics he is a Democrat. He has been quite successful as a farmer and is one of the progressive young men of the county.

John P. Smith, citizen and farmer of Fayette County, was born in Maury County, Tenn., August 29, 1837, and is the son of John and Rebecca (Buizwell) Smith, natives of North Carolina. The father was born in 1803 and the mother in the same year. The father died in Fayette County in 1857 and the mother in 1863. The parents in early life moved from North Carolina to Maury County, Tenn., and lived there over twenty years. In 1856 the father went to Texas, but not being pleased with the country immediately returned and settled in Fayette County, ten miles southwest of Somerville where he died. He was always a farmer and a sound Democrat and with his wife, who was a very devout woman, was an influential member of the Methodist Episcopal Church South. Our subject was the sixth of ten children; after finishing his education he commenced farming quite young. His parents moved to Fayette County when he was eighteen. In 1861 he entered the Confederate Army and enlisted in Company B, Thirteenth Tennessee Regiment of Infantry in Cheatham's division, and was at the battles of Belmont, Ky., Shiloh, Richmond and Perryville, Ky., Murfreesboro, Chickamauga, Mission Ridge, and in the battles that occurred between Dalton and Atlanta, and at Franklin and Nashville. At Corinth, Miss., he received a furlough in January, 1865, and did not again enter the service but resumed farming. March 29, 1865, he married Miss Mary B. Alexander, born in Fayette County November 15, 1840. Two sons and three daughters have been born to them; one daughter died. Their names and ages are as follows: Willie T., born January 8, 1866; Zula W., born January 20, 1867; Hattie M., born March 23, 1869; Ada J., June 4, 1873; Arthur A., March 13, 1878. Mr. Smith is a Democrat and with his wife belongs to the Methodist Episcopal Church South. He is a man of good judgment and fine integrity.

Samuel G. Sparks, editor and proprietor of the *Reporter and Falcon*, at Somerville, Tenn., was born in Jonesboro, Tenn., July 25, 1837, and is the son of Dr. James L. and Mrs. Margaret C. Sparks, natives of Virginia and Tennessee. Our subject received his education at Jonesboro, at Martin Academy and at Washington College, and when young was in the printing business with his father, who owned and edited the *Railroad Journal* at Jonesboro, Tenn., but was afterward in the mercantile business until 1860, when he moved to West Tennessee and located at Somerville, and was appointed deputy chancery court clerk, serving in that capacity until 1862, when he went into the Confederate Army, in the Thirty-eighth Tennessee Regiment, and served until the war closed, and then went to Memphis, remaining there a short time, when he returned to Somerville. In October, 1866, he established with his brother, J. L. Sparks, the Somerville *Falcon*, and two years later bought his brother's interest in the paper, and was the proprietor and editor of it until 1879, when he sold it and moved to Ripley, Tenn., where he engaged in the mercantile business until 1880, then moved to Brownsville, Tenn., and purchased the Brownsville *Bee*, but soon after moved the office to Somerville, and in connection with R. H. Yancey commenced the publication of the Somerville *Reporter*. In March, 1881, Mr. Yancey withdrew and Mr. Sparks became sole editor and proprietor of the paper. In June, 1883, he also bought the *Falcon*, and united the papers, and now issues the *Reporter and Falcon*. May 16, 1866, Mr. Sparks married Mary C., daughter of Isaac B. and Mrs. Margaret R. McClellan, of Somerville. Two sons have been born to this marriage: Samuel L. and Robert M. Mr. Sparks is a prominent Democrat and a member of the I. O. O. F., K. of H., and with Mrs. Sparks holds membership in the Methodist Episcopal Church South. He has been a very successful newspaper man, and is an able writer and is extensively known.

Charley A. Stainback, attorney at law at Somerville, was born in Fayette County, Tenn., August 27, 1851, and is the son of Ashley D. and Katharine E. (Palmer) Stainback, who were natives of Virginia. Our subject was raised and educated on a farm. In 1870 he commenced the study of law under T. A. Blare, of Iuka, Miss., and in 1871 he entered the Cumberland University at Lebanon, Tenn., and graduated in law there in 1872; then located in Somerville, where he has since given his time to professional duties, and has rapidly built up an extensive practice, and is well known as a lawyer. In 1876 he married Laura Blakeley, daughter of Drewry and Mary E. (Morgan) Blakeley, of Arkansas. Four sons have blessed this union: Ashley D., Charles A.,

Jr., Blakeley and Ingram M. Mr. Stainback is an ardent Democrat, and is deeply interested in the success of his party. He stands well in the community, and is an enterprising citizen and a successful lawyer.

Julius A. Summers, an enterprising merchant of Williston, Fayette County, was born in Iredell County, N. C., April 16, 1839, and is a son of Hezekiah and Elizabeth (Baggaly) Summers, both natives of Maryland. The father was born in 1803 and died in North Carolina in 1859. The mother was born in 1812, and died in North Carolina in 1868. They married in 1828. They moved to North Carolina in early life. The father was a mechanic. Our subject is the third of nine children; he received a good education at Statesville, N. C., and farmed two years after leaving school; then traveled for a tobacco firm, Stevenson & Bro., of North Iredell, until the war. In the spring of 1861 he entered the Confederate service, enlisting in Company H, Fourth Regiment of North Carolina, R. S. Ewell, captain, and was received in Anderson's brigade and Rhode's divisions. Mr. Summers was with the army in Virginia, Maryland and Pennsylvania, and participated in the battles of Manassas, Seven Pines, Bull Run, Fredericksburg and Cold Harbor, Anderson's Ferry, Chancellorsville and Gettysburg. After the return of Lee's army he was in all of the battles fought between Lee and Grant. Mr. Summers was severely wounded May 16, 1863, and was disabled for six months; then returned and remained with his command until the surrender. He entered as a private and on December 12, 1861, was promoted first lieutenant of his company, and in January, 1863, was made adjutant of his regiment, which rank he held at the time he was wounded. After the war he farmed a year in North Carolina, then moved to Fayette County and settled eight miles southwest of Somerville and three miles west of Williston and farmed until 1879, when he established a store at Williston and has continued the mercantile business ever since. January 29, 1869, Mr. Summers married Miss Callie E. Burnett, a native of North Carolina, born October 30, 1846. They have had three children, all boys. Mr. and Mrs. Summers and the children are members of the Methodist Church. He is a Democrat in politics, and a man of good business qualifications and strict integrity.

Edward W. Tatum, a prominent citizen of Somerville, Fayette County, was born in Guilford County, N. C., December 9, 1810, and is a son of Rev. Henry and Elizabeth (Bruce) Tatum. The father was of English descent, born in Brunswick County, Va., in 1781, and died in Guilford County, N. C., in 1857. The mother was of Irish descent, born in Guilford County, N. C., and died in that county in 1872. The father when still young went to Guilford County, and in 1804 married there, and spent the rest of his life there, where he was a useful and popular preacher in the Primitive Baptist Church; he was also a farmer and a merchant. Our subject was the third of eight children. After acquiring a good education he clerked several years in his father's store, and was then proprietor of a tobacco factory in Guilford County for a few years. In 1838 he immigrated to Tennessee and settled in Fayette County ten miles west of Somerville and has since lived in the county, where he has been engaged in the mercantile business for twenty-five years, thirteen at Oakland, where he first settled, then three years at Macon, when he moved to Somerville, continuing the business for several years, and is still a resident of Somerville. Mr. Tatum lost heavily by the war, but is now in fine circumstances; he is an upright man of fine business principles. In 1871 he was elected county register, and held the office for sixteen years. He is a Democrat and a consistent member of the Missionary Baptist Church. Mr. Tatum has been married three times; first September 26, 1833, to Miss Elizabeth F. Peebles, who died June 4, 1848; three sons and a daughter were born to this union, one son is dead. The mother was a Primitive Baptist. February 10, 1849, he married Miss Rebecca Copeland, who died September 6, 1850; they had one daughter who died in infancy, and April 8, 1851, Mr. Tatum married Mrs. Elizabeth B. (Menees) Manning, and she died March 28, 1884, a member of the Missionary Baptist Church. Two sons and three daughters were born to this marriage; one daughter is dead. The second wife was a Presbyterian. Mr. Tatum is very popular in his town and is a man of broad views and generous impulses.

James T. Terrence, citizen and farmer of Fayette County, was born in Giles County, Tenn., May 5, 1829, and is a son of Hugh and Nancy (Granger) Terrence. The father was born in Mecklenburg County, N. C., May 16, 1786, and died in Fayette County, May 13, 1874. The mother was born in Pulaski, Giles Co., Tenn., in 1801, and died in Fayette County, February 6, 1874. They were married in Pulaski, and lived in Giles County several years. In 1834–35 they moved to Fayette County, and settled in the Twelfth District, fourteen miles south of Somerville where they spent the rest of their lives. The father was a tanner by trade, and both parents consistent members of the Methodist Episcopal Church South. Our subject was the fourth of twelve children. After finishing his education he spent fifteen years in the tanning trade, and in 1855 purchased a farm, and since then has been an enterprising industrious farmer. He began life poor but by his energy has accumulated a nice estate; he now owns 400 acres of good land in Fayette County, a cotton-gin, etc. In 1861 he entered the Confederate Army in

Company B, Fifty-fourth Tennessee Regiment, known and designated at the time as the Macon Grays. At first they were in Cheatham's brigade, then in his division, and in the battles at Belmont, Columbus, Shiloh, Guntown, Miss., Richmond and Perryville, Ky. At the latter place he was severely wounded and disabled for six months, and returned home. A short while before the surrender he re-entered the service, joining Burnett's cavalry, and was surrendered at Memphis in the spring of 1865. March 16, 1865, he married Adelia A. Anderson, born in Fayette County June 24, 1840. No children have been born to them. Mr. Terrence is a true Democrat, and stands very high in the estimation of all who know him. Mr. and Mrs. Terrence both belong to the Methodist Church.

Iverson J. Walker, farmer and resident of Williston, Fayette Co., Tenn., was born in Caswell County, N. C., November 20, 1823, and is a son of Job and Sarah (Garrison) Walker, both natives of Orange County, N. C. The father was born in 1778, and died very suddenly in Fayette County, in 1852, from heart disease. The mother was born in 1795, and died in Fayette County in 1861. They married in North Carolina in 1810. In 1848 they moved to Fayette County, and settled near the point where Williston now stands, and spent the rest of their lives. The father was quite a successful farmer; he never united with any denomination but was a man of good morals, and a great friend to the cause of religion. The mother was a Presbyterian. Our subjec, is the sixth of seven children. He was chiefly educated at Leasburg, N. C. When twenty-five years old he moved with his parents to Fayette County, and has since made it his home. He lived with, and cared for his parents until they died. In 1853 he came in possession of the old homestead. Mr. Walker has been an active man all of his life; he now owns 340 acres of good land in Fayette County and 320 in Crittenden County, Ark. May 3, 1854, he married Miss Sarah A. Currie, born in Haywood County, Tenn., June 25, 1831. They had six sons and four daughters, four sons and two daughters living: Iverson J., born June 13, 1861; Sallie M., married to H. P. Hobson, and living in Somerville; Lea E., born March 8, 1868, and living with her parents; Wilber I. born July 12, 1870, living with his father. Mr. Walker is a Democrat and with all of his children belongs to the Methodist Church. Mrs. Walker is a Cumberland Presbyterian. Mr. Walker is a moral kind-hearted man, and an eminently just one.

Americus V. Warr, M. D., a well known retired physician and citizen of Rossville, is a native of Wayne County, Tenn., born near Clifton, April 9, 1835, and is the son of James and Emily (Bishop) Warr, both natives of North Carolina. The father was born in 1800 and died in Fayette County in 1876. The mother was born in 1812 and died in Wayne County in 1849. They married in North Carolina and in 1825 moved to Tennessee and settled in Wayne County, sixteen miles from Waynesboro. In 1854 the father married again in North Carolina a younger sister of his first wife, and in 1855 moved to Fayette County and settled two and a half miles northwest of Rossville where he died at the age of seventy-six. He was a successful farmer and an old line Whig, and for thirty years was a class leader in the Methodist Church. Our subject is the sixth of eight children; he was educated chiefly at Bingham Classical School at Orange County, N. C. In the fall of 1856 he went to the Medical University of Louisiana and took his first course of lectures. In the fall of 1857 he entered the medical department of the University of Pennsylvania where he received his diploma in 1858. After graduating he commenced the practice of medicine in Fayette County and soon had an extensive practice, but declined practicing after his marriage, which occurred February 8, 1860, to Miss Geraldine Isbell, born in Fayette County April 28, 1842. She was an intelligent, cultured lady, educated at the Marshall Female Institute, at Marshall, Miss. Five sons and a daughter were born to them; the daughter, Geraldine, is the only one living. Since the war Mr. Warr has been engaged in farming and the mercantile business, and supplemented his collegiate education with extensive travel in the United States, having visited every State in the Union but four. From 1872 to 1879 he was a merchant at Rossville; since then he has been engaged in settling his business and looking after his extensive farming interests; he now owns 4,000 acres of land in Fayette County and nearly the entire town of Rossville. His reputation as a Free Mason is of a national character. He has taken all degrees in Masonry, and has filled all of the offices from Worshipful Master to Grand Master of Tenn. In his political views he is a Democrat but was a Whig before the war. Mr. Warr is a consistent member of the Presbyterian Church, Mrs. Warr of the Methodist. He contributes freely to both churches, and they are important factors in the social circle of their community, exerting a wide influence for good.

John T. Watkins was born in Fayette County in February, 1853, and is the only one living of a family of two sons and a daughter, born to Benjamin and Sallie (Winfrey) Watkins. The father was a Virginian; he married in Fayette County and engaged in agricultural pursuits until a short time before his death when he sold his property in Fayette County and moved to Arkansas, where he died in 1861, the mother having died in our subject's infancy. John T. Watkins accompanied his father to Arkansas and after his death made his home with a relative in Texas until 1870, when he returned to Fayette County and located on his present farm of 675 acres, six miles northwest of Somerville. In 1880 Mr. Watkins married Sallie Salmon, a native of Fayette County, and two daughters have been born to their marriage, both living: Ethel and Fannie Kent. Mr. Watkins is one of the energetic, progressive citizens of the county; he owns a nice estate, is liberal in disposition and honest in all things, and a man of good social position.

A. Weber, an enterprising merchant of Hickory Withe, Fayette County, was born in March, 1841, in Shelby County, Tenn., and is of a family of two sons and two daughters born to N. and Catharine Weber, our subject and one sister being the only surviving members. The parents were born and married in Germany, and soon after marriage came to America and located at Memphis, where the father was a house carpenter. The mother died in 1848, and in 1850 the father married again; the last wife is still living; he died September 28, 1855. Our subject remained at home until the war, when he entered the Confederate service in the Fifteenth Tennessee Infantry, with which he served as drum major until the war closed, participating in the Georgia campaign and the battles of Belmont, Shiloh, Chickamauga, Missionary Ridge and many others. After the war Mr. Weber returned to Memphis, but July 1, 1865, he commenced merchandising at Hickory Withe, under the firm name of A. Weber & Co., until 1869, when the firm name became Weber & Wilson until 1873, then changed to Weber & Ivy from 1873 until 1885, when the present partnership of A. Weber and R. H. Bone was formed. They carry a most complete stock of general merchandise, valued at $6,000. They have recently built a large and handsomely furnished storehouse, being the best in the county. In November, 1866, Mr. Weber married M. F. Ivy, a native of Fayette County; three sons and seven daughters have been born to them, of whom two daughters died in infancy. The names of the children are William A., Clara E., John A., Elizabeth and Isadora (twins), Fannie and Anna (twins, deceased), May and Clara. Mr. Weber is a Cumberland Presbyterian, and in politics a Democrat. He is a useful and highly esteemed citizen of Fayette County.

William B. Wilkinson, M. D., a retired physician and a progressive farmer of Fayette County, was born near Petersburg, Dinwiddie Co., Va., January 16, 1824, and is a son of Wyatt and Mrs. Nancy (Lloyd) Wilkinson, both being natives of Virginia. In 1825 they immigrated to Alabama and located in Limestone County, where they spent the rest of their lives. The father was a successful farmer, and both parents were consistent members of the Methodist Church. Our subject was the second of three children, and was well educated at La Grange College, Ala., when it was under Bishop Robert Paine. After completing his literary education he entered the Medical College of Pennsylvania at Philadelphia, where he received a diploma in 1845, then located in Fayette County in the Twelfth District, and commenced the practice of medicine, but after a successful effort for a year in that direction, not liking the responsibility of the work, he retired from the profession, and for the next four years gave all of his time to farming. From 1851 to 1861 he was without a permanent home and engaged in various enterprises. In 1860 he purchased the place where he now lives and moved to it the next year, and has met with great success as a farmer; he now owns over 1,400 acres of land in Fayette County. February 2, 1859, he married Margaretta L. Locke, who was born in La Grange, Fayette County, January 25, 1840. They had eleven children—seven sons and four daughters—of whom three sons and two daughters are dead. Dr. Wilkinson is a Democrat, taking an active interest in the success of his party. Mrs. Wilkinson is a worthy member of the Methodist Episcopal Church South, and both are highly esteemed by all who know them.

William A. Williamson, a banker and farmer residing at Somerville, Tenn., and one of the most influential citizens of the town, was born in Person County, N. C., March 7, 1814, and is the son of James and Susan (Paine) Williamson. James Williamson emigrated from Scotland to America and located in North Carolina in the latter part of the eighteenth century, and was a very prominent citizen of that State for many years; he represented Person County in the Legislature, and died in 1832. The mother died in 1828. William A. Williamson was raised on a farm, and educated at Hillsboro, N. C. In early life he was in the mercantile business, and in 1838 moved to Tennessee, locating in Somerville, and was in no regular business until 1845, when he purchased a very large tract of land and gave his time to farming, which he has since been extensively engaged in, owning now over 4,000 acres of land well improved and very valuable; he has given a great deal of attention to the raising of fine stock. Mr. Williamson was president of the State Bank at Somerville until the war, and since then has been connected with the Union & Planter's Bank at Memphis, having been vice-president of it since its organization. October 3, 1844, he was married to Ann Brown, a daughter of Dr. Thomas and Eliza (Lewis) Brown, of Columbia, Tenn., and by this marriage had seven children: Cordelia, Mildred, Orlando, Thomas, Susie, Robert and Alexander. Mildred, Robert and Alexander are dead. The family belong to the Presbyterian

Church, and Mr. Williamson is a F. & A. M., and in politics a Democrat. He is a kind-hearted, generous man and possesses fine business capacity and is well known all over West Tennessee, and has done much to advance the interests of his town and county, where he has the friendship and confidence of every one.

James Wilson, a pioneer farmer and resident of Fayette County, was born in Campbell County, Va., December 16, 1813, and is the only surviving member of a family of three sons and a daughter born to William H. and Agnes (Bayley) Wilson, who were both natives of Virginia, where they married; and in 1817 they moved to Maury County, where they farmed until they died in 1822. The father, in about 1810, before his marriage, moved to Giles County, Tenn., and for several years acted as deputy sheriff there. After the death of his parents, our subject remained at home with an aunt until twenty-one years of age, then in 1835 moved to Fayette County, locating in the immediate neighborhood of his present home, seven miles northwest of Somerville, his aunt accompanying him, and he has since then been identified with the agricultural interests of the country. He owns 550 acres of good land. In 1853 Mr. Wilson married Ann E. Hall, daughter of William E. Hall now an aged citizen of Brownsville but formerly a pioneer of Fayette County, where he located in 1832. A son and a daughter were born to this union, and are still living: William H. and Sidney. Mrs. Wilson and daughter are members of the Methodist Church. Mr. Wilson was formerly a Whig, but is now a Democrat. From his long citizenship in Fayette County, he is well posted in regard to the history and progress of the county, and has a large circle of friends and acquaintances.

Frank A. Wilson, a merchant of Hickory Withe, Fayette County, was born December 31, 1824, in Anderson County, S. C., and is one of three sons and a daughter born to David and Elizabeth (Wilson) Wilson. Our subject and a brother are still living. The parents were born in Newberry County, S. C., married and farmed there a few years, then moved to Anderson County where the mother died in 1828. The father then married Lucretia Dollor, and by this marriage had a son and a daughter; the son is living. In 1832 they moved to Illinois and farmed in Hamilton County, where this wife died in January, 1834. The father afterward married Martha Kettle, of Gallatin County, Ill., and one son and two daughters were born to this marriage, all of them living. This wife died in 1870 and the father died in 1874 in Hamilton County, Ill. Our subject remained with his parents until twenty-two years old, then moved to Fayette County, Tenn., and commenced merchandising at Hickory Wythe. March, 1862, he enlisted in the Thirty-eighth Tennessee Infantry (Confederate Army), and two years later went into the Fifteenth Tennessee Calvary under Gen. Forrest, where he remained until the war closed. In 1869 Mr. Wilson bought an interest in the store of A. Weber, but at the end of three years he commenced merchandising on his own responsibility. November, 1880, he sold his stock and commenced burning brick and farming until October, 1885, when he again went into the mercantile business at Hickory Withe, and now carries a stock valued at $1,800 January 29, 1850, he married Hadassah Boyd, of Fayette County. They had one son who died in infancy. Mrs. Wilson died March 1, 1879, and in 1883 he married Cordelia Boyd. He is a prominent member of the Presbyterian Church, and upright in all business transactions.

Hon. Thomas B. Yancey, United States marshal for the western district of Tennessee, was born in Fayette County, Tenn., October 10, 1843, and is a son of Alexander L. and Elizabeth (Bragg) Yancey, both natives of North Carolina. Our subject was reared and educated in his native county. He also graduated in medicine and dentistry at Baltimore College, Baltimore, Md., and entered the practice of his profession at Somerville in Fayette County, where he continued with the best of success until appointed to his present position in September, 1886. Dr. Yancey served two years as private in the Confederate service and two years on the staff of Gens. Preston Smith and Vaughan, ranking as first lieutenant and later as captain. November, 1884, he was elected to the State Legislature, serving one session of 1885–86. He is a Democrat in politics, and as such has been elected to the offices he has held. He is a member of the I. O. O. F. and also of the Episcopal Church. In April, 1871, he married Narcissa J. Warren and to them were born three sons and three daughters.

HARDEMAN COUNTY.

G. N. Albright, of the well known firm of Edwards & Albright, merchants and millers of Cedar Chapel, was born February 14, 1840, in North Carolina, where his parents also were born, raised and wedded. His father, James R., was a merchant in his early life, and afterward a farmer; was successful in both. For twenty years he was a magistrate. Previous to the war he was a Whig, and then a Democrat. He married Miss Sallie Albright, by whom he had five sons and one daughter. Both were earnest and respected members of the Methodist Church. They lived to a good old age, and were laid to rest in their native State when their lives were spent. Our subject, G. N., is of German-Irish descent; his ancestors came from Pennsylvania. He was raised on a farm, and received a liberal education. In 1861 he volunteered in Company F, of the Sixth North Carolina, Confederate troops. For about three years he served as second lieutenant. He received a serious wound at the battle of Fredericksburg, disabling him for seven months. At Rappahannock Station, Va., he was captured and held prisoner for eighteen months, being confined at various points—first at Johnson's Island, then Point Lookout, Fort Delaware, Morris Island, Fort Pulaski—and back to Fort Delaware where he was released. For forty-two days he was fed on bread and water. This was the work of retaliation. In 1865 he came to West Tennessee, which has since been his home. The same year he married Barbara E. Thompson, who died in 1877. She was the mother of two sons and three daughters and a devout member of the Presbyterian Church. In 1879 Mr. Albright wedded Miss Mollie Walden, by whom he has one son. He belongs to the Presbyterian Church and Mrs. Albright to the Methodist. For a number of years he was engaged in farming and operating a saw-mill; in 1886 he embarked in the present business. He has been quite successful in life, owns 200 acres in Fayette County. He is an industrious upright man, a worthy citizen and a stanch Democrat.

Hon. Chamberlain H. Anderson, present chairman of the county court of Hardeman County, was born in Chesterfield County, Va., June 3, 1820. He is the oldest of a family of twelve children born to Benjamin B. and Nancy H. (Dance) Anderson, both natives of the same State and county as that in which C. H. was born. They came to Hardeman County in 1835, settling ten miles south of Bolivar, where they spent the remainder of their lives. Both were members of the Missionary Baptist Church. The father was of English descent, born in 1792, a millwright who thoroughly understood the business; a Whig in politics. He took part in the war of 1812 and died in 1848. The mother was born in 1796, and departed this life in 1846. The subject of our sketch was educated in an old field school. He remained at home assisting his father in the mill and on the farm, until he was twenty-five years of age. In 1845 he was united in wedlock to Miss Elizabeth W. Perry, who was born in 1823. Their union was blessed with six children, four of whom are living, one son and three daughters. Mrs. C. H. Anderson died in 1884, a true Christian woman and esteemed member of the Methodist Church. Mr. Anderson is a member of the old Presbyterian Church. He is a life-long Democrat. He has been a magistrate for about forty-five years; served as register of Hardeman County ten years, and chairman of the county court about eight years.

In 1879 he represented his district, consisting of Hardeman and Madison Counties, in the State Senate. For fifty-one years he has been a resident of the county.

Washington L. Baird, M. D., is a prominent physician of Hickory Valley, a native of Fayette County, Tenn., born April 16, 1839, the sixth of eight children born to Capt. Charles and Nancy T. (Robards) Baird, who were both of Scotch-Irish descent. The father was a native of North Carolina, born July 16, 1797, and in early life came with his parents to Robertson County, Tenn. He was a Democrat in politics, for a number of years was captain of the State militia and a member of Primitive Baptist Church. His death occurred in Fayette County February 11, 1871. The mother was a native of Tennessee, born March 7, 1807; she was a member of the Primitive Baptist Church and died in Fayette County, September 17, 1867. Washington L. received a good education in youth and having selected the medical profession, attended lectures at the Memphis Medical College, In 1860 he began the practice of his profession with an elder brother in Dallas County, Ark., remaining there one year, when he returned to Tennessee and began practicing in Springfield. September 26, 1861, Dr. Baird married Miss Callie V. Cunningham, a native of Davidson County, born in 1842, and to them have been born six children, one son deceased. In the spring of 1862 he moved to Dallas County, Ark., where he practiced medicine until the fall of 1863 when he enlisted as a private of volunteers and remained with Maj.-Gen. Holmes one year. The entire company to which he belonged was captured, but he escaped capture while on duty as quartermaster. He then came to Tennessee and joined Gen. Forrest and remained with him until the close of the war. He then returned to Fayette County, remaining a short time with his father; then returned to Arkansas, for two years; then returned to Tennessee and after practicing at different points, settled in Hickory Valley where he has since remained. Dr. Baird has two married sisters whose husbands are distinguished men: Lamiza A., whose husband is Judge Joseph C. Stark of Springfield, Robertson County, and Emma H., whose husband is Louis T. Cobb, now a member of the State Legislature and represents the Twelfth Senatorial District. Dr. Baird is a Democrat in politics and a prominent member of the Methodist Episcopal Church which he has served as recording steward seven years.

J. A. and A. J. Barrett, the proprietors of a prominent dry goods store of Bolivar, are natives of Hardeman County. Their parents, John and Salina (Birkhead) Barrett, were born in North Carolina and came to West Tennessee when small with their parents, who were among the very early settlers. After marriage Mr. Barrett located in Hardeman County; was one of the best known and most enterprising agriculturists in the section. He belonged to no church. He was a Democrat. His career ended in 1885. Mrs. Barrett, who is still living, is a devout member of the Methodist Church; she has been the mother of nine children—five sons and four daughters. Three of the boys, Anderson, Thomas and Kindred, served in the Confederate Army. The second, after passing safely through all the dangers and hardships of four years' warfare, met a sad and shocking death. He was killed by the "Home Guards," who mistook him for a man for whom they were lying in waiting. J. A., the senior member of the firm, was born March 12, 1852. He received a good education in the common schools. When about eighteen years of age he began the mercantile business as salesman. Failing in health he went west, and spent about four years in roaming. In 1880 he returned to Bolivar greatly improved, and sold goods in the house which he now occupies. In 1885 the existing partnership, under the name of Barrett Bros., was formed. A. J., the junior member, was born March 12, 1857. His early education was acquired in the common schools; afterward he attended the Henderson High School and Conference School at Montezuma. After his return he spent four years as a clerk, two years as traveling salesman and six years in Arkansas. Since 1885 he has been engaged with his brother as above stated. The Barrett brothers are warm Democrats, and wide-awake, accommodating, able, business men. They are having a flourishing trade. Their ancestors were of Scotch-Irish extraction.

Dr. Henry Biggs, a resident and practicing physician of Grand Junction, was born August 9, 1822, in Gibson County, Tennessee. His parents were Luke and M. (Bennett) Biggs, both natives of North Carolina. The father was of English descent, born in 1795; the mother was of English-Irish origin, born in 1798. They immigrated to Stewart County, Tenn., in 1819, and a year later to Gibson County, where the father departed this life in 1858, and the mother in 1859. The subject of this sketch was raised and worked on his father's farm until nineteen years of age, when he engaged in the same occupation for himself. A year later he became an overseer, and in 1845 began the study of medicine under tuition of Dr. A. Biggs, a resident of Arkansas. He entered the Botanical Medical College at Memphis, Tenn., in 1847, graduating in 1849. He immediately began the practice of his profession at La Grange, Tenn. In 1850 he went to California, where for seven months he was interested in mining. About that time cholera became epidemic in Sacramento City, whither the brave doctor went, practicing in a private hospital on Jay

Street. After the disappearance of the disease he returned to La Grange, receiving an extensive patronage. In 1853 he entered the Eclectic Medical College at Philadelphia, Penn., receiving a diploma the next year. Again he went to La Grange, where he remained ten years, and met with great success. After a year's practice in Memphis he engaged in the drug business in La Grange, where he was also interested in molding and farming, together with his profession. In 1868 he closed out his business, and in 1869 went to New York and matriculated in the Bellevue Hospital Medical College one term. During this time he visited all the seats of medical progress in that city. He returned to Memphis, practicing for one year. His office was on Main Street. In 1871 he went to La Grange; one year later to Saulsbury, where he remained until 1875, when he located at present place of residence, where he has had a large and profitable practice, in connection with which he is interested in agriculture. He is a good and substantial citizen. Although he has met with several financial misfortunes, he is now in easy circumstances, all made by his own efforts. He is a Republican. In 1869 he was elected to the State Legislature to fill an unexpired term. He is a member of the Methodist Episcopal Church, and in good standing with the Masonic lodge at La Grange. The Doctor was united in marriage in March, 1855, to Mrs. Cassandra Nevels. This union resulted in the birth of James William, now a resident of Arkansas. Mrs. Biggs died, and in 1873 the Doctor united with Julia W. Mason, of Georgia. There is no issue.

Robert R. Black, farmer of Hardeman County, is a native of South Carolina, born October 10, 1831, the third of nine children born to Amos and Lucy (Foster) Black, both natives of South Carolina. They were married in South Carolina in about the year 1825, and in 1836 they immigrated to Tennessee and settled in Madison County, where they lived seventeen years. In 1853 they moved to Hardeman County and there spent the remainder of their days. The father was of Irish descent, born in 1804. He was a Democrat in politics, a tiller of the soil by occupation, and a prominent member of the Cumberland Presbyterian Church, and died in Hardeman County in September, 1877. The mother's ancestors came from England; she was born about the year 1806, was a member of the Cumberland Presbyterian Church and died March 23, 1857, in Hardeman County. Robert R. received a good education in youth and in early life began farming. At five years of age he came with his parents to Tennessee and has ever since made it his home. In 1853 he came to Hardeman County and after living at different places, in 1865 he purchased the farm where he now resides. Mr. Black began life poor but by close application to business, and industry and economy has secured a fair portion of this world's goods, owning 800 acres of good land in his county, and a water grist-mill and cotton-gin on Mill Creek. May 10, 1855, he married Miss Ann E. Toone, a native of Hardeman County, born February 5, 1839, and to them have been born six sons, five now living. Mr. Black is a Democrat and he and wife are members of the Cumberland Presbyterian Church.

William J. Blair, farmer and magistrate of Hardeman County, is a native of South Carolina, born October 19, 1836, the second in a family of twelve children born to Thomas and Editha (Black) Blair. The parents were married in South Carolina about 1831 or 1832 and in 1836 immigrated to Tennessee and settled in Madison County, where they lived some time when they came to Hardeman County. The father was a native of South Carolina, born in 1808 of Scotch-Irish descent, and was a Democrat in politics and a farmer by occupation. He was a member of the Cumberland Presbyterian Church, of which he was elder for a number of years. He died in Madison County in 1872. The mother was also a native of South Carolina and it is thought her ancestors came from Germany. She was born about the year 1810 and died in Hardeman County in 1866 a worthy member of the Cumberland Presbyterian Church. William J. has made farming his principal occupation in life but at one time was engaged in school-teaching. He was reared in Madison County but in 1855 moved to McNairy County where he lived four years, when he immigrated to Rusk County, Tex., where his wife died. He remained there one year and in 1860 returned to Tennessee and in 1863 enlisted in Company C, Seventh Tennessee Regiment Mounted Infantry, under Gen. Forrest's command and remained with him until the fall of 1864, when he was severely wounded at Collierville, Tenn. He was left near Salem, Miss., with a family named Powell who tenderly cared for him until he recovered. After a partial recovery he returned home and was immediately captured by the Federal forces and was sent as a prisoner of war to Camp Chase, Ohio, but was finally paroled at Vicksburg in the spring of 1865. He then returned home and for eight years was engaged in teaching school. In 1870 he purchased the farm where he now lives and has been successful in acquiring a competency of this world's goods, owning 500 acres of good land. Mr. Blair has been three times married. His first wife was Miss Nancy Suggs whom he married February 8, 1854. She was a native of North Carolina, a member of the Missionary Baptist Church and died July 18, 1860, the mother of two children. December 23, 1868, he married Miss Elizabeth Steward, a native of Madison County, and a member of the Cumberland Presbyterian Church. She died in March, 1873. They were the parents of one daughter. October

R. M. Bostwick M.D.
HARDEMAN COUNTY.

11, the same year, Mr. Blair married Miss Minerva Steward, a sister of his second wife and to them have been born four children. He is a Democrat in politics and has served his county as deputy sheriff. Mr. and Mrs. Blair are members of the Cumberland Presbyterian Church.

Jesse Blalock, planter, of Hardeman County, is a native of Granville County, N. C., born October 5, 1814, son of William and Katie (Cash) Blalock. The parents were natives of North Carolina, and there lived and died both in the same year. When Jesse was an infant he was left with strangers, but through his own efforts secured a good practical education, and was bound out to J. W. Philpott, who died before our subject reached his majority, and not receiving any compensation for all his years of hard work Mr. Blalock was left with nothing but an honest heart and name, and an ambition that prompted him to industry and labor. In May, 1833, he married Miss Rosana Lee, a native of North Carolina, born October 5, 1812. This was a happy union for forty years and the wife died October 5, 1873. In 1836 Mr. Blalock purchased a little farm near where he now lives, where he remained a short time, then moved to Fayette County, near New Castle, where he lived a short time and after living in different places until December, 1850, he then moved where he now lives, twelve miles west of Bolivar. He now owns 500 acres of good land under a good state of cultivation. To his first marriage ten children were born, nine of whom lived to be grown. July 21, 1874, he married for his second wife Miss Bettie Hudson, a native of Hardeman County, born May 20, 1850, and to them have been born two daughters: Pauline, born August 31, 1875, and died September 30, 1877, and Annie May, born November 19, 1877. In politics Mr. Blalock is a stanch Democrat, and he and wife are prominent members of the Methodist Episcopal Church South, and to the interest of which he is a very liberal contributor.

Robert Montrose Bostwick was born near Charlotte, N. C., January 21, 1834, the youngest child and fifth son of William Merida and Caroline (Graham) Bostwick. Their family consisted of five sons and two daughters. William was born in South Carolina, and as he died while his children were quite small but little is known of the Bostwick connection. He married Miss Graham near Charlotte, Mecklenburg Co., N. C. She was a daughter of Gen. George Graham, who was born December, 1757, in Chester County, Penn. He was a son of James Graham (great-grandfather to R. M.), who at the age of eighteen came from the north of Carlington Bay, County Down, Ireland, about the year 1733. According to a family tradition James was a descendant of a close kinsman and follower of the fortunes and disasters of the celebrated Montrose, who took a conspicuous part in the civil wars of Scotland during the reign of Charles I. When the English Army prevailed in Scotland Montrose fled to Holland, and his adherents (among whom was a clan of the Grahams) passed over into the North of Ireland, where many of the descendants now reside. James Graham died, leaving his widow with several young children. She moved to Mecklenburg County, N. C., when George was but ten years of age. He received such education as was common to the youth of that period. The college at Charlotte, now known as the Davidson College, was in its zenith. George attended the first public meetings held in Charlotte, at the beginning of the Revolutionary war. He was too young to have a voice in the councils, but was deeply interested. He was in attendance May 20, 1775, when independence was declared, an official copy of which was sent to Congress by Capt. James Jack. In the summer and autumn of 1776 George served under command of Gen. Rutherford, in the campaign against the Cherokee Indians. While in the Nation he was one of the party selected to pursue Scott and Hicks, two British traders, who lived there and were believed to have instigated the Indians to war. The early part of 1780 he served in a campaign as lieutenant, under Maj. John Sharpe, of Tennessee, who was his captain. They had the intrenchments made and the abatis placed before Charleston ere the town was besieged. Their term of service expired and they were relieved by another detachment of militia only two days prior to the time the city was invested. After Buford's defeat, when Mecklenburg became the frontier and the men were almost continually under arms, Lieut. George Graham was present at every call of his superiors. He was under Gen. Rutherford's command at the battle of Ramsoms, August 6, 1780. He was lieutenant of a company under command of Capt. James Knox, at the battle of Hanging Rock. He had command of a detachment of infantry who accompanied Col. Davis' cavalry in the attack on a party of Tories at Nahub's plantation at Naxhaw a few days previous to the arrival of the British at Charlotte. When they entered that place on the 26th of September, 1780, Capt. James Thomson, George Graham and others went with Gen. Davidson and the artillery of Phifer's. Finding in a day or two, that the enemy was not advancing and probably would continue in that place for some time, they, by their general's permission returned. Being well acquainted with the country, collected a party numbering fourteen, and October 3 defeated Maj. Doyle, who commanded a foraging party of upward of 500 at McIntyre's, on the Beatties Ford road. After Tarleton's defeat, when Lord Cornwallis was pursuing Gen. Morgan, George Graham joined our cavalry as a volunteer on February 1, 1781; was in the battle of

Cowan's Ford, where Gen. Davidson met his death. In the spring of same year George was appointed adjutant of a regiment called State troops, raised by South Carolina for the period of ten months, and under command of Gen. Sumter. While in this service, George was in numerous skirmishes with the British and Tories. He was at the taking of Orangeburg, and with the State troops and Washington cavalry when they were detached to attend the movements of Lord Rawdon when on his way to relieve Ninety-six. Three or four days before he arrived at that place and when Gen. Greene retired, he covered his retreat. In the military department, shortly after the Revolutionary war, George Graham was appointed major of the First Regiment of Mecklenburg troops, and afterward rose through the different offices until he was promoted to rank of major-general of the Fourth Division of both Carolinas' militia, which he held until 1825. In 1784 he was united in marriage to Miss Cathay, by whom he had two sons and three daughters. One son died when young, and the other after reaching manhood. The eldest daughter, Mary Graham, married George Caruth. The second daughter wedded William Merida Bostwick, the third daughter became the wife of William McCree, of Mecklenburg, N. C. Mrs. Graham died in 1798, and George afterward married Mrs. William Potts, of Providence. There was no issue.

In 1786 Mr. Graham was elected sheriff of Mecklenburg County, and continued in that office until 1794. The following year he was elected senator, to represent the county in the General Assembly. He was re-elected annually, almost without opposition until 1801, when he received the appointment of clerk of the supreme court, retaining that office until 1825, when failing health forced him to resign. The best evidence of the high opinion entertained for this worthy man's integrity, patriotism and honor, was the varied and responsible offices of trust which he was for so many years called upon to fill. He discharged his numerous and laborious duties with distinction, fidelity and satisfaction to all. He was a brother of Gen. Joseph Graham, who was the father of William A. Graham, governor at one time of North Carolina, and afterward candidate for Vice-President of the United States on the ticket with Winfield Scott. Mrs. Stonewall Jackson was the daughter of Mr. Morrison, a Presbyterian minister of eminence, and the granddaughter of Gen. Joseph Graham. The subject of this sketch, Robert Montrose Bostwick, emigrated with his parents from Mecklenburg County, N. C., in 1837, to Marshall County, Miss., where he resided until a few years after the death of his parents, which occurred about 1839 and 1840. He began the study of medicine under the instruction of his brother-in-law, Dr. N. C. Whitlow, when about the age of nineteen. He attended the medical lectures at the University of Louisville, Ky., the fall and winter of 1855-56 and 1856-57, graduating in the spring of the latter year. For about one year he practiced his profession in North Mississippi, then located at Hickory Valley, Hardeman Co., Tenn., where he had an extensive practice until the beginning of the late civil war. He entered the One Hundred and Fifty-fourth Senior Regiment of Tennessee Volunteers, under command of Gen. Preston Smith. Dr. Bostwick acted as assistant surgeon until 1864, at which time he received his commission for the same, and remained in that capacity until the close of the war. He was wounded at Lovejoy Station, Ga. After the restoration of peace he resumed his practice at Saulsbury, of which place he is still an esteemed citizen. January 21, 1869, he was united in wedlock to Mrs. Fannie Guy Oates, who by her former marriage had two sons: William Leroy and Martin Guy Oates. To Mr. and Mrs. Bostwick one son and three daughters were born: Robert Graham, whose birth occurred March 26, 1870; Marie Louise, born October 9, 1873; Luta Paulina, born September 11, 1876, and Fannie Guy, born March 9, 1878, died February 9, 1887. Dr. Bostwick has been most successful in his practice, receiving an extensive and lucrative patronage. He is universally popular and recognized as one of the most skillful and eminent practitioners in the county. He is an active and consistent member of the Presbyterian Church (Old School). He is prominently connected with the Masonic fraternity, K. of H. and also with the K. & L. of H. He is a Democrat and self-made man. Mrs. Bostwick is the third daughter of Martin Winston Guy (dec'd), who inherited Scotch-Irish blood from his mother and English from his father, whose ancestors first settled in Pennsylvania. The mother's maiden name was Esther Sharpe. Martin was born July 25, 1803, in Statesville, Iredell Co., N. C. He was the third son of Dr. Joseph A. Guy, who emigrated from North Carolina to Franklin County, Ala., which was then known as the Cherokee Nation. Here the Doctor died. He was a prominent physician and surgeon of his time. His wife survived him several years, dying at the advanced age of eighty-two. Their family consisted of five sons and four daughters. Martin W. Guy married Hester Ann Hardy December 9, 1829, near Tuscumbia, Franklin Co., Ala. To them were born three sons and four daughters, of whom only two are living, and are residents of the State. Mrs. Hester (Hardy) Guy died August 15, 1847, at the age of thirty-two years. Six of her children were living at that time. Her mother's maiden name was Sheppard, a lady of English origin. Martin W., while a resident of Alabama, was for a number of years sheriff of Franklin County; it was a responsible and lucrative position, and he filled it with fidelity to his country and distinction to himself. He left the office with a reputation for integrity which has been equaled by few of his successors, and surpassed by none. In 1836 he moved to Hardeman County, Tenn., and purchased land from an Indian whose name was Isaac Love. Mr. Guy was one of the pioneers. By his industry and enterprise contributed greatly to the development of the country. His occupation was that of a farmer, which calling he followed until infirmities and advanced age rendered him unable to discharge the numerous and active duties of an agricultural life. He was always in sympathy with the tillers of the soil, by whom he was highly regarded. He succeeded in amassing a very comfortable estate from the natural resources of the farm. He was reared by a Christian mother, who imparted to him the teachings of the Old School Presbyterian Church, of which she was a devout member, and which has been the prevailing religious sentiment of the family. Politically he was a Whig, and supporter of John Bell when he was presidential candidate in 1860. Mr. Guy was a strong Union man, strenuously opposed to the secession of the States. Believing it to be his duty to his country, posterity and himself, he firmly adhered to his convictions, though ever in sympathy with the unfortunate people of the South. He was a patriot more than a partisan. Living as he did in a section which was continually disputed ground between the contending armies, finding his property greatly damaged and his life endangered, he sought refuge within the limits of the city of Memphis, where he remained until the termination of the war. He then returned to his farm. He was one of the twelve chosen men who composed the first United States grand jury of the Federal court, which assembled in Memphis. This body was instructed to find a true bill against Gen. N. B. Forrest for treason against the Government. Col. Guy opposed this proceeding with all the vehemence of his nature. He was denounced by Judge Trigg as a traitor. The Colonel asked the privilege of being allowed to write his defense against the charge. The request was granted, and the paper read before the Federal court, giving in detail his reasons. He then begged to be relieved and was, after receiving strong terms of condemnation from the judge, who in subsequent years realized his own error and as an honorable and just man, asked pardon of Col. Guy, assuring him of the high regard for him and his decision. The Colonel died in Memphis, April 21, 1885, in his eighty-second year. The article of defense above mentioned, and which had been carefully preserved for twenty years, was found after his death among his papers, with the special request that it should be published in the Memphis *Appeal.* It was as follows:

A Personal Vindication of Martin W. Guy, and the Reason Why

During the War He Refused to Serve on a United States Grand Jury, which Found a True Bill Against the Late Gen. N. B. Forrest for Treason. In discharge of the duties incumbent upon me as one of the grand jurors of this district, I am asked by my fellow jurors to concur with them in finding a true bill of indictment for Tennessee against Maj.-Gen. N. B. Forrest of the Confederate Army, as he is notoriously in arms in defense of the Southern Confederacy and very recently has been in this county and a portion of the troops have penetrated this town, captured prisoners and made war upon the troops of the United States. This forms a strong and striking case, requiring an indictment for treason in the opinion of my fellow jurors. I have given this subject all the consideration of which I am capable, with an anxious desire to do my duty. The presiding judge in his charge to the jury, uses this language: "In making this diligent inquiry, your highest aim within the sphere of the duties assigned you, should be simply to promote the end of public justice." With this highest aim to promote public justice, I cannot concur with my fellow jurors for the following reasons: First, the Government of the United States is a voluntary compact between sovereign, equal and independent States, forming a compact for certain specified limited purposes. This compact, or partnership, is the constitution of the United States. In 1861 a portion of the States to this Federal compact, each in its sovereign capacity withdrew from the Federal Union and created another union and government called Confederate States, the States still adhering to the old Union called United States, denying the power and right of the seceding or withdrawing States to withdraw and form a separate Confederacy. As there is no umpire to decide this high question peaceably, the States calling themselves United States have resorted to umpire of the sword, to compel the seceding States to return to the old compact. There is no warrant in the constitution for making war upon sovereign States. If the published debates of the framers of the constitution are to throw any light upon the subject, the power of the Federal Government to make war upon a sovereign State is expressly and emphatically repudiated. Whether the remaining States to the old compact have a right to make war on the seceding States or not, they are, nevertheless, making war on the seceding States. The seceding States under their new form of government, Confederate States, are defending themselves against the war made upon them by the States still adhering to the old compact. With this view of the case I am not prepared to say that Maj.-Gen. N. B. Forrest is making war upon the United States. He is a citizen of one of the seceding States. They claim they have a right to secede; that they have seceded and made another government, and that they are simply acting in self-defense, not making an aggressive war on the States called the United States. I am not prepared to say whether they are right or not. Second, I am a citizen of the State of Tennessee. The citizens of the State of Tennessee against my vote, against my wishes, against my judgment, against my acts (while it was an open question, I had a right to vote and act) by an overwhelming majority voted to secede from the old confederation and join the new. I cannot separate myself from my State, if I would. Against my judgment they have withdrawn from the old Union. A majority of its citizens determined to belong to the new union, that is an impossibility! The war has been raging for more than three years with varying success. After more than three years' war, I have no evidence before me that a majority or even a tenth part of the citizens desire to return to the old Union. The facts would seem to justify a different conclusion. Nashville, Memphis, Knoxville and perhaps two or three counties in East Tennessee are under the control of Federal authorities. Such places are held by the arms of the Federal Government, while all the balance of the States are in sentiment with them, and the greater portion of the fighting population is in arms against them. This Federal judicial district embraces all of West Tennessee, while in fact and in truth its jurisdiction and processes would not be acknowledged and could not be enforced over and beyond the corporate limits of the town of Memphis, or at least outside of the limits of the Federal pickets, about three miles square. The construction of this grand jury is significant. The law contemplated that they should be selected from different counties, while in truth and in fact they are all from the town of Memphis. With these facts before me, with war raging over the length and breadth of the land, I am not prepared to join in bills of indictments against my fellow citizens of Tennessee and arraign them for treason and have them tried for their lives. They have as much right to their opinions as I have to mine. I differ with them as to the policy of their acts. But who is to decide which is right and who is wrong? I cannot pronounce them traitors. The line of separation between traitors and patriots is almost invisible. It depends upon success. Washington, Hancock and other Revolutionary fathers were called traitors. After seven years of war they succeeded, and in all coming time they will be called patriots, notwithstanding they rebelled against their government. Third, the presiding judge, with much emphasis, warns us that we are public functionaries, standing between the accuser and the accused; that we are the great security to the citizen against unfounded and vindictive prosecution, and the grand-jury room, therefore, is no place for the exhibition of personal animosities, or the gratification of individual malice. The moment that these, and less seductive influences of fear, favor or affection are permitted to invade the sanctity of the jury-room, grand juries cease to answer the purpose of their institution and become instruments of oppression and wrong. If the sage suggestions are necessary in peace, how potent they become in times like these, "when" (to use the language of the Court) "the whole country has become the victim of a delirium which strikes at the foundation of our political organization.

Grand jurors are but men, liable to err, as other mortals. Can they—when the country is deluged with blood, when father is arrayed against son, and brother against brother, when the whole country is seized with delirium—calmly, philosophically and wisely lift themselves against the surging passions of the hour, and rightfully discharge these duties to themselves, their God and their countrymen? Fourth, I cannot believe we shall promote the highest aim of our duties, the end of public justice, by holding courts and instituting charges against those who differ with us in opinions. If we commence wholesale charges and indictments for treason against all those who are opposed to us, in retaliation they will commence the same against those who think as we do throughout the South—these many thousand wise and good union loving men, who deeply deplore the course which the Southern States have thought proper to pursue, and with uplifted hands are imploring God Almighty for a return to union and peace. Shall we commence here a system which will certainly involve these noble patriots in speedy and certain destruction? The war is not yet ended. The man don't live who can see through it, or when or how it is to end. We are told the race is not always to the swift, nor the battle to the strong! The slightest incidents in life control the destinies of states, empires and individuals. No man living can tell what to-morrow will bring forth. The incidents of war may drive the Federal authorities out of Tennessee. If we sit here, hatch charges against our fellow men, what becomes of us in turn? Fifth, in view of all things, while the land is raging with delirium, I cannot believe we shall subserve the ends of public justice by instituting terrible inquisitions and indictments against our fellow citizens. Especially is it important that we desist at this time. A presidential election will come on before the people of the United States in less than sixty days. The war is now working to points beyond which, in the opinion of many, it cannot much further go. Out of these may come peace, union, liberty, fraternity. Is it wise to stir up strife when all good lovers of mankind hope that strife shall cease? If these things must be done, if the guilty must be punished, in the name of all that is holy, let us wait until the angry passions and delirium of the hour shall cease, and men selected from all parts of the judicial circuit come together, and unmoved by prejudice, passion, hatred, fear or revenge, calmly weigh these matters of high import and act rightly. Sixth, we have recognized Maj.-Gen. Forrest, the Confederate, even men on the high seas termed pirates and belligerents. Can we recognize them as belligerents and then institute these proceedings against them? Had Gen. Forrest been captured, would we have held him prisoner and tried him for treason, or would we have held him a prisoner of war, finally exchanged him, and turned him loose to come up against us in arms? Seventh, may I now ask that you, Mr. Foreman, make known to the court my position, and let my position be filled by another more worthy and competent. I, since sitting in your body, have suffered much bodily pain, as I am much afflicted. If I may be permitted to retire by leave of the court, I shall carry with me no unkind feelings toward any member of this jury; but, on the other hand, I believe you to be gentlemen who have a high regard and desire to promote what you think the best interest of the State, and our common country. For the officers comprising this grand jury, from my limited acquaintance, in the discharge of your duties, I entertain the most profound respect, and I must say a word in behalf of my worthy friend and old countryman from Hardeman County. I have known him well for the last twenty-five years. A nobler or more honorable heart God never put into man than he possesses. A friend to the widow and orphans, the poor man in affliction or in prison, or an outcast, has ever found Pitser Miller a friend. The friendless he was always desirous to relieve and comfort in distress. May all such noble men live to a ripe old age, as the benefactors of our country. Gentlemen, I am now in your hands; I hope that you will have charity enough in your souls. Although you may think I am in error, if so then I am honorably so, so help me God.

MARTIN W. GUY.

Rev. N. A. D. Bryant was born in Moore County, N. C., in 1816, in which State his father, Elisha Bryant, was born in 1792. The Bryants, or Bryan as the name originally was called, are among the oldest and most honored families in the South. They are of Welsh origin; the ancestors immigrated to America about 1675, and settled on the Roanoke River, in North Carolina and Virginia. They are connected by marriage and intermarriage with the Whitfields and Boones; Daniel Boone, of historical fame, being a member of the latter mentioned family. The grandfather, Michael Bryant, about 1785 visited Moore County, N. C., where he wedded Miss Leah Graham, a woman of rare beauty and fine attainments. The subject of this sketch, in company with an older brother, M. A. Bryant, who was a civil engineer, came to Montgomery, Tenn., in 1837. During a portion of that and the ensuing year, they both worked on a farm, the brother surveying, and our subject teaching school. In 1839 they went to Arkansas, visiting the famous "fountains of health," the Hot Springs. At that day no elegant hotel or palatial bath house was to be seen; the only improvement was five rude pole pens, partly covered, and one spring was boxed with rough boards, at the base of the hill. A few miles northwest, on Cane Creek, they found a colony of people, some of whom had been there for forty years. Our subject taught, on the Sabine River; M. A. was employed at Iron Sulphur Springs, both receiving large salaries. It soon became known that the Rev. N. A. D. was licensed to preach the gospel; and on Cane Creek, beneath a large brush arbor, the whole colony assembled to hear the maiden sermon of the youthful and earnest "boy preacher." So gratified were the people, that by their unanimous request he delivered two more sermons later on. He returned to Tennessee, and entered the traveling ministry of the Methodist Episcopal Church. At the annual conference, he was put on the North Alabama Circuit. His first appointment was at Decatur, the seat of wealth and refinement. He was met in that large and elegant house of worship, by a vast and cultivated congregation, all anxious to hear the young, new minister. He disarmed the critic, and made such an impression upon his listeners, and so widespread became his reputation for sincerity and eloquence, that whenever it became known that he would fill the pulpit, he was greeted by an enthusiastic and mighty assemblage. Mr. Bryant is one of the most able and influential ministers of the Methodist Church. He is of so earnest, firm and yet sympathetic a nature, that he has the power of calling back to the fold the most hardened sinner, of comforting the afflicted, and guiding the young into the paths of truth and morality. In 1845 our subject was united in marriage to Susan E. Joslin, of Dickson County, Tenn., a granddaughter of Benjamin Joslin of Davidson County. The fruits of this union was John Clarke, who died in infancy; William S., now a resident of Hardeman County; Thomas Lafayette, a well known divine, now living in Texas, and James Hart, who is connected with the United States mail service in Cincinnati. In 1854 Mrs. Bryant departed this life at Durhamville, Tenn. Mr. Bryant, in 1856, wedded Miss Virginia C. Ingram, a daughter of the late W. P. Ingram of Hardeman County. To this marriage five children were born: Nannie Taylor, wife of Rev. A. T. Hendrix, now in Hopkins County, Tex.; Charles Wesley, also resident of same State and county; Mattie McNeill, who died in infancy; Joseph Johnson, living at home, and Sue Idella, who is in Texas, with Mrs. Hendrix. In 1855 Mr. Bryant purchased the Person farm, in Hardeman County, where, in 1857, he moved his family this being the first time that wife, children, servants and chattels were all in one place. Two years later Mr. Bryant bought the homestead of the late Rev. D. W. Hullenn. This is a beautiful place, highly cultivated and improved, in a healthful locality in sight of Grand Junction. January 1, 1860, the family took possession of their new home, where they have since resided. In 1870 Mr. Bryant formally withdrew from the traveling ministry, since which time he has been a local minister, having no special pastorate. In connection with the religious duties, he has been engaged in agricultural pursuits. In 1883 he made an extensive tour through Texas, and in 1885, accompanied by Mrs. Bryant and their infant child, again visited the Lone Star State.

F. M. Cargile, a resident and leading merchant of Saulsbury, was born June 2, 1832, in South Carolina, of which State his parents were also natives. The father, James Cargile, was of Scotch descent. He immigrated to Alabama in 1832, from there to Mississippi in 1841, and to Texas in 1858, where he died in 1884; and the mother, Annie (Parsons) Cargile, in 1872. Our subject worked on his father's farm until he attained his majority, when he began agricultural pursuits on his own responsibility, so continuing in a flourishing condition until the outbreak of the war. He entered the Confederate service as a private, July, 1861, in the Twenty-second Tennessee Infantry. At the reorganization he was transferred to the Twelfth Tennessee Infantry, and was elected first lieutenant, which rank he held during the remainder of the service. July 22, 1864, at Atlanta, Ga., he was shot through the upper portion of the head, disabling him from further duty. With one exception, he participated in every engagement in which his company was drawn. The South had not a braver or more gallant soldier. After the war and entire recovery from his wound, he resumed farming. In 1872 he embarked in general merchandising and the cattle business at Saulsbury, where he has been very prosperous. He is a self-made, enterprising and esteemed man. He began life after the war with nothing but a will of iron and ability. By industry and judicious management he has accumulated considerable property and means. He is a sincere member of the Missionary Baptist Church, the Masonic order and K. of H.; is also a stanch Democrat. December 18, 1858, he married Mary F., daughter of Wm. B. H. and Elizabeth Gatlin. To Mr. and Mrs. Cargile five children were born: James Robert, Ruth, Elizabeth (died December, 1872), Ida and Francis Marion.

Roger S. Clark, a resident and prosperous merchant of Saulsbury, was born July 22, 1849, in Hardeman County. His parents were Jackson and Sallie (Lyle) Clark. The father was born January, 1824, in Alabama, and immigrated to Tennessee at an early day, locating near Saulsbury, where he resided until his death, which occurred December 8, 1857. The mother was born April 15, 1824, in North Carolina. She is beloved by all who know her and is still living with her son, our subject. The grandfather, Cornelius Clark, was born in 1763, and is supposed to have left Scotland and settled in Georgia when a comparatively young man. He took a prominent part in the war of 1812. The exact position he held is not known, but was evidently an officer of high rank. He died in Alabama. The grandfather Lyle was of Irish descent, a native of North Carolina, born in 1800, and came to Tennessee in 1826, locating in Hardeman County, where he lived a number of years. He died in Fayette County, July 22, 1885. Roger was a mere child when bereft of his father. He remained with his mother until 1870, when he went west. He traveled most of the time, visiting nearly all the Western States, and returned home January, 1873. The next five years he was salesman for different firms, and in 1878 engaged in merchandise business for himself, in which he has been very successful. Since 1875 he has had charge of the postoffice, and was appointed postmaster in 1877. He began life without capital, but by untiring energy and judicious management is now in easy circumstances, having accumulated considerable means and property. He is a respected member of the Missionary Baptist Church, of the Masonic order, the K. & L. of H. He is a true Democrat. November 5, 1874, Mr. Clark was united in marriage with Miss Sarah E., daughter of W. W. Elliotte. Their union resulted in the birth of five children, two of whom are living: Pear T. and Jewel E.

Napoleon B. Cross, farmer of Hardeman County, is a native of Madison County, born May 4, 1840, the fourth of eight children born to Richard D. and Sarah (Springfield) Cross, both natives of Chatham County, N. C. They were married in North Carolina, February 23, 1832, and in 1839 immigrated to Tennessee, settled in Madison County and lived there eleven years. In 1850 they moved to Hardeman County and settled ten miles west of Bolivar. The father was born April 7, 1809, and died in Hardeman County April 29, 1874. The mother was born May 21, 1811, and the next year after her husband's death she moved to the home of her daughters, Emily and Eddie; the former is the widow of Thomas A. Green, who died in 1872. Napoleon B., after receiving a good education, selected farming as his occupation, and in 1868 came in possession of the old homestead, which he purchased in 1879.

He owns 1,200 acres of land, and December 11, 1867, was united in marriage to Miss Lizzie Jarmon, a native of Hardeman County. To them have been born the following family: Robert D. born September 7, 1868; Napoleon R., born December 6, 1874, and John B., born April 30, 1881. In 1861 Mr. Cross enlisted in Company E, Seventh Tennessee Regiment Cavalry, was received into Gen. Forrest's command and remained under him throughout the war, taking part in the battles of Harrisburg, Miss., Brice's Cross-roads, Miss., Fort Pillow, Tenn., and several others. He received two wounds, one at Britton's Lane in 1863, the other at Harrisburg in 1864. Received his honorable discharge in the spring of 1865 at Memphis. Mr. Cross is a Democrat, and although not a member of any church is in sympathy with the Methodist Episcopal Church, of which his wife is a worthy member.

H. P. Day, register of Hardeman County, was born in Robinson County, March 7, 1833, a son of William and Martha (Brewer) Day. The father was born in South Carolina in 1790; was of Scotch-Irish descent. He immigrated to Alabama and later to Middle Tennessee, where he married, and came to Hardeman County in 1846. He was a farmer by occupation, a Democrat in politics. He was not connected with any church but was a most excellent and honest man. He departed this life in 1855. His wife was of English origin, born in Knox County in 1800. She was a true Christian woman, and member of the Methodist Church. Her death occurred in 1866. She was the mother of four sons and four daughters, and for twenty years previous to her death she was blind. The subject of our sketch was raised on a farm. He received a good education in the common schools of the county. He was an affectionate and devoted son, and assisted his parents as long as they lived. In 1861 he enlisted in Company B, Thirty-third Tennessee Infantry, Confederate service. For three years he did active and faithful service, was never captured and but once wounded, but in the fourth year, 1864, his left arm was shot off on the New Hope Line, Ga., which of course disabled him. In 1865 he married Miss Eliza J. Coggins, a native of North Carolina, born July 13, 1843. To this union four girls were born. Mr. and Mrs Day are consistent members of the Missionary Baptist Church. Mr. Day is an earnest and influential Democrat. He was elected to his present position in 1886. For thirty-six years he has been a resident of the county, where he is well known, and esteemed as one of the most worthy citizens and reliable men.

G. W. Dowdy, a member of the firm of Dowdy & Cargile, of Saulsbury, was born in August, 1842. His parents were B. F. and Susan (Akin) Dowdy. The father was born in Virginia, July 8, 1816, and immigrated to Tennessee about 1836, locating at La Grange, Fayette County. He was married February 12, 1839, to Miss Akin, who was born in North Carolina November 8, 1824. Her death occurred April 27, 1880, her husband dying December 31 of same year. The subject of this sketch is of Scotch-Irish descent. He attended the Woodland Academy until the outbreak of the late war. He entered the Confederate service, in Company K of the One Hundred and Fifty-fourth Regiment Infantry. At Murfreesboro he received a shot on the top of the head. It was the only serious wound he had during his gallant and faithful service. After the surrender he returned home and engaged as salesman. In 1872 he and his present partner established a general merchandise business at this place, since which time they have been exceedingly prosperous. Mr. Dowdy is an honorable, enterprising and substantial citizen, who has accumulated his possessions by hard work and economy. He is a member of the Missionary Baptist Church and treasurer of the K. of H., and a stanch, earnest Democrat. In May, 1866, he was wedded to Miss Sallie E. Whitlow. Their union resulted in the birth of Theodore, Nicholas, Frank, Ernest, Julius, Joe, Laurie and Mary Susan. Mrs. Dowdy is of an old and highly respected family. Her father, Nicholas (Cowan) Whitlow, was born in Limestone County, Ala., near Athens, September 28, 1821—a son of Jesse and Sarah (Cowan) Whitlow, married in 1820 in Alabama. Mary Jane Bostwick was born near Charlotte, Mecklenburg Co., N. C., July 25, 1827—the daughter of William and Caroline Elizabeth (Graham) Bostwick. Mr. and Mrs. Whitlow were married in Tippah County, Miss., July 23, 1844. They had a family of four sons and six daughters. Dr. Whitlow, who was for thirty-three years a practicing physician, died June 8, 1877, and his widow departed this life, July 17, 1881.

Edwin R. Drake, a prominent farmer of the Fourth District, was born in Southampton County, Va., February 6, 1839. His parents were John and Mary (Doyle) Drake, both natives of Virginia. The father is of English descent, born in 1807. After marriage, and in 1842, they came to Hardeman County. The family consisted of six children, five of whom lived to reach maturity. Mr. Drake has never united with any church, but has always led an honest, upright life. Previous to the war he was a Whig, but has since affiliated with the Republican party. For nearly eighteen years he served as magistrate—by occupation, a farmer, in which he was most successful. In 1863 he moved to Illinois. He is nearly eighty years of age. His wife, who was born in 1814, departed this life in 1881. The grandfather Drake was a gallant soldier of the Revolutionary war. Edwin R., our subject, was reared on a farm and received a good, common-school education. He was a kind and devoted son, remaining at home and assisting his parents until his twenty-fourth year, when he engaged in farming. In 1864 he married Miss Frances M. Kinney, born April 17, 1840, in Haywood County. Their union resulted in the birth of two children: George W. and John R. (deceased). In national politics Mr. Drake is a thorough Republican, but in county affairs votes for the man, not the party. He has always been successful in his agricultural pursuits; by hard work, he now owns 314 acres of good land. He is an esteemed and worthy man.

C. A. Duncan. Among the early settlers of Hardeman County was William B. Duncan, a native of South Carolina, who came to this county on a hunting expedition in 1814. He was so well pleased with the country that in 1820 he returned, bringing his family, among whom were Henry W. and Thomas. The former is spoken of in another sketch. Thomas was born in Rutherford County, Tenn., in 1807. He married Mrs. Nancy Gray, born in 1797. To this union five children were born, four of whom lived to be grown. Mr. Duncan was a farmer and a Democrat. He died in 1858. His wife's death occurred in 1855. Both were members of the Methodist Church. The Duncan family is of Scotch-Irish descent. The only living son is Calvin A., our subject; was born October 25, 1836, in Marshall County, Miss., where his parents lived a short time. His early life was spent on a farm. He received a good common-school education. At the age of eighteen he began his career as a farmer. In 1861 he enlisted in Company G of Tenth Arkansas Infantry, Confederate service. He was severely wounded at the siege of Port Hudson by the bursting of a shell, a portion striking him on the head. It was thought at first that he was dead. He was disabled for nine months, and for thirteen months held a prisoner. A year after his entry into the army he was promoted to rank of third lieutenant and later to first lieutenant. After peace reigned once more, he commenced life again without a cent. For two years he clerked in a store in Whiteville, and then opened a saloon, continuing in the business four years. Later he embarked in general merchandising in which he has since been engaged, and with unusual success. In connection with his mercantile business, he is interested in farming to a considerable extent. In 1871 he married Miss Sallie Andrews, born in 1852. They have no children, but are raising two orphans. Both Mr. and Mrs. Duncan are active and liberal members of the Cumberland Presbyterian Church. For forty-five years Mr. Duncan has been a resident of Hardeman County, and twenty years closely associated with the commercial interest. He is known throughout the section as a man of fine business qualifications and honor. He is charitable and popular, and a stanch Democrat.

Stephen N. Duncan, a farmer and mechanic of Whiteville, was born August 6, 1851, in Hardeman County. His parents were Henry W. and Margaret (Ruddell) Duncan. The father was born in 1800. He had been twice married previous to his union with Miss Ruddell. By his first wife he had one child, and eight children with the second wife. When about twenty years of age he settled in the western district, where Whiteville now lies. His chief occupation was farming. He also operated a grist and saw-mill, and kept a landing on Hatchie River. He began life a poor man, but by industry and good management amassed quite a snug fortune, and became the possessor of 1,900 acres of good land. He was a a consistent, conscientious Christian. From religious principles, he never owned a slave. He met a sad and shocking death by drowning in Hatchie River in 1869. Mrs. Duncan was born in Kentucky in 1822, and died in 1852, leaving only one child, Stephen, our subject. He was but ten months old when his mother died. He was raised by his uncle, R. K. Ruddell. He received such educational advantages as the common schools of that day afforded. At the age of sixteen he began life for himself. After running a saw-mill for two years in Arkansas, he returned home and commenced farming. In 1873 he married Alice P. Andrews, who was born August 10, 1853. Of the three children born to this union only one is living—Mussie D. Mr. and Mrs. Duncan are respected members of the Methodist Church. In 1880 they located in Whiteville, where Mr. Duncan has since been engaged in mechanical pursuits, although still interested in farming. He owns 240 acres of fine productive soil. All of his life has been spent in Hardeman County, where he is well known and highly esteemed. He is one of the few surviving members of a prominent and once large family.

Wiley Durden, a resident and merchant of Saulsbury, was born March 28, 1836, in North Carolina, of which State his parents were natives. They were William and Elizabeth (Sauls) Durden. The father was born in 1806 and immigrated to Tennessee in 1837, locating in Hardeman County, where he resided until his death, February 12, 1855. The mother was born in 1797, and died August 22, 1854. Our subject was raised on a farm, upon which he worked until 1859, when he obtained a situation as salesman for J. M. Richardson, in the merchandise business, remaining in the position until the late war. He entered the Confederate service in 1863, in Col. J. C. Neely's regiment. In 1864 he returned home and became clerk for McCullen & Bostwick. In 1867 he and R. M. Wright bought out the firm for which he had been working. The new firm was styled Wright, Cox & Co., changed in 1868 to Wright & Durden and, with the exception of one year, has so continued. They are now among the leading and most prosperous merchants of the place, having, by their fair dealing and courtesy to patrons, built up a large and profitable trade. Mr. Durden was married, November 15, 1870, to M. E. Tucker, of Somerville, Tenn. Their union has been blessed with two children: Edward Tucker and Willie Gwynne. Mr. Durden is highly respected by the entire community, and known as a man of fine business capacity, enterprise and honor. He began life at the close of the war without a cent, and is now the owner of some valuable property and considerable means. He is a stanch Democrat.

David E. Durrett, a leading merchant of Bolivar and an old resident of the county, was born April 15, 1835, in Albemarle County, Va., a son of Robert D. and Mary D. (Wood) Durrett, both of whom were natives of the same county and State as David. The father was born in 1796. He remained in his native State until after his marriage. He came to Hardeman County in 1836, and settled ten miles west of Bolivar. In the same year his wife died. Mrs. Durrett was the mother of nine children— six sons and three daughters—of whom but two are living. Mr. Durrett's second union was with Mrs. Polk, by whom he had one child. Mrs. (Polk) Durrett dying in 1844, ten years later Mr. Durrett returned to Virginia, and married Mrs. Terrell, who bore him one child. He was a farmer by occupation. He participated in the war of 1812, and was a Whig. He and his first wife were members of the Presbyterian Church. His death occurred in 1883. The subject of this sketch was raised on a farm. His educational advantages were rather limited, despite which fact he is possessed of no small amount of knowledge and information. At the age of fifteen years he obtained a situation as salesman in a store, continuing in the business until the war. In 1861 he enlisted in the Confederate service, Company E, Seventh Tennessee Cavalry. At the battle of Britton's Lane his left limb was broken by a minie-ball, which crippled him for life, and has necessitated the use of crutches. In 1865 he opened a store at Clover Port, and one year later located in Bolivar, where he formed a partnership with Hugh Harkins, Sr. They established a house, the firm being known as Harkins & Durrett. They did an extensive and profitable business, and were recognized as one of the most substantial and reliable firms in the county. The death of Mr. Harkins, in 1885, dissolved the partnership which had continued so harmoniously for such a number of years. In 1866 Mr. Durrett married Miss Mary E. Walton, who was born in August, 1843. Their union was blessed with five children, four of whom are living. Mrs. Durrett is an estimable Christian woman, and an earnest member of the Presbyterian Church. Mr. Durrett is not connected with any church.

For half a century he has been a resident of the county, thirty years of which time he has been actively and directly engaged in the business interest of Bolivar; not once has he failed nor asked an extension of time. In connection with merchandising he carries on farming. He is a man of indisputable integrity, and a worthy citizen.

W. W. R. Elliotte, Jr., a leading merchant of Saulsbury, was born May 22, 1839, in Tippah County, Miss. His parents are W. W. R. and Jemima W. Ferguson. His father was born August 14, 1813, at McMinnville, Tenn., a son of William and Elizabeth (Wilson) Elliotte, both natives of North Carolina, born respectively in 1767 and 1775. They immigrated to Tennessee at a very early day and located in Rutherford County, where they lived a number of years. The father died in Henderson County in 1836, and the mother in 1862. W. W. R., Sr., who is of Scotch-Irish descent, was raised on a farm. In 1856 he engaged in the wholesale and retail family grocery business, afterward adding a fine drug stock. In February, 1885, he was burned out, and lost a great deal. He is an old and honored citizen, and highly respected. He is a member of the Methodist Episcopal Church South, and belongs to the Masonic order. Previous to the late war he was a Whig, but since that time has belonged to no party. November 1, 1838, he was married to Miss Jemima W. Ferguson. To them a family of nine children was born: Daniel F.; Mary A. E., wife of L. T. Barden; John W., C. G., Emily, Francis, Virginia T., Alice B. and the subject of this sketch, W. W. R., Jr., who is the third son. When quite young he entered the merchandise business, continuing as a salesman until 1874, at which time he embarked in general merchandise and cotton trade at Saulsbury, and to the present date has been very prosperous. He was married October 29, 1874, to Maggie Brown, of Tippah County, Miss. She is a daughter of Lawson W. and Elizabeth Brown, both natives of Mississippi. To Mr. and Mrs. Elliotte four children have been born: Lizzie J., Lawson W., Ida May and an infant. Mr. Elliotte is a worthy and substantial citizen, and a self-made man, who has accumulated his property by economy and industry. He is an esteemed member of the Methodist Episcopal Church South, and a strong Democrat.

William W. Farley, county court clerk of Hardeman County, is a son of Franklin B. and Mary (Parr) Franklin. Both were born, reared and married in North Carolina. In 1833 they came to Fayette County, Tenn., where they remained until 1848, and then moved to Shelby County. The father was a farmer by occupation and a Whig in politics. They were both members of the Methodist Church and lived to a good old age. Our subject was born January 18, 1827, in Caswell County, N. C., was reared on a farm and had the very best educational advantages his county afforded. At the age of twenty-one he began for himself by clerking in a dry goods store. After six years' experience he began merchandising, which he continued some time. He then engaged in agricultural pursuits. In 1851 he married Mary J. Redd, daughter of Maj. P. B. Redd, an educator of Haywood County. This union was blessed by the birth of one son, William E., a farmer of Hardeman County. Mrs. Farley is a member of the Cumberland Presbyterian Church. Before the war our subject was a Whig but since that event he has been a Democrat. In 1876 he was elected sheriff, which office he held as long as the law permits (six years). He was then elected to the office of county court clerk and is now discharging the duties of that position. He also carries on his agricultural pursuits and has 630 acres of valuable land. For forty years he has been a resident of Hardeman County, and the official positions he has held speak well for his popularity in the county. He is a man liberal in his support of schools, churches and other worthy enterprises. His father was of German-Irish extraction.

Judge James Fentress, general solicitor for the Illinois Central Railroad Company, was born July 27, 1837, the second of a family of five children born to David and Matilda (Wendel) Fentress, whose ancestors came from England at an early day and located in Virginia. As the families increased they sought new and different homes, some coming to Tennessee. The grandfather, James Fentress, was speaker of the House of Representatives for a number of years. The maternal grandfather, David Wendel, of Murfreesboro, was the only Whig postmaster allowed to retain his office during Jackson's administration. David Fentress married at Murfreesboro, moved to West Tennessee, where he made his home, and practiced law. He was considered one of the most talented and able lawyers in the entire section. He was at one time representative of Hardeman County in the State Legislature. Mrs. Fentress was a consistent and highly respected member of the Presbyterian Church. Mr. Fentress died in 1856, at the age of fifty-six years. Mrs. Fentress is still living, and in her seventy-eighth year. Her family consists of Dr. David W., of Texas; Francis, a lawyer of Bolivar; Kate, wife of Albert T. McNeal; Sallie W., wife of Jerome Hill, who is head of the firm of Hill, Fontaine & Co., of St. Louis, and the subject of this sketch, who after having the best of educational advantages at home, completed his course at the University of Virginia. After reading law for three years, he was admitted to the bar in 1859, since which time he has given most of his attention to his profession. The year of his admission to the bar he was united in marriage to Miss Mary T. Perkins, who was born January 16, 1842. This union resulted in the birth of ten children, of whom six are living: Mary W.; Matilda, wife of Girault Farrar, a lawyer of New Orleans; James, David, Calvin and Ethel. When the late war broke out between the North and South Judge Fentress entered the Confederate service as a volunteer May 15, 1861, as lieutenant. He soon became captain of Company B, Fourth Tennessee Infantry. In 1862 he resigned his commission and entered the cavalry service as private in Company E, Seventh Tennessee, and so continued until the close of the war. During his four years of active service he was neither wounded nor captured. Judge Fentress is a Democrat in politics. In 1870 he was a member of the State Constitutional Convention, and took a prominent part in the revision of the Constitution. The same year he was elected chancellor of the Tenth Chancery Division of Tennessee, and resigning in 1872, returned to the practice of his profession. In 1876 he was appointed general solicitor of the Illinois Central Railroad Company for Kentucky, Tennessee, Mississippi and Louisiana. He makes New Orleans his winter headquarters, spending the summer at his beautiful country residence near Bolivar. He is also chief attorney for the Mississippi & Tennessee Railroad Company, general solicitor for the Canton, Aberdeen & Nashville Railroad, for the Yazoo & Mississippi Valley Railroad, for the West & East Railroad, for the New Orleans Belt Line, and serves in the same capacity for several other railroad companies of less importance. The Judge advocates travel as a means of attaining the highest culture. Both he and his family have visited all the different countries of Europe and have also traveled extensively in America. They are a cultivated, refined and interesting family, always recognized as among the first in the land. Judge Fentress and his estimable wife are members of the Presbyterian Church.

Francis Fentress, a member of one of Tennessee's oldest and most honored families is a well known and leading attorney at law, of Bolivar, is a native of the place, born May 28, 1840, the son of David and Matilda (Wendel) Fentress. His early education was received in Hardeman County; at the age of sixteen he entered the Bandusia Seminary of Nashville, and later attended the La Grange Synodical College, completing the Freshman and Sophomore courses in one year. He graduated at the University of Mississippi in 1861. The same year he entered the Confederate service as a volunteer, enlisting in Company E, Seventh Tennessee Cavalry, serving until the close of the war. After the restoration of peace, 1865, he began the reading of law under the guidance of his distinguished brother, Judge James Fentress, and was admitted to the bar the following year, since which time he has practiced in Bolivar. In 1870 he married Miss Bettie, daughter of Gen. R. P. Neely. Mrs. Fentress was born September 2, 1849, and died in 1881, leaving three children: Elizabeth, Frank and Louise. Mr. Fentress' second marriage was with Miss Bettie Bradley, of Franklin, Tenn., who was born June 12, 1857. To their union one child has been born, Margaret. Mr. Fentress is one of the best informed and most prominent lawyers of Bolivar. For nineteen years he has been local attorney for the Illinois Central Railroad, also the Memphis & Charleston Road. He is a "sky blue" Democrat, being at present chief superior of elections in the western district of Tennessee, appointed by Judges Jackson and Hammond of the United States circuit and district courts. Mr. Fentress has passed his life almost entirely in the home of his nativity where he is universally esteemed. He and his wife are earnest members of the Presbyterian Church.

Squire Daniel A. Ferguson, a prominent resident and retired merchant at Saulsbury, was born January 8, 1825, in Franklin County, Va., of which State his parents were also natives. His father, Daniel Ferguson, was born August 4, 1782, and immigrated to Tennessee in 1836, locating in Hardeman County, where he died March 27, 1858. He was an officer of high rank in the war of 1812. The mother, Jemima (Saunders) Ferguson, was born, and spent her life in her native State. She died in 1835. Our subject's early life was passed on a farm. In 1857 he embarked in the merchandise business at Saulsbury, where with the exception of about six years, he continued until 1882. He was one of the most successful merchants of the county for many years, and considered a man of best business qualifications. In 1849 he was elected magistrate, and served about ten years in that capacity. He was the first mayor of the town, holding the office for eight or ten years. No man in the community is better or more favorably known. He has great force of character. He began life with comparatively nothing, but is now in most comfortable circumstances, and owns some fine property. He is a Mason and a Democrat. April 29, 1847, he married Miss Frances E., daughter of James and Mary (Jones) Smith, of Tippah County, Miss. To the union two children were born: James and Mary Frances, both deceased. Mr. and Mrs. Ferguson are zealous and consistent members of the Methodist Episcopal Church South.

James P. Ferguson, magistrate of the Second Civil District of Hardeman County and merchant of Hickory Valley, is a native of this county born September 28, 1845, the third of seven children born to Joel and Sarah (Flynt) Ferguson, both natives of Middle Tennessee, the father of Rutherford County, and the mother of Lincoln County. They came in early life to Hardeman County and were there married in 1833. The father was born in 1804, was a farmer, a Democrat, and a worthy member of the Methodist Episcopal Church. He died October 1, 1862. The mother was born in 1810, was a member of the Cumberland Presbyterian Church and died in 1885. James P. received a good practical education, after which he engaged in farming interests for six years. In 1873 in partnership with a brother-in-law, D. W. McAnulty, he established a store in La Grange, Tenn., where they remained one year, when they moved their stock of goods to Hickory Valley, and in about a year's time Mr. Ferguson sold his interest and for the next three years was not engaged in any special business. In 1877 he was employed by the old firm as bookkeeper and remained with them five years, after which he again became a partner, but on account of ill health was compelled to abandon mercantile life for a time. October, 1885, with a younger brother, Z. L. Ferguson, he established a store at Hickory Valley and has since been one of the active business men of the place. He owns one-half interest in this store and 275 acres of land in Hardeman County. December 10, 1867, Mr. Ferguson married Miss Mary L. Moorman born in 1839, a daughter of Rev. R. A. Moorman of Hardeman County. To this union have been born four children—one son and three daughters. He is a Democrat, a member of the Cumberland Presbyterian Church, and for eighteen years has served this church as elder. Mr. Ferguson is mayor of the town and notary public, the duties of which are the same as county court clerk.

William D. Galloway, a well-to-do farmer, and for four years magistrate of the Ninth Civil District of Hardeman County, was born in this county June 1, 1842, the second of six children born to Robert and Martha (McCrory) Galloway. The father was born in Limestone County, Ala., February 19, 1817. He was a life-long farmer, a Whig in politics, and a worthy member of the Methodist Church. The mother was a native of North Carolina, born in Mecklenburg County November 13, 1820. She was a member of the Missionary Baptist Church. William D. after securing a good education began early in life as a farmer. He has always made his native county his home with the exception of the time he served in the Confederate Army. In 1876 he settled on 200 acres of land, but in 1882 moved to where he now resides. Mr. Galloway has been an active business man all his life and now owns 750 acres of land in Hardeman County. January 13, 1876, he married Miss Sarah McCammon, a most worthy lady and daughter of George and Elizabeth McCammon, both still living in Hardeman County. Mrs. Galloway was born in

Hardeman County October 5, 1853, and she and husband are the parents of these children: Nona G., born April 6, 1877; Bunyan, October 8, 1878; Kelcie, February 6, 1880; Edgar, April 8, 1881; David, October 5, 1882, and Wilmer, July 9, 1884. Mr. Galloway is a Democrat in politics, and he and wife are members of the Missionary Baptist Church.

Col. G. W. Garrett, a prominent resident and prosperous merchant of Pocahontas, was born March 5, 1840, in South Carolina, of which State his parents were also natives. His father, Henry Garrett, was born March 5, 1808, and moved to Mississippi in 1851, locating in Tippah County, where he is living at present, extensively engaged in agriculture. The mother, Mrs. Elizabeth (Cauley) Garrett, was born in May, 1812. Col. Garrett's ancestors were Scotch-Irish. He entered the Confederate service in 1861, at the age of nineteen, in the Third Mississippi Infantry, which was afterward consolidated with the Twenty-sixth and Twenty-third. He was second lieutenant of Company C, and was gradually promoted until he reached the rank of colonel. During his brave and gallant service he did not receive a serious wound, but was captured twice, first at Fort Donelson, when he was imprisoned at Johnson Island for five months. He was again taken prisoner at Nashville, and confined at that place until the surrender. After peace was restored he returned home and engaged in farming which he continued for a year, at which time he formed a partnership with Halcomb, the firm being styled Halcomb & Garrett. One year later it was changed to G. W. Garrett & Bro., the same as at the present time. They have met with unusual success, having by their fair dealings and accommodating manners secured a large and profitable trade. January 9, 1866, the Colonel married E. J., daughter of Dr. R. L. and Annie Bouten, of French descent. To Col. and Mrs. Garrett five children have been born: Minnie, Ottie, Hallie, Georgie and Lloyd. Col. Garrett is a true, worthy and esteemed citizen, a man of best social standing and an earnest member of the Missionary Baptist Church, also of the K. of H. He is a stanch Democrat and prohibitionist.

George S. Gibson, a well known and enterprising planter of Hardeman County, was born in Davidson County, Tenn., October 27, 1801, the second child in a family of eleven born to Jesse and Elizabeth (Parmley) Gibson. The parents were married near Knoxville, Tenn., about the year 1799, and soon after they moved to Davidson County, where they lived for a short time and then immigrated to Kentucky. The father was a native of Virginia, born about the year 1777; was a planter, and died in Kentucky about 1847. The mother was born in South Carolina, but the date of her birth is not known. She was several years younger than her husband and died in Hardeman County February 7, 1854. George S. received a good common school education and early in life turned his attention to farming. In 1826 he came to Tennessee and settled in Hardeman County, one of its first settlers. He was almost without money, and began at once a life of hardships and toil. By energy and economy after years of hard labor he was able to purchase a home, and in 1828 bought the farm where he now lives. Mr. Gibson was a heavy loser by the war, but now owns 220 acres of land. January 31, 1828, he married Miss Nancy Henson, a native of Madison County, Ky., born September 10, 1810, and to this union have been born ten children—seven sons and three daughters. Mr. Gibson was constable and deputy sheriff of his county for ten years, and has all his life been a Democrat. Although not a member of any church his views are in sympathy with the Missionary Baptist Church. Mrs. Gibson is a member of the Methodist Episcopal Church.

Robert Hannah, a resident and farmer of the Thirteenth District, was born July 12, 1819, in Ireland, the eighth of ten children born to James and Margret Hannah. The mother died in Ireland and the father in Tennessee. The subject of this sketch immigrated to America in 1852, locating first in Arkansas where he engaged in farming and a portion of the time overseeing hands. In 1861 he came to Hardeman County, purchased land and resumed farming in which he has always been very successful. He was married the first time about 1855 to Elizabeth Myrick. At the birth of the first child the mother died and the infant soon followed. In 1859 Mr. Hannah united with Leean Ransey. This union resulted in the birth of seven sons and four daughters. The second wife departed this life in 1882 and a year later Mr. Hannah wedded Eddie Puckett, of this county. The fruits of this marriage are two boys. All the family belong to the Methodist Episcopal Church South. Mr. Hannah is one of the most substantial men in the county, is worth a considerable sum. He had the misfortune to lose several thousand a few years ago, by security. All his means have been accumulated by economy and hard work without the aid of an education. He is a self-made man whose word is as good as gold, and he richly deserves the esteem in which he is held by the community. He is a strong Democrat and deeply interested in educational institutions and all worthy enterprises.

Orris Harris, magistrate of the Third Civil District and farmer of Hardeman County, is a native of Southampton County, Va., born February 5, 1832, the sixth of a family of ten children, three of whom are now living, born to Hardy and Elizabeth (Peete) Harris, both natives of Southampton County, Va. They were married in Virginia, May 25, 1820, and came to Tennessee in 1842 and settled in Hardeman County.

The father was a merchant and planter by occupation, and a Democrat in politics. He was born January 19, 1793, and died in Hardeman County, September 28, 1844. The mother was born April 10, 1802, and after her husband's death she broke up housekeeping and lived with her children. She was a member of the Missionary Baptist Church and died in Fayette County, August 2, 1882, while on a visit to her daughter, Mrs. Hardin. Mr. Harris secured by his own efforts a good education and selected farming as his occupation through life. He came with his parents when ten years old to Hardeman County, and with the exception of seven years has ever since lived here. In 1869 he purchased the farm where he now lives and owns 365 acres of land well improved. August 30, 1858, Mr. Harris married Miss Lucilla W. Price, a native of Hardeman County, and second cousin to Gen. S. Price, born April 10, 1842. To them have been born nine children, four now living. In the spring 1861 he enlisted in Company F, Seventh Tennessee Regiment Cavalry under Gen. Forrest's command, remaining with him during the war. He participated in the battles of Belmont, Mo., Corinth, Miss., Fort Pillow, Guntown and numerous others. He is a Democrat but before the war was an old time Whig. For the last sixteen years has held his present office, that of magistrate, and is a member of the Methodist Episcopal Church South. Mrs. Harris and two daughters are members of the same denomination.

R. R. Harriss. Among the early settlers of Hardeman County was James B. Harriss, a native of Kentucky, born in 1810. His educational advantages were very meager, but by coming in contact with the business world he became well informed in all practical affairs. When young he came to this county and here met and married Mary Robb, also a native of Kentucky, born in 1819. They had eleven children, seven of whom are now living. He was a Democrat in politics, and had the honor of holding several county offices. For six years he was sheriff, was also county court clerk, and magistrate. His chief calling in life was farming, though for about ten years he was interested in merchandising. Although he started in life on a small beginning he was successful and at the time of his death, which occurred in 1877, was the owner of 2,400 acres of land. Six years afterward the mother followed him. Of the seven surviving children, two sons are in Arkansas, one son in Texas and two sons and two daughters in this county. One of the daughters, Ann. C., is the wife of William R. Kearney, the other daughter, Ophelia, is the wife of William A. Franklin. The two sons living in this county are Robert R. and Charles H., both born and reared in this county, and are among its rising young farmers. Both are Democrats in politics. Few families have lived in Hardeman County longer then the Harrisses and few deserve a more honorable mention in the pages of its history.

Theophilus Higgs, a prominent farmer of Hardeman County, is a native of Halifax County, N. C., born June 29, 1822, the youngest of eight children and the only one now living, born to Theophilus and Mary P. (Brantly) Higgs. The father who was a farmer by occupation, was of French descent born in about the year 1786, in Northampton County, N. C., and died when our subject was about three years old, in Halifax County, N. C. The mother was of Irish origin born in Halifax County, April 2, 1789, and died in Hardeman County, Tenn., September 13, 1869. They were married in Halifax County, and the father was an honored and esteemed man and a Democrat in politics. Our subject secured a good academical education and having selected farming as his occupation in life, at an early age began tilling the soil. In 1848 he came with his mother and two sisters to Tennessee and settled in Hardeman County and has ever since made it his home. In 1849 he purchased the farm where he now lives, and since then has been one of the active and enterprising farmers of the county. Before the Rebellion he was very successful and had secured a handsome competency. The results of the war left him somewhat impoverished but he has since, by industry and economy, been fairly successful and now owns 400 acres of land under a good state of cultivation. January 31, 1856, Mr. Higgs married Miss Margaret Cheairs, a native of North Carolina, born June 5, 1835. To this union have been born seven children—five sons and two daughters—one son and one daughter deceased. In political views he is rather inclined to the Independent party, but is somewhat in sympathy with the Democrats. Mr. Higgs is not a member of any church but a firm believer in Christianity. Mrs. Higgs is a member of the Methodist Episcopal Church.

Benjamin V. Hudson, a leading and well known druggist of Bolivar, was born October 11, 1859, in Hardeman County. He was the youngest son of Thomas W. and Elizabeth C. (Reaves) Hudson. When young, both parents came to the county, where they were married. Both were members of the Methodist Church. The father was a man of considerable means and an extensive planter; he owned about 1,100 acres of valuable land. For many years he held the position of county surveyor. In 1862 he died leaving a wife, two sons and four daughters. Mrs. Hudson is still living; is about sixty-two years of age. Previous to her union with Mr. Hudson she was married to Mr. McKinnie, by whom she had two children. The subject of this sketch was raised on a farm and received his early education in the common schools. He afterward spent some time at the University of Tennessee. He clerked in a drug store at Whitesville about two years, and the same length of time in Bolivar. He then attended two courses of lectures at Baltimore, Md., for the purpose of thoroughly understanding pharmacy, preparing himself for the business he was to embark in. In 1883 he purchased the drug stock of Coleman & Co., and enlarged it until it now ranks among the leading houses of the county. He is an energetic, enterprising young man, and has built up a large first-class trade. He is an active and earnest member of the Methodist Church, and a Democrat. His brother is teaching school in Arkansas.

George T. Ingram, one of the leading grocery merchants of Bolivar, was born in Hardeman County, October 10, 1851; he was the only child of Thomas and Mary Ingram, both of whom were born and raised in Hardeman County, and were consistent members of the Cumberland Presbyterian Church. The father was a farmer by occupation, and a stanch Democrat. He was a highly respected man. His death occurred when he was but thirty-two years of age. Mrs. Ingram moved to Texas in 1856. There she married Dr. A. A. Prewitt, by whom she bore one son, J. A. Mrs. Prewitt died in 1860, at Jefferson, Tex. Our subject, George T., was principally raised in his native county, where he received a good common education. At the age of nine years he had to begin life for himself. He was possessed of more determination and force of character than many of his seniors and he managed to overcome the difficulties which surround the young and inexperienced. After reaching manhood he clerked for three years, at the same time handled notes, bonds, and conducted various transactions. In 1875 he established a grocery store, and by courtesy to patrons, and close attention to his affairs, has an extensive and profitable trade. He is one of the board of directors of the bank of Bolivar. He is a stanch Democrat, but takes no active part in politics. He has resided in the county about twenty-five years; nearly half of that time he has been connected with the business circles, and no man in the community has a better record, or is more esteemed. In 1879 he married Miss Priscilla Nuckolls. Of the three children born to them, Mary and George T. are living, Neither Mr. nor Mrs. Ingram are church members, but they are a conscientious, charitable and upright couple universally respected.

Squire M. H. Jernigan, a well known resident and farmer of the Thirteenth Civil District, was born in Hardeman County December 4, 1834. His parents were Arthur A. and Sarah (Howell) Jernigan, both natives of North Carolina. The father was born in 1804 and immigrated to Tennessee at an early date, locating in Hardeman County, where he died about 1859. The mother was born in 1814; was a relative of the late distinguished Rev. R. B. C. Howell, of Nashville, Tenn. Her death occurred in 1884. There was an extensive connection of children and grand-children, numbering in all about eighty-five. Our subject is of Scotch-Irish descent. He was raised on a farm; was working on his mother's place at the outbreak of the late war. His educational advantages were of the most inferior character. When he attained his majority he could scarcely write his name, but by study, application and reading a good class of literature, has become well informed and fairly educated. In 1863 he entered the Confederate service, and was soon captured and was imprisoned at Alton, Ill.; shortly afterward he was sent to Fort Donelson, making the length of his confinement about seventeen months. He was released but a short time before the surrender, after which he returned home and engaged in farming and school-teaching alternately. He was elected in 1875 to the office of magistrate, to fill the unexpired term of R. N. Mitchell, and has served since that time. July, 1865, he married Miss Smithie E. Tennyson, of Mississippi. To their union five children were born: Loudella D., the wife of M. J. Brannam of Gibson County; Martha D., wife of A. J. Brannam of this county; Arlington Lee, Hiram A. and Mary Rosella, whose death occurred August 14, 1873. Mr. Jernigan is a respected member of the Missionary Baptist Church. He belongs to the Masonic order at Rose Creek, McNairy County, and is a stanch Democrat. He is of high social standing, a self-made, substantial and worthy man.

William M. Johnson, Esq., is among the old and respected settlers of Hardeman County. He was born January 29, 1819, in Williamson County. His parents were Andrew M. and Mary (Guthrie) Johnson. The father was born in 1794 in Brunswick County, Va., and came to Tennessee with his parents when a small child. He was married in Davidson County, 1816, and eight years later moved to Rutherford County, and in 1833 located in Hardeman County, where the remainder of his life was spent. He was of English descent; a farmer by occupation; a Whig in politics. He served gallantly under command of Jackson against the Indians and in the battle of New Orleans. His family consisted of seven sons and four daughters; five of the children are living. He died in 1851. He and his wife were both connected with the Methodist Church. Mrs. Johnson was of French-Welsh origin; born in Nashville, Tenn., in 1797. Her father was one of the earliest settlers, and first tinner and coppersmith of that place. Her death occurred in 1843. Our subject was raised on a farm. His educational advantages were limited. At the age of nineteen he began to learn the tinner's trade, which he followed some six years, and then turned his attention to farming. He has met with a great deal of success. He began life with comparatively nothing, but by judicious management, enterprise and industry, now owns about 1,800 acres of valuable land. Previous to the war he was a Whig—an uncompromising Union man. He is an ardent and influential Democrat. In 1867-68 he represented Hardeman County in the State Legislature. He has been a resident of the county for more than a half century; a member of the county court for twenty-one years. He is recognized as one of the most enterprising, charitable and esteemed men in the community. In 1862 he married Mrs. Margaret Johnson, *nee* Lacy. She was born December 25, 1839. To this union three children have been born: Lou, Belle and Myrtle. Mr. Johnson and his daughters are Methodists. Mrs. Johnson has not united with any denomination. By her first marriage she had one child, Nettie.

J. H. and E. M. Jones, proprietors of the Hardeman Woolen Mills, are the sons of Paul T. Jones, who was born in North Carolina in 1828, and came with his parents to Hardeman County in 1832. They settled on the farm upon which the West Tennessee Insane Asylum is now situated. He received an excellent and thorough education, completing his course at Lagrange College, Alabama. In 1848 he was married to Miss Jennie M. Wood, who bore him four sons and two daughters. In 1863 Mrs. Jones died a respected member of the Presbyterian Church; five years later he married Miss Mary Kirkman, with whom he had four sons and two daughters. Mr. and Mrs. Jones are consistent members of the Presbyterian Church. Previous to the war Mr. Jones was a Whig, and is now a stanch Democrat. At the close of the war he was appointed magistrate by Brownlow, and was afterward elected to the same office. He was the founder of the once lively village of Leatherville, in Hardeman County, where he operated a saw and grist-mill, a tanyard and woolen-mill, the last of which is successfully run by his two sons whose names appear at the head of this biography. The woolen factory was established in 1868 by the father, who had charge of it until 1874, when the present senior member took the management, and four years later was joined by his brother. Both of these gentlemen were born and raised in Hardeman County. They are energetic, wide-awake men, who have by their ability and integrity been unusually prosperous in their business. They are universally known and popular.

Isaac and Samuel Kahn, under the firm title of Kahn Bros., are leading dry goods merchants of Bolivar, and the sons of Henry and Louise (Newberger) Kahn, both natives of Germany where they grew up and were married. Soon after they immigrated to America and located in Bolivar, where he opened a dry goods store and was engaged in this business until 1863. He then moved to Louisville, Ky., where he carried on the same business a short time and then retired in 1868. He was a Democrat in politics, and a remarkably successful merchant. He died in 1880. The mother is still living in Louisville and is sixty-five years of age. They had five children—four sons and one daughter. In 1868 the four sons came to Bolivar, opened a large dry goods house and for fifteen years were in partnership. In 1883 Marcus Kahn left the firm and a year later Jacob Kahn withdrew, leaving the firm as it now is. Twice the store has been burned and each time a more extensive one has been built. Isaac, the senior member of the firm, was born July 20, 1849, in Bolivar where he received his early education and afterward attended the Male High School at Louisville, Ky. After completing his education he came to Bolivar and has since been engaged in business at this place. In 1880 he married Emma Rosenthal, by whom he had two sons—Henry and Claude Mellville. Samuel, the junior member of the firm, was born in 1852 in Bolivar, and received the same educational advantages as his brother, Isaac. In 1881 he married Miss Tillie Frank, and to this union were born three children: Annie, Louise, and an infant. Both brothers are stanch Democrats in politics. The firm of Kahn Bros., have had the leading dry goods business in Bolivar since 1868 and are prominent among the first business men of the town.

William R. Kearney, a well known miller and farmer of the Sixth District, was born September 17, 1832, in Bolivar, Tenn., and is a son of Philip and Sarah (Ramsey) Kearney, both of Irish descent. They came to Hardeman County when quite young and here were married. To them were born three sons: William R., John H. and Philip; the last two mentioned are dead. The father, after making several moves, finally settled in Holmes County, Miss., where he died. He was a Democrat in politics. His widow returned to Hardeman County and married Robert H. Walton, by whom she had two children: Mary E., wife of D. E. Durrett, and Charles A. Mrs. Walton was a consistent member of the Missionary Baptist Church and died April 2, 1886. The grandparents came direct from the Emerald Isle. Our subject was reared in his native town, and received a very limited education. When about twenty years of age he began life for himself. After a year spent in Louisiana, and another in Kentucky he returned to Bolivar and with his brother in 1854, purchased a grist-mill, in which business he has since been engaged. In connection with the mill, which is the best in the county, he is largely interested in agricultural pursuits, owning about 1,500 acres of valuable land. The mill was burned once but was soon replaced by a better one. In 1865 Mr. Kearney married

M. L. Davis, who was born in 1842. She was a most estimable woman and an earnest member of the Cumberland Presbyterian Church. She died in 1868 leaving one son. Five years later Mr. Kearney wedded C. A. Harriss, who was born October 6, 1844. This union resulted in the birth of five children, four of whom are living. For over half a century our subject has lived in Hardeman County and is recognized throughout the entire section as a man of fine business capacity, and an honest, upright citizen. He is a stanch Democrat in politics, and he and wife are members of the Missionary Baptist Church.

Mrs. Sallie R. Kent, nee Polk, was born in Hardeman County, Tenn., in the year 1821 and is the daughter of William and Elizabeth (Dodd) Polk. Mrs. Kent came of an illustrious family, her father being an uncle of President J. K. Polk. William Polk was a native of North Carolina and in 1837 he moved to Walnut Bend, Arkansas, sixty miles below Memphis. In 1843 our subject married Dr. Joseph Kent, a son of ex-Gov. Kent of Maryland. Dr. Kent was a native of Prince George County, Md., born in 1805, and practiced his profession in the city infirmary of Baltimore for seven years. He was an Episcopalian in his religious belief, and his death occurred in 1862, in Arkansas. Seven children were born to their marriage, two now living: Joseph and Olivia Polk Kent. Mrs. Kent had the best of educational advantages in her girlhood, having been educated at Salem, N. C. Olivia married James Bass, a native of Middle Tennessee. Dr. and Mrs. Kent's generosity was proverbial within the pale of their acquaintance, being ever ready to bestow kindnesses on all worthy applicants. In 1863 Mrs. Kent left her home in Arkansas for the purpose of educating her children in the schools of St. Louis, Mo., and in 1864 her home valued at $35,000 was destroyed by fire, besides valuable books to the amount of $3,000. After the visitation of this dire calamity, a home was offered her by her sister, Mrs. Abner Taylor, who lives in Madison County. Mr. and Mrs. Taylor were a great comfort to her in this great distress and too much cannot be said of their kindness. In 1870 Mrs. Kent moved to New Castle, Hardeman County, where she still lives, respected by all who know her, for excellent qualities.

John W. Kinney, a respected and well known farmer, of the Second District, was born August 14, 1838, in Haywood County, Tenn. His parents were George W. and Lucinda J. (Tucker) Kinney. When young they both came to the western district, settling in Haywood County, where they were wedded. In 1860 they moved to Hardeman County. Both belonged to the Methodist Church. Of the fourteen children born to their union, only four sons and three daughters survive. The father was of Irish descent, an old school Democrat, as are his sons. All of his life he was an industrious, energetic farmer, and accumulated some 1,700 acres of fine land. He died in 1883, since which time the mother has made her home with her children. The subject of this sketch was reared on a farm and received his education in the common schools. On reaching manhood's estate, he took charge of his father's business, conducting it for seven years. In 1866 he married Miss Letitia F. Goodwin, who was born August 29, 1848. Their union has been blessed with eight children, four of whom are sons. Mr. and Mrs. Kinney are consistent and earnest members of the Missionary Baptist Church. After marriage he settled in Mississippi where he farmed until 1880, when he returned to Hardeman County. He has been quite successful in agricultural pursuits and now owns about 600 acres of good land. He is an enterprising and worthy citizen.

Joseph L. Lax, farmer, is a native of the county where he now resides, born February 3, 1837, a son of Berryman and Virginia O. (Farmer) Lax. Both were of English descent and natives of Halifax County, Va. They were married in their native State and soon after immigrated to Tennessee and stopped in Bedford County for two years and then moved to Hardeman County and were among its first settlers. The father was born about the year 1792. In 1858 he immigrated to Arkansas where he died in 1874. He was a Whig in politics and he and wife were members of the Missionary Baptist Church. The mother died in Hardeman County, June 27, 1853. Joseph L., after securing a good education, began farming and has always made Hardeman County his home excepting the time spent in the war and two years spent in the States of Arkansas and Mississippi. In June, 1862, Mr. Lax enlisted in Company C, Forty-second Mississippi Regiment Infantry; was received in Gen. Heath's division, participating in the battles of the Wilderness and others. He was captured at Cold Harbor and was sent as a prisoner of war to Point Lookout. In 1865 he returned home and resumed farming, and now owns 700 acres of land. December 7, 1859, Mr. Lax married Miss Ann E. Cook, born in Montgomery County, N. C., August 20, 1837, a daughter of William and Martha Cook. Mr. Lax is a believer in Christianity, but not a member of any church. Mrs. Lax and her mother are members of the Missionary Baptist Church.

John T. Low was born June 19, 1851, two miles southwest of Saulsbury, Hardeman Co., Tenn. He is a son of E. E. and Mary A. (Aitken) Low. The father was born in Perry County, Ala., August 24, 1824, and immigrated to Hardeman County, Tenn., January, 1831, and was married September 5, 1847, to Miss Aitken, of Hardeman County, Rev. Samuel Lambeth officiating. To this union four sons were born, three of whom died in childhood. E. E. Low joined the Masonic fraternity in 1848, Berlin Lodge, No. 170, in town of Berlin, Hardeman County, and the Royal Arch Chapter and Council Masons in La Grange, Fayette Co., Tenn. September, 1854, he became a member of the Baptist Church at Rock Springs, Hardeman County, the pastor being Rev. L. Savage. September, 1855, he engaged in commercial business at Saulsbury. He formed a copartnership with John M. and J. J. Chambers; the firm was styled E. E. Low & Co. They met with considerable success and were regarded as men of ability and integrity. J. J. Chambers was a prosperous merchant and farmer, always a true Democrat. In 1861 a company was organized and called the Saulsbury Grays. J. M. Richardson was made captain. H. A. Guynn first lieutenant, E. E. Low, second lieutenant and Jesse Barden, third lieutenant. A company called the Hatchy Hunters, of Bolivar, Tenn., with R. H. Wood of that place as captain, was consolidated at Trenton, Gibson County, into the Twenty-second Tennessee Volunteers, Thomas J. Freeman as colonel of the regiment. After serving about four months Mr. Low resigned his commission as lieutenant and joined the company as a private. In the fall of 1862 the conscript law took effect and he being over thirty-five years of age was released from duty at Tupelo, Miss. He returned home. In November of the same year, while leading a quiet and peaceable life, he and several others were taken by the Federal soldiers and imprisoned at Alton, Ill. His fellow prisoners were M. M. Thurmond, T. B. Bowdon, William Gannon and T. B. Low, his brother. January, 1863, without charges or trial he was released and lived as a citizen until the following fall, when he went south with C. W. Phelps, an old comrade of the Twenty-second Regiment and enlisted in the Fourteenth Tennessee Cavalry, Col. J. J. Neely's regiment, under command of Gen. N. B. Forrest. Mr. Low was commissary of the regiment until the latter portion of December, 1864, after the battle of Franklin, Tenn., or better known as Hood's raid. He was taken sick near Nashville, Tenn., with pneumonia and left three or four miles north of Franklin with James P. Moore, a citizen. In March, 1865, he went to Memphis by boat, and obtained a situation as clerk for Pearce, Park & Co., at that place. In the fall of that year he entered into business at Saulsbury in partnership with J. J. Chambers, T. C. Moore and J. D. Ussery, the firm being known as Moore, Ussery & Co. In the fall of 1866 he retired from business, devoting the remainder of his life to his family. In 1873 Saulsbury Grange was organized with E. E. Low as Master. He died July 4, 1886. He was one of a family of twenty-two brothers and sisters. His father, Thomas Low (grandfather John T.) was born in

Randolph County, N. C., January 22, 1768. He immigrated to Georgia when quite young, then to Alabama, and January, 1831, came to Hardeman County, Tenn. The next year he formed a M. D. society in that county. His death occurred March 9, 1846, and the community lost a useful and esteemed resident. His father (great-grandfather of subject) was John Low; he married Charity, a sister of the distinguished Gen. John Butler and a niece of Gen. William O. Butler, a noted and gallant officer with Gen. Zachary Taylor in the Mexican war. The mother of John T. Low was born January 29, 1826, in Russellville, Ala. Her father, John Hall Aitken, was a native of Edinburg, Scotland. He immigrated to America in 1817. In 1821 he married Miss Mary F. Rutherford, of Russellville. His death occurred April, 1827. March, 1828, Mrs. Aitken, with her two children, William and Mary, and her father, Samuel Rutherford, immigrated to Hardeman County, Tenn., and settled where the town of Grand Junction now lies, or about two and a half miles south of the railroad crossing. Samuel Rutherford was born in Gochland County, Va., in 1763 and located in Russellville, Franklin Co., Ala., in 1818. John T. Low, the subject of this sketch, was raised on a farm and received such educational advantages as the average country boy and schools of that day gave, until about his nineteenth year or the close of the war. He then entered the Union University at Murfreesboro where he remained two years, returning home in 1872. He became interested in agriculture and has devoted his time to that pursuit in which he has met with prosperity. In connection with his chief pursuit he has done a portion of the surveying for Hardeman County since 1875. He is a man of the best social standing, influence and indisputable integrity. He is prominently connected with the Masonic order, being a Royal Arch Mason. His membership is at Saulsbury Lodge, No. 48. He is a stanch, true Democrat. He is an enterprising farmer, and extensive dealer in fine blooded stock and cattle. He is liberal and always ready to assist all charitable institutions or worthy and beneficial enterprises. He was married in Texas, December 23, 1874, to Josie Guy, the only daughter of Dr. J. H. and Ranie (Carlton) Guy. Mrs. Low was born December 5, 1856, in Haywood County, Tenn. To this union four children have been sent : Willie Carlton, born November 14, 1876; Ranie Mary, born October 10, 1877; Johnnie T., born June 14, 1881, and departed this life January 5, 1885; Josie Irene, born October 14, 1885. Mr. and Mrs. Low are devoted and exemplary members of the Missionary Baptist Church. Mr. Low joined in 1868.

Hon. J. A. Manson, a resident of Saulsbury, was born July 28, 1842, in McDonough, Ga. His parents were Dr. F. E. and Mary

B. (Bethune) Manson. The father was born March 19, 1800, in Virginia, and immigrated to Georgia about in 1820, where he was prominently connected with the political affairs of that day. He was a member of the Legislature a number of terms, being a Representative at the time Georgia seceded. His death occurred in 1874. The mother was born in Georgia, in 1810, and departed this life in 1852. She was a sister to the distinguished Gen. James Bethune of Pennsylvania. Our subject received an excellent education at Emory College, Oxford, Ga., where he was at school when the war broke out. He entered Company A, Cobbs, Ga., as private. In 1863 was promoted to rank of lieutenant; November 29, 1863, he received a wound from the explosion of a hand grenade, at Knoxville, and was disabled for about thirty days. April 6, 1865, he was captured, and imprisoned at Johnson's Island, where he was held about two months. After his release he resumed his studies at college, graduating in 1867. He taught school at Bolivar, La Grange and Saulsbury until 1880. In the meantime, 1873, he received the degree of A. M. He was elected to represent Hardeman County in the State Legislature, in 1876. He served with so much credit and distinction that he was chosen each succeeding term until 1884. In 1885 he became speaker of the house. July, of the same year, he was appointed deputy revenue collector, which position he still holds. He is a strong Democrat, and very influential. He is intelligent, enterprising and honorable. He has, by his own efforts, accumulated considerable fine property and means. He is a sincere member of the Methodist Episcopal Church South, and prominently connected with the Masonic order, K. of H., and K. & L. of H. June 28, 1870, he married Miss Fannie E., daughter of W. W. Elliotte, Sr. To Mr. and Mrs. Manson an interesting family, consisting of three boys and two girls, have been born: Joseph A., Minnie J., Frank E., Mary J. and Grover Cleveland.

David W. McAnulty, a prominent merchant of Hickory Valley, is a native of Hardeman County, born October 14, 1847, the elder of two children born to Joseph S. and Margaret A. (Woods) McAnulty. The father is a native of North Carolina, born May 12, 1821, and came with his parents to Hardeman County in 1835, where they lived the remainder of their lives. He is engaged in agricultural pursuits and has been successful in securing this world's goods. He is a Democrat and a member of the Cumberland Presbyterian Church. The mother is a native of Hardeman County, born May 14, 1833, and is a worthy member of the Cumberland Presbyterian Church. David W., by his own efforts secured a good practical education, after which he was engaged in the farming interests on his father's farm. In 1865 he became a salesman in the store of J. H. McClellan & Co., of La Grange, Tenn., where he remained one year, and the year following was connected with the firm of Graves & Gaither in the same capacity. December 10, 1867, Mr. McAnulty married Miss Martha R. Moorman, an accomplished daughter of Rev. R. A. Moorman of Hardeman County. They are the parents of eight children, six of whom are living. For about five years after his marriage, Mr. McAnulty was engaged in farming, with fair results, but in 1873 established a store in La Grange in partnership with a brother-in-law, J. P. Ferguson, which he continued one year. In 1874 they moved their stock of goods to Hickory Valley, and since then Mr. McAnulty has been of the enterprising and energetic business men of that place, now owning one-half interest in the store which is valued at $10,000, besides 300 acres of land. He is a Democrat and contributes liberally to the support of the Cumberland Presbyterian Church, of which he and wife are members.

Joseph A. Mathews, planter of Hardeman County, is a native of Abbeville County, S. C., born January 15, 1830, the thirteenth of fourteen children born to Joseph C. and Margaret (Brough) Mathews. The father, of Irish descent, was born in Abbeville County, S. C., and his occupation was farming and tanning. He was a Democrat in politics and an elder in the Presbyterian Church for many years. He died in his native county in about 1854. The mother was also a native of Abbeville County, S. C., and a member of the Presbyterian Church, and her death occurred in 1860. Joseph A. secured by his own efforts a practical education and for several years followed the tanner's trade in South Carolina, but in 1848 immigrated to Tennessee and settled in Fayette County. He here followed the same business for four years but in 1852 bought four horses and began teaming from West Tennessee and northern Mississippi to Memphis. In the summer of 1860 he took a prospecting tour through Arkansas, Texas and Louisiana, but did not buy and soon returned to Fayette County and gave his attention to farming. In 1865 Mr. Mathews purchased the place where he now lives in Hardeman County, where he moved the next year, and now owns 850 acres of land in this county. September 15, 1857, he married Miss Ellen Morrow, a lady of highly respected family, born in Greenville County, S. C., June 22, 1822. She was a member of the Presbyterian Church and died February 27, 1880, leaving two children: William M., a young lawyer of much promise, and Jennie, a young lady of many accomplishments. December 1, 1881, Mr. Mathews married Miss Fannie Campbell, a most worthy lady, born in Mississippi, May 15, 1860. Mr. Mathews is a Democrat, and he and his wife are members of the Methodist Episcopal Church South.

William A. May, merchant and planter of Hardeman County, is a native of Fayette County, born December 6, 1861, one of two children born to William A. and Mildred (Davis) May. The parents were natives of Virginia and were married in New Castle, Hardeman Co., Tenn., in about 1857. The father was born about 1815, was a Democrat, a merchant and planter, and died in Fayette County, Tenn., in 1885. He was a prominent member of the Missionary Baptist Church. The mother was born about 1840, was a highly cultured lady, a member of the Methodist Episcopal Church. Her death occurred in Fayette County, June 2, 1877. The subject of this sketch received good educational advantages, was educated at Culleoka, Tenn., and University of Alabama. After completing his education he was engaged in farming interest for two years with good success. In 1879, in partnership with W. T. Scott, he established a store of general merchandise in Hickory Valley, and has since been an active and successful business man. Mr. O. B. Polk has recently entered this firm. Mr. May owns one-third interest in this house. He also owns 3,000 acres of land in Hardeman and Fayette Counties. February 26, 1884, he married Miss Annie Morgan, an accomplished lady, a native of Memphis, Tenn. They have a child, William A., born January 15, 1885. Mr. May is a Democrat in politics, and he and his wife are members of the Presbyterian Church.

John E. McCaskill, farmer is a native of Hardeman County, born October 24, 1837, the third of five children born to Taylor and Nancy McCaskill. The parents were natives of North Corolina, where they married in about the year 1832 and in 1835 they immigrated to Tennessee and settled in Hardeman County, where they spent the rest of their days. The father was of Scotch descent, born in 1809, was a farmer, a Democrat in politics, and a worthy member of the Missionary Baptist Church. His death occurred in Hardeman County, August 10, 1841. The mother was of English origin, born February 16, 1812. She was a member of the Cumberland Presbyterian Church and died at Hardeman County, April 9, 1883. John E. received a good practical education and began early in life as a farmer, and except the time spent in the Confederate Army has always made Hardeman County his home. In the spring of 1861 he enlisted in Company B, Fourth Tennessee Infantry, and was received into Cheatham's division, and participated in the battles of Perryville, Murfreesboro, Chickamauga, etc. He was wounded at Jonesboro, Ga., in August, 1864, and was compelled to return home, when he again resumed farming. In 1865 he purchased half of the farm where he now lives from his brother, and now owns 240 acres of good land in his county. May 1, 1866, Mr. McCaskill married Miss

Cynthia Sutton, a native of Hardeman County, born November 25, 1849. Unto this union have been born ten children—seven sons and three daughters—one son deceased. Mr. McCaskill is a Democrat, and he and wife are strict members of the Cumberland Presbyterian Church.

Thomas E. Mercer, an enterprising merchant of Toone and member of the firm of Mercer & McGlathery, is a native of Madison County, Tenn., born February 5, 1844, the fourth of eight children, four now living, born to Thomas B. and Catharine (Crisum) Mercer. The parents were married in Madison County about the year 1830 and in 1843 came to Hardeman County, where they have since lived. The father was born in Currituck County, N. C., in December, 1816, is a farmer, a Democrat, and a member of the Missionary Baptist Church. The mother is a member of the same church, born in Middle Tennessee in 1818. Our subject's education at seventeen was interrupted by the breaking out of the war, when he enlisted in Company B, Thirty-third Tennessee Regiment Infantry; was received in Cheatham's division and participated in the battles of Shiloh, Perryville, Ky., Murfreesboro and of Chickamauga. At the latter place he received a severe wound which caused him much suffering. After a partial recovery he returned to the service but was officially placed on the retired list at Greensboro, Ga., in July, 1864. Mr. Mercer then returned to Tennessee and re-entered school, and after completing his education he was engaged as clerk in different mercantile houses for five years. In 1869 he formed a partnership with a brother, W. A. Mercer, and James Little and opened a grocery store in Toone which he continued with some changes in the firm for seven years. In 1876 he and brother opened a store of general merchandise, but in 1883 the brother sold his interest to F. M. McGlathery, now one of the firm. Mr. Mercer also owns 300 acres of land in Fayette, Madison and Hardeman Counties. September 6, 1870, he married Miss Lizzie Cartwright, a lady of Fayette County, born in 1843, and to them have been born eight children, six now living. Mr. Mercer is a Democrat and a member of the Missionary Baptist Church. Mrs. Mercer is a member of the Methodist Episcopal Church.

Frank M. McGlathery, of the firm of Mercer & McGlathery of Toone, is a native of Alcorn County, Miss., born June 13, 1847, a son of Samuel E. and Nancy S. (Surratt) McGlathery. The parents were married in northern Alabama in 1839, and moved the same year to what is now Alcorn County, Miss., where they have since lived. The father is of Scotch descent, a native of Lincoln County, Tenn., born February 10, 1818. He was engaged in farming until the year 1880 when for four years he sold goods in Corinth, Miss., but since then has lived a retired life. He is a

Democrat and a prominent member of the Methodist Episcopal Church South. The mother was born in Alabama June 10, 1821, and is of French ancestry. She is a member of the same church as her husband. Frank M. enjoyed fine educational advantages, receiving a good academical education, after which he clerked in his uncle's store at Boonsville, Miss., one year. In 1869 he entered the firm of A. J. Borroum & Co., druggists at Corinth, Miss. In 1870 he secured a position as assistant depot agent at Bolivar, Tenn., and at once began the study of telegraphy and soon became an expert in that branch of railroad work. November, 1872, Mr. McGlathery was appointed operator and agent at Voiden, Miss., and in May, 1873, was transferred to Toone, Tenn., where he was connected with the railroad business for eleven years. He then resigned and has since given his attention exclusively to mercantile interests, and now owns one half interest in a stock of goods valued at $15,000 or $20,000. May 1, 1872, Mr. McGlathery married Miss Mattie E. Mercer, who was born May 14, 1850. Mr. and Mrs. McGlathery are the parents of six children—three sons and three daughters—two sons deceased. Mr. McGlathery is a Democrat and he and wife are influential members of the Methodist Episcopal Church South.

J. R. Miller, a prosperous farmer and well known resident of the Fourth District, was born July 28, 1853, in the house where he now resides. His parents were John and Mary E. (Bradford) Miller. The father was born in Haywood County, in 1827, the mother in same county, in 1831. They were wedded in 1847, and soon afterward moved to Hardeman County. They had four sons and four daughters, five of whom are living. Both parents were consistent members of the Methodist Church. The father was a stanch Democrat. His chief occupation was farming, which he carried on to a great extent. For twelve years he was interested in merchandising. In all financial matters he was one of the most successful and shrewd men in the county. He was prosperous in all his undertakings. He met a sad and distressing death in 1879; while coming out of a house in Centreville he was shot and instantly killed by an unknown party. The cause of the deed remains enshrouded in mystery. The mother died in 1886. Our subject, owing to delicate health, received but a meager education. When quite a young man he began his career as an independent farmer. In 1877 he married Miss Rebecca Franklin, who was born August 3, 1856, in Hardeman County. She is a sincere member of the Methodist Church, and the mother of two children: Robert P. and John F. Mr. Miller is a conservative in politics, but takes no active part and seldom votes. For three years he has been constable, but does not aspire to offices of public trust. He has always been an enterprising and fortunate agriculturist, owning over 500 acres of land in the best portion of the county. He is deeply interested in the raising of fast, blooded horses. He has Clipper, Tom, Hal, and Highland breeds.

Martin Moore, a prominent farmer of the Fourth District, was born April 11, 1819, in Pitt County, N. C., in which State his parents were born, raised and married. His father, William Moore, while a resident of his native State, was a magistrate for a number of years, and a constable until he was forced to sell the household goods of a family. He was of so kind and sympathetic a disposition, that he resigned rather than perform such duties. He married Miss Frances Forrest, of English origin, by whom he had five sons and three daughters. In 1835 he moved his family to Tennessee, locating in the western district, Haywood County. He was a prosperous farmer and Jeffersonian Democrat. His death occurred in 1836, and his wife's in 1873. Both were Christian people, true and honorable, but never united with any church. The grandfather Forrest was a faithful soldier of the Revolutionary war. Our subject was raised on a farm; his educational advantages were inferior, but by his own efforts and application he has acquired an extensive amount of practical information. At the age of fourteen he began life for himself. After working as a laborer for ten years, he engaged in agriculture on his own responsibility. By hard work, economy and good management he has prospered to such an extent that he now owns 1,700 acres of land. He belongs to no church, but is liberal to all denominations, charitable institutions, and all who are in distress. For forty-three years he has made his home in Hardeman County, where he is well known as a worthy, honest man. He is a stanch Democrat. In 1841 he married Miss Martha E. Sammons, who was born January 20, 1822. Their union resulted in the birth of twelve children, five of whom live. The oldest son, Geo. W., was wounded at Perryville, Ky., from the effects of which he died in prison. Benjamin F. was a professor in the Medical College, at Little Rock, Ark. Mrs. Moore was an earnest member of the Primitive Baptist Church. Her death occurred in 1864. In 1868 Mr. Moore wedded Mrs. Elizabeth E. Brogden, by whom he had one son, deceased. Mrs. Moore is a Cumberland Presbyterian.

James A. Moore, Esq., one of the leading farmers of the Fourth District, was born August 8, 1837, in Hardeman County. His parents were William A. and Mary A. (Coates) Moore, both born in Halifax County, Va., the former in 1808 and the latter in 1810. They were married in their native State, residing there until 1836, when they moved to Hardeman County. To their union four sons and four daughters were born, only one surviving. Mr. Moore was an old school Whig, and after the war a Democrat. He never aspired to office of public trust, but preferred the quiet life of a farmer, in which occupation he was prosperous. In 1884 he died, a consistent member of the Missionary Baptist Church, to which his wife also belongs. Mrs. Moore makes her home with her only child, our subject. The grandfather Moore was a major in the war of 1812. J. A. Moore, Esq., was raised on a farm, and educated in the common schools. In 1861 he volunteered in Company E, Seventh Tennessee Cavalry. After a year's service, and while home on a furlough, he was elected first lieutenant of Company F, Fourteenth Tennessee Cavalry, Confederate Army, holding that rank until the close of the war. During his active and gallant service, he was neither wounded nor taken prisoner. After the restoration of peace he returned to the farm. In 1865 he married Miss Margaret A. Mitchell, who was born January 17, 1843. Their marriage resulted in the birth of seven children—two sons and five daughters. Squire Moore and his estimable wife are active and respected members of the Missionary Baptist Church. Squire Moore is a stanch Democrat. In 1882 he was elected magistrate, which office he still fills. As an agriculturist he has been very successful. He owns about 580 acres of good land. He is well known throughout the entire county, and universally esteemed.

Rev. R. A. Moorman, M. D., a well known retired physician and a popular preacher in the Cumberland Presbyterian Church of Hardeman County, is a native of Campbell County, Va., born April 8, 1808, son of M. C. and Easter (Alexander) Moorman, both natives of Campbell County, Va. They were married in that county, and afterward immigrated to Alabama, where they spent the remainder of their lives. R. A. is the third of six children born to this union, and the only one now living. He received an academical education in his native State, and at the age of nineteen came to Hardeman County, Tenn. In 1831 he entered the medical school at Lexington, Ky., where he received his diploma, and after his graduation he returned to this county, and commenced the practice of his profession, where he was a physician of fine reputation until the beginning of the war. In 1836 Dr. Moorman obtained license to preach in the Cumberland Presbyterian Church, and for fifty years has been a faithful minister in this church. While he has been a physician and minister he has also been engaged in farming, and now owns 640 acres of good land in this county. Rev. Moorman has been twice married; for his first wife he married Miss Martha A. Morgan, May 21, 1838, and to this happy union were born eight children—four sons and four daughters. This excellent woman was born in Hardeman County in about 1821, and died March 24, 1857. October 24, 1858, he married Mrs. N. T. (Young) Watson, who was a native of Madison County, and died January 16, 1884. One daughter was born to this union. Both wives were members of the Cumberland Presbyterian Church.

John T. Morrow was born in Greenville County, S. C., October 4, 1829, the youngest of fourteen children born to Col. William and Jane (Reid) Morrow, both natives of South Carolina. The parents were married in South Carolina about 1812, and in 1834 they came to Tennessee, and settled in Fayette County, where they spent the remainder of their days. The father was of Irish descent, born in 1778, was a farmer, and a member of the Presbyterian Church. He was colonel of the State militia, and a soldier of the war of 1812, and died in Fayette County in 1864. The mother was of Scotch ancestry, born in 1787, a member of the Presbyterian Church, and died in Fayette County in 1873. John T. attended the country schools of Fayette County, and afterward turned his attention to farming, and after forty years spent successfully in Fayette County, he came to Hardeman County and purchased the farm where he now lives. He was a heavy loser by the war, but has regained much of his loss, and now owns 1,150 acres of land. September 14, 1854, Mr. Morrow married Miss Margaret F. Marsh, a daughter of Daniel H. and Mary Marsh, born in Chatham County, N. C., September 20, 1835. Her parents made a settlement in Hardeman County at an early day. Mr. and Mrs. Morrow are the parents of nine children—four sons and five daughters—three now living, two sons and one daughter. Mr. Morrow is a Democrat, and he and wife and daughter are members of the Presbyterian Church.

Bartley H. Moss, a prominent citizen and well-to-do farmer, of Hardeman County, is a native of McMinn County, East Tenn., born September 15, 1836, the sixth of nine children born to Eli and Dicy (Brock) Moss. The parents were natives of South Carolina, and were married in that State. Early in life they immigrated to Tennessee, and settled in McMinn County, where they spent the remainder of their days. The father spent his life in agricultural pursuits, at which he was fairly successful. He was a Democrat in politics and a man who had many warm friends who honored him for his integrity and appreciated him for his kindness of heart. Bartley H. secured a good academical education and having selected farming for an occupation, at an early age began tilling the soil. He lived in McMinn County until the year 1873, when he came to Hardeman County and settled eleven miles southwest of Bolivar where he now lives. He began life rather poor, but by industry, economy and close application to business has secured a competency, now owning

220 acres of land well cultivated. About thirty years ago Mr. Moss was united in marriage to Miss Eliza Martin, who was born in McMinn County about 1836. They are the parents of nine children—four sons and five daughters—all living. Mr. Moss in his political views is rather inclined to the Republican party. Though not a member of any church he is a firm believer in the Christian religion and is an honored and respected citizen of his community.

P. H. McKinnie, M. D., is one of the prominent physicians of Hickory Valley, a native of the same county where he resides, born February 3, 1844, a son of Rev. Arthur and H. D. (Lee) McKinnie, who were natives of North Carolina. The father is a native of Wayne County, born in 1811; was a local preacher in the Methodist Episcopal Church and rendered that church much valuable service. He was also a farmer, at which he was very successful. His death occurred in Hardeman County. The mother was born in Rockingham County in 1810 and died in Hickory Valley in 1886. They were married in Hardeman County. P. H. McKinnie is the youngest of seven children born to his parents and received a good collegiate education. In the fall of 1862 he entered the Confederate States Army and enlisted as a private of volunteers in Company E, Seventh Tennessee Regular Cavalry, and was received in Gen. Forrest's command under Brig.-Gen. James R. Chalmers. He participated in the battles of Hernando, Miss., Moscow, Tenn., Harrisburg, Miss., Union City, Tenn., Nashville and Franklin; returned home in 1865 and took the oath of allegiance at La Grange, and soon after entered the school at New Castle where he attended one year and then entered the college at Georgetown, Ky., and having chosen the medical profession went in the fall of 1873 to the medical college at Louisville, Ky., where he duly received his diploma in 1880. He then returned to Hardeman County, and located in Hickory Valley, where he soon built up a large practice and has since been a popular and successful physician. February 29, 1876, he married Miss Susan M. Scott, born February 27, 1861, in Hardeman County, and to them has been born the following family: Claude S., born October 24, 1877; Arthur S., born April 28, 1882, and William H., born April 13, 1884. Dr. McKinnie is a Democrat in politics and a consistent member of the Missionary Baptist Church. Mrs. McKinnie is a member of the Cumberland Presbyterian Church.

Edward A. Mullen, planter, of Hardeman County, was born in York County, S. C., February 1, 1827, the oldest of a family of eleven children born to Alexander and Jane (West) Mullen. The father was born in Ireland about 1786, and came to America when twelve years of age. He was a farmer all his life. The mother was of English-Irish descent, born in South Carolina about 1793, and died January, 1877. They were married in South Carolina, and in 1829 immigrated to Tennessee, and after two years they settled in Madison County, where the father died March 13, 1853. Edward A. came to Tennessee when an infant and has spent his entire life in farming in Madison and Hardeman Counties. In 1851 he settled where he now lives, which is one of the best portions of Hardeman County, and owns 1,000 acres of land in this and Madison County. December 13, 1849, Mr. Mullen married Miss Eliza Summers, a native of Madison County, born July 31, 1827. She was a member of the Missionary Baptist Church and died April 11, 1879. May 15, 1881, he married Miss Adaline Westbrook, who is a member of the Missionary Baptist Church. In 1862 Mr. Mullen entered the Confederate Army, was received under Forrest's command and served under him until the fall of 1864, when he returned home on account of ill health. He is a Democrat and a believer in the Christian religion.

Gen. Rufus P. Neely, an early settler of Hardeman County, is the son of Charles and Lousa (Polk) Neely. The father was born in Virginia in 1787, and when young moved with his parents to Middle Tennessee. The mother was born in North Carolina in 1787, and was the daughter of Col. Ezekial Polk, of Colonial distinction, and the originator of the Polk families in Tennessee. They were among the early settlers of Maury County. The parents of our subject reared a family of four children, all of whom are living. At the breaking out of the war of 1812 Charles Neely, as captain, led a company under Jackson, and while on this campaign he saw a beautiful scope of country near Tuscumbia, Ala., where he moved after the war. He followed farming for a livelihood. In 1820 he passed away while yet in the prime of life. His young widow returned to Maury County, Tenn., and in 1822 came to Hardeman County before Bolivar was started, and when not more than half a dozen families lived in the county. Here she married Dr. C. C. Collier, by whom she had three children, all of whom are deceased. She died in 1869. Our subject was born November 26, 1808, in Maury County, near Spring Hill, and inherited Irish blood from both father and mother. He secured a good academic education, and in 1821 came to Hardeman County on a pony loaded with bacon, in company with Ezekial Polk, before mentioned. Mr. Polk had purchased extensive tracts of land and came to locate them. In 1829 our subject married Elizabeth Lee, and the result of this union was ten children, five of whom are living—one son, a physician at Bolivar, and four daughters. Mr. Neely is a Democrat in politics, and has held the offices of register, county court clerk, and has served in every clerkship in the county. In the Legislature of 1839-40 he represented Henderson County. In the days of militia the General held the position of brigadier-general, and when the trouble arose between Texas and Mexico he offered the services of his command, but his forces were authoritatively disbanded, inasmuch as it was contrary to the law of nations for the Government to allow her troops to participate. In 1839 the General led a company to assist in removing the Indians to their territory. He offered the services of his command in the Seminole war and also in the war with Mexico, but there being a surplus of troops his were left out by lot. In 1861 he enlisted as captain of Company B, Fourth Tennessee Infantry (Confederate Army), and in May of the same year was promoted to colonel of his regiment. During his service he was three times imprisoned, twice at Alton, Ill., and once at Camp Chase, Ohio. For many years he has been intimately connected with the railroad interests of the South. He it was who built the Mississippi Central, of which he was president for several years and receiver by appointment of Gov. Porter; he was president of the Memphis & Knoxville Road, and is now one of the board of directors of the Mississippi & Tennessee Road. For sixty years he has been a resident of Hardeman County, and is one of its most highly respected citizens.

Dr. James J. Neely, Jr., a prominent physician of Bolivar and a son of Gen. R. P. and Elizabeth (Lee) Neely, was born September 12, 1848, in Hardeman County. He was reared on a farm and received his early education at Bolivar, but subsequently attended the University of Mississippi, finishing the sophomore year. In 1863 he enlisted in Company E, Seventh Tennessee Cavalry (Confederate Army), and during eighteen months of service never received a wound nor was he taken prisoner. In 1868 he began the study of medicine under Drs. Moore and Tate, of Bolivar, and entered Bellevue Hospital Medical College, graduating from that institution in 1872. He then located in Bolivar, and has enjoyed a good practice. In 1876 he married Julia A., daughter of Judge Thomas Smith of Memphis. To this union were born three children: Rufus P., Jr., Thomas S. and Francis F. Mrs. Neely is a member of the Episcopal Church. Mr. Neely is a stanch Democrat in politics, and has had the honor of holding the position of health officer of the county and local surgeon of the Illinois Central Railroad. For fourteen years he has been practicing his profession in Bolivar and has met with good and well deserved success, as his many patients now living can testify.

Thomas M. Newsom, circuit court clerk of Hardeman County, was the sixth of a family of eleven children born to Michael J. and Mary C. (Cosbey) Newsom. The father was a Virginian. He moved to Middle

Tennessee when quite a young man. There he was married. During his residence in that section of the State he assisted in the laying of the corner-stone of the State Capitol. About 1850 he settled in Hardeman County, where the remainder of his life was spent. He was a prosperous agriculturist, owning some 700 acres of valuable land. For six years he was magistrate and served eight years as constable. He was a stanch Democrat. He died in 1871, a consistent member of the Methodist Church, to which his wife also belongs. Mrs. Newsom is still living on the homestead. She is about sixty-three years of age, a true Christian woman, beloved by all who know her. Of her family of children ten are living. Our subject, Thomas M., was born in Hardeman County, March 17, 1858. He was raised on a farm. In his early years his educational advantages were very meager, but later he received the benefits of a much better class of schools. At the age of eighteen he began teaching school, which he continued for about eight years, meeting with considerable success, and giving entire satisfaction to his patrons. In 1886 he was called to the important and honored position which he now holds. Thus far he has proved to be a most efficient officer, and his friends have no doubts concerning his future discharge of duties. He is an ardent Democrat, a genial, intellectual gentleman, well known and highly respected.

John S. Norment, one of the oldest and best known residents of Hardeman County, was born in the county January 31, 1828. His parents were Nathaniel E. and Sarah (Menifee) Norment. The father was a Virginian of English descent; the mother was of English-Dutch extraction, born in Knox County, Tenn. When quite young they moved to Alabama, where they were married and lived until 1826, when they came to Tennessee, settling near Whiteville, Hardeman County. To their union seven children were born, two of whom are living. Both parents were Methodists, but late in life Mrs. Norment united with the Cumberland Presbyterian Church. Her death occurred in 1881. Previous to Mr. Norment's marriage with Miss Menifee, he had been twice married. By his first wife he had two children, and by the second wife four children. He was one of the most prosperous farmers of the section in which he lived, and built the first and only cotton factory in the county. He departed this life in 1839. The subject of this sketch was raised on a farm, receiving such education as the common schools of that day afforded. At the age of nineteen he engaged in agricultural pursuits, to which he has given his attention since that time. For a short time previous to the war he was interested in merchandising. He is a consistent member of the Cumberland Presbyterian Church, a liberal contributor to all charitable, religious or worthy enterprises. He was an old time Whig, and is now a stanch Democrat. Few men in the county are older or more respected residents than he. In 1847 Mr. Norment married Miss Nancy Burford, born March 10, 1829. To them six sons and five daughters were born. Mrs. Norment died in 1874, a sincere Christian, an estimable woman and devout member of the Methodist Church. Her parents were Dr. Jonathan and Nancy (Chaffin) Burford. The father was a native of North Carolina. Early in life he moved to Alabama, where he was at one time clerk of the court. In 1828, after his marriage, he came to Hardeman County, where he was a successful practicing physician until failing health caused him to retire from active life. He was an old school Whig. His death occurred in 1849. Mrs. Burford was a Virginian, the mother of ten children, of whom only two are living. She died in 1838. Both were members of the Methodist Church.

Rev. William M. Norment, one of the leading and best known ministers in the Cumberland Presbyterian Church, was born September 21, 1829, near where Whiteville now stands. His parents were Nathaniel E. and Sarah (Menifee) Norment. The subject of this sketch was raised in the country, receiving a liberal education in the best schools in the community. When sixteen years of age he took a year's work at the Cumberland University. At the early age of nineteen he married Miss Martha B. Miller, born November 6, 1831, in Virginia, and brought her to Hardeman County when a mere child. This union resulted in the birth of twelve children, of whom two sons and five daughters are living. The mother and family are all members of the same denomination of which he is a clergyman. After marriage Mr. Norment settled on a farm. He had devoted considerable time to theological study and in 1852 entered the ministry, being ordained two years later, in which noble work he has since been engaged for the past thirty-four years with most favorable and satisfactory results, laboring zealously from a sense of duty, always putting aside pecuniary considerations. In connection with his ministerial duties he was interested, for several years previous to the war and immediately afterward, in mercantile business in Whiteville. He has also run a saw-mill for a number of years. He is still engaged to some extent in farming. He owns about 250 acres of valuable land.

Hon. Jesse Norment, attorney at law and proprietor of the Bolivar *Bulletin*, was born Aug. 20, 1849, in Hardeman Co. where he has been raised and received his education in the common schools. He is a son of John S. and Nancy S. (Burford) Norment, also natives of the same county. The mother was born March 10, 1829, and departed this life in 1874, an exemplary Christian, an affectionate wife and mother. The father was born January 31, 1828. He is one of the prosperous agriculturists and most worthy residents of the county. The grandparents on both sides were among the earliest and most respected settlers of Hardeman County. The subject of this sketch entered the Lebanon law school in 1869 and was admitted to the bar one year later, since which time he has been having an extensive and lucrative law practice in his native county. He is a strong and influential Democrat and for several years has led a public life. He first served as mayor of Bolivar, discharging the duties of his office in a highly commendable manner. In 1882-84 he represented Hardeman and McNairy Counties in the State Senate, and in 1886 had the honor of being re-elected, which was a practical demonstration of the regard in which he is held by the people. He is an able lawyer, an efficient public servant and a courteous, popular man. In 1873 he married Miss Sallie Black, who was born January 21, 1855, in Bolivar, Tenn. Their union has been blessed with four interesting children: Hamilton, Nancy E., Jesse B. and Maggie. Mr. and Mrs. Norment are members of the Cumberland Presbyterian Church.

William Nuckolls, an old and highly esteemed resident of Hardeman County, was born August 15, 1804, in Robertson County, Tenn. His parents were Richard and Temperance (Walton) Nuckolls; both were natives of Virginia and came to Middle Tennessee about 1798. They had a family of five sons and two daughters, our subject being the youngest and only surviving one. He received a very limited education. In 1824 he located in Hardeman County where he has since resided. In 1852 he wedded Zarilda Cotton, who was born in 1818. To them were born six children, of whom two sons and two daughters are living. Mr. Nuckolls was for a short time magistrate, having received his appointment from Brownlow. He has been a Democrat nearly all his life and during the war was a strong Union man. His chief occupation has been the saw-mill business in which he has amassed quite a snug fortune. He is also interested in farming. He began life without capital but by industry and attention to his affairs is now the possessor of about 2,600 acres of fine land. He has lived in Hardeman County many years and is universally regarded as an able, substantial and worthy citizen. Neither Mr. nor Mrs. Nuckolls have ever united with any denomination.

John W. Nuckolls, M. D., a well known physician and extensive planter, a resident of Toone, Hardeman Co., Tenn., is a native of the county where he resides, born December 7, 1840, the fourth of nine children, eight now living, born to Starling and Narcissa (Whitaker) Nuckolls. The father was of Welsh descent, born in Virginia in 1784, but when a child came to Tennessee and settled in Robertson County. He was engaged in farming and the milling business and was a prominent man of his day. He died in 1860. It is thought the mother was a native of Lincoln County, Tenn. She was much younger than her husband and died in Hardeman County in 1876. John W. in the fall of 1861 entered the Confederate States Army and joined what was known as Capt. J. J. Neely's company of cavalry and was received in Forrest's command. He served two years under him but was captured in December, 1863, and was held as a prisoner of war several weeks in Bolivar, but was finally released upon taking the oath of allegiance. December 5, 1867, he married Miss Fannie R. Anderson, daughter of Edward Anderson, of Hardeman County. She was born in 1845, and they are the parents of eight children, six now living. Immediately after his marriage he began the study of medicine, and in 1870–71 attended the Medical College of Nashville, after which he returned home and began practicing in connection with Dr. J. R. Anderson establishing a drug store at the same time. Dr. Nuckolls dissolved partnership with Dr. Anderson after two years' connection. He now owns a fine residence in Toone valued at $5,000, besides 4,000 acres of land in Hardeman and Madison Counties. Dr. Nuckolls is a Democrat in politics and his religious views are in sympathy with the Missionary Baptist Church.

Noah C. Nuckolls, one of the leading livery men of Bolivar, is a son of William and Zarilda (Cotton) Nuckolls, and was born September 8, 1855, in Hardeman County. He was reared on a farm and had good educational advantages. After reaching manhood he spent some time in Texas, Middle Tennessee and Arkansas. He then returned to Hardeman County and farmed till 1885, when he moved to Bolivar and opened a livery stable, which he is now operating with evident success. Though in business only a short time Mr. Nuckolls has succeeded in gaining his share of the patronage of the county. Mr. Nuckolls' fine rigs for the accommodation of the public are to be had at the very lowest prices. Those having had any business transactions with him have found him pleasant and prompt in all his dealings.

T. A. Parran, farmer of Hardeman County, was born June 18, 1829, in Memphis and received a rather limited education. On reaching manhood he began his career as a farmer, which he has continued up to the present. In 1848 he married Maria Wood, a native of Hardeman County, born in August, 1830, and to them were born three children: David, Anna and Thomas C. Both he and wife and all the children are members of the Presbyterian Church. In politics Mr. Parran has always been a Democrat. He is not one who aspires to places of public trust, but performs the duties of a public-spirited citizen. He holds the position of alderman of the town of Bolivar. In 1875 he came to this town and has been engaged to some extent in selling machinery in partnership with his son David. His chief occupation is superintending his plantation, which consists of 1,200 acres. He has made this county his home the principal part of his life, and is considered an excellent citizen. His parents, Thomas O. and Anna (Carr) Parran, were natives of Calvert County, Md., and Albemarle County, Va., respectively. They were married in Memphis and to this union was born one child, a son. By occupation the father was a journalist, having established one of the first newspapers of Memphis. He died while in the prime of life, and his widow soon followed him.

James M. Pettigrew, a prominent farmer of Hardeman County, was born in Haywood County, Tenn., October 24, 1843, a son of Samuel E. and Nancy (Nicholson) Pettigrew. The father was born in Virginia, and the mother in North Carolina, but were brought to this county when very young, and here they married. To them a family of eleven children were born of whom one son, and one daughter are living. The father when only a boy served under Jackson, at New Orleans. He was a stanch Democrat. Although not a church member he was an honest and esteemed man. By trade he was a carpenter and assisted in building the first houses in Bolivar. After living in this county many years, they moved to Haywood County, where the mother died in 1859. During the war the father went to Arkansas where he died. The subject of this sketch was raised on a farm, receiving a good common-school education. He began life for himself at the age of seventeen. Some time afterward he engaged in the grocery business. In 1870 he married Mrs. L. L. Miller, *nee* Doyle, who was born May 19, 1841. By her first marriage she had two children, of whom Mary is living. To Mr. and Mrs. Pettigrew seven children were born, five of whom are living: Carrie B., James C., Joseph V., Edna L. and Nannie P. Soon after marriage Mr. Pettigrew moved to Humboldt, Tenn., engaging in the cultivation of fruits. In 1879 they returned to Hardeman County, settling at Centerville, where they have a fine farm, consisting of about 665 acres. He is an industrious, prosperous and most worthy citizen. He and his estimable wife are members of the Missionary Baptist Church.

W. A. Pledge, a resident and undertaker of Grand Junction, was born December 1, 1823, in Virginia, and immigrated to Tennessee in 1849, locating in the immediate vicinity of his present residence, where he has since lived. His parents were Archie and Mary E. (Garthright) Pledge, both natives of Virginia. The father was born January 1, 1782, and came to Hardeman County in 1850, where he died June, 1858. The mother was born in 1791, and departed this life in 1861. They were respected, good people. The subject of this sketch on his arrival to this place entered upon his present occupation, in connection with various branches of mechanical trade. November 1, 1849, he married Elvia J. Yancy, a native of North Carolina, whose parents came to Tennessee about 1837. This marriage resulted in the birth of Olivia, wife of E. L. Estep, present proprietor of the Stonewall Hotel; Joel A., whose death occurred in 1862, and William W., died in 1878. Mr. Pledge entered the Confederate service in 1862, in Company G, Thirteenth Tennessee Infantry. July 22, 1864, at Atlanta, Ga., he was shot in the right shoulder, which disabled him for further service, but his feelings were so strong, that he did not return home until the surrender. He is a stanch Democrat, and has been an active, consistent member of the Missionary Baptist Church since 1842. He is in good standing with the Masonic order and K. of H. He is one of the most substantial and worthy citizens in the entire community.

Oscar B. Polk, an extensive planter of Hardeman County, is a native of the county where he resides, born March 1, 1849. He came of the old Polk family of State and national fame, and was a near relative of James K. Polk. For sketch of parents see biography of Thomas Polk. Oscar B. received good educational advantages in youth afterward attending the St. Louis University and the Oxford College of Mississippi. After completing his education he engaged in agricultural pursuits on his father's farm until 1871 when his father died. He then took charge of the farm which was a large cotton plantation and fine success attended his efforts. November 25, 1879, Mr. Polk was united in marriage to Mrs. Ada C. Lowe, whose maiden name was Boyle, an accomplished lady, a native of Hardeman County, born in 1852. Mr. and Mrs. Polk are parents of two children: Oscar B. and Ada C. Mr. Polk has been an active business man all his life and is perhaps the most extensive planter in the county. He also owns a third interest in the firm of Polk, May & Scott at Hickory Valley, and owns over 5,000 acres of land in Tennessee, Arkansas and Texas. He is not a member of any church but a believer in the Bible and a man of good moral character. Mrs. Polk is a member of the Roman Catholic Church.

Thomas Polk, a well known merchant of New Castle, Hardeman Co., Tenn., is a native of the county where he resides, born November 27, 1852, a son of J. J. and T. J. (Bowels) Polk. The father was a native of North Carolina, born in 1808 and died in Hardeman County, September, 1871. The mother was born in Virginia, in 1816, and died in Hardeman County in 1879. In early life the father immigrated to Tennessee and settled in Hardeman County, where he spent the remainder of his life as a farmer, and was one of the most extensive planters in the county. He was a Democrat in politics, and he and wife were devout members of the Methodist Episcopal Church. Our subject came of one of the most eminent families that has ever made a home in Tennessee, J. K. Polk, the President, being one of its illustrious members, Thomas secured a good education in his youth, and after farming until 1872 he then established a store in New Castle, and since then has been an active merchant and has secured a fair competency. He now owns a stock of goods valued at $10,000, and owns 800 acres of good land in the county. July 15, 1874, Mr. Polk married Miss Willie Roders, a highly cultured lady, a native of Louisiana, born March 1, 1855. To this union have been born four children: John J., born April 28, 1875; Florence E., born May 17, 1877; Sarah T., born August 20, 1879, and Lola M., born November 27, 1881. Mr. Polk is a Democrat and he and wife are influential members of the Methodist Episcopal Church South.

Dr. Thomas E. Prewitt, a leading and skillful physician and surgeon of Grand Junction, was born July 31, 1838, in South Carolina, of which State his parents were also natives. His father, James Prewitt, was born November, 1797, and moved to Hardeman County in 1845, and there died in 1875. His wife was Elizabeth Hill, born in 1804 and died in this county October, 1869. The grandfather Prewitt's name was David. The maternal grandfather was an Englishman by birth and an extensive agriculturist of South Carolina, where he resided for many years. Our subject is the sixth of nine children. He was raised on a farm, attending the schools in the vicinity. At the age of nineteen he entered Bethel College, at McLemoresville, Carroll County, where he continued for three years. He then returned home and began the study of medicine with his brother, Dr. N. H. Prewitt. In 1859 he began a course at the Jefferson Medical College, Philadelphia, Penn., and graduated at the University of Nashville, February, 1861. The spring of the same year he began practicing at Grand Junction. Soon afterward the late war broke out, and with others he entered the Fourth Tennessee Infantry, Confederate service. In a short time he was made surgeon of artillery, and the spring of 1862 was assigned surgeon of the Twelfth Tennessee Infantry, which he retained until the surrender. After peace was restored he went to Arkansas, locating in Drew County, where he remained until 1875, when he moved to present place of residence, forming a partnership with his brother, Dr. Nathan Prewitt, who was medical railroad inspector, employed by the National Board of

Health. Dr. Thomas E. Prewitt was surgeon of the Illinois Central Railroad, and inspector of the State and National Boards of Health during the yellow fever siege of 1879, and is now director of the board of health at Grand Junction, which position he has filled for past eight years. He is one of the most popular and successful physicians and surgeons in the county, and has performed some wonderful operations with most favorable results. He is of good social standing, highly respected, a member of the Methodist Episcopal Church South, and prominently connected with the Masonic order and K. of H., also a stanch Democrat. July, 1866, the Doctor wedded a daughter of Judge Dudley Dix Daniel of North Carolina, Miss M. E. Daniel. To this union seven children were born, five of whom are living: Dudley, James H., Malcolm Lee Roy, Bennona F. and Thomas W.

T. P. Pulliam, a well known farmer of Hardeman County, is a native of Montgomery County, N. C., born October 6, 1822, the sixth of sixteen children born to Silas and Sarah (Morgan) Pulliam, both natives of Montgomery County, N. C., where they were married. In 1837 they immigrated to Tennessee and settled in Hardeman County. The father, who was a farmer, was a Democrat in politics and was born in 1787 and died in Hardeman County December 4, 1873, a worthy member of the Methodist Episcopal Church. The mother, who was several years younger than the father, was a devout member of the same church as her husband; she died in about 1862. T. P. secured by his own efforts, a good academical education and at an early day began farming. At the age of fifteen he came with his parents to Hardeman County, and except about six years spent elsewhere he has made this his home ever since. In 1874 he settled where he now lives, sixteen miles southwest of Bolivar. Mr. Pulliam has been a man of unusual energy all his life and has been very successful as a planter. He began life poor but with a good name, and by industry and economy has secured a fine competency. Although he lost considerable by the late war, he yet owns, clear of all incumbrances, upward of 800 acres of good land in his county. December 19, 1854, he married Mrs. Martha J. (Reagan) Hinson, a native of Hardeman County, born April 6, 1828. They are the parents of nine children, five now living. Mr. Pulliam is a stanch Democrat and is a member of the Methodist Episcopal Church South. Mrs. Pulliam and three children are members of the same church.

Prominent among the early settlers of Hardeman County were William and Tabitha (Coburn) Reynolds, both natives of North Carolina. In 1824 William came to Hardeman County and helped clear the forest from the spot where the town of Bolivar now stands. Some time after this he married and settled in this county, making it his permanent home. Their family consisted of seven children, only three now living. The father was a Democrat before the war and a strong out-spoken Union man afterward. For a calling in life he followed manufacturing and selling furniture. He died in 1878. The mother is still living, is over three score and ten years of age and is a member of the Cumberland Presbyterian Church. William H., the eldest son of William and Tabitha (Coburn) Reynolds, was born June 21, 1837, in Bolivar, where he received his education. At the age of eighteen he took charge of his father's business, learning the cabinet-maker's trade, at which he has worked ever since. In 1867 he married Jennie Estes, and the fruits of this union were six children, five of whom are living. In 1859 William H. went to Arkansas, where he remained for some time. In 1866 he returned to Bolivar and since then has been engaged in the undertaking and furniture business. In 1884 he opened a grocery and hardware store and is engaged in this business at the present. He is also somewhat interested in farming. He is a Democrat in politics and for forty-nine years has made this county his home. Twenty years of that time he was intimately associated with the business interests of Bolivar. Although not a church member, he is liberal toward churches, schools and all other worthy enterprises. He also took an active part in raising the funds and helped survey the grounds, etc., for the new asylum. He is of Scotch-Irish origin.

Dr. Abraham Rhea, a leading and skillful physician of Whiteville, was born February 25, 1830, in Maury County, Tenn. His parents were Matthew and Mary (Looney) Rhea, both natives of Sullivan County, Tenn. The father was of Scotch-Irish extraction. He was married and resided in Maury County until 1836, when he moved to Fayette County and there passed the remainder of his life. His family consisted of thirteen children, only five of whom are living. He and his wife were consistent members of the Presbyterian Church. Mr. Rhea was a man of great culture and intellect. He had a thorough liberal education and was considered a fine classical scholar. In early life he completed a law course but never practiced to any great extent. After abandoning his profession he taught school awhile, then turned his attention to farming, but spent a great portion of his time with his books, of which he was very fond. He made the first map of Tennessee, taken from a survey of the State. At Somerville there is also a map he drew of Fayette County. He died in 1870 at the age of seventy-five years. Mrs. Rhea, who was of English descent, departed this life in 1884, having attained the full ripe age of eighty. The grandfather, Mathew Rhea, was an officer of the Revolutionary war; for his gallantry, had the honor of being presented with a very fine sword by the distinguished Gen. Greene. The great-grandfather, Joseph Rhea, was a graduate of the University of Glasgow, Scotland, and was a Presbyterian minister. The subject of our sketch spent his early days on a farm; later he lived in Somerville, where his literary education was received. At the age of eighteen he began the study of medicine under the guidance of Dr. A. F. McKenzie. In 1853 he graduated at the Memphis Medical College. After several years of extensive practice, he became a great sufferer from rheumatism and afterward sold drugs for three years. In 1861 he volunteered in Company B, of the Thirteenth Tennessee Infantry, Confederate service. After serving some fourteen months, he stood an examination and was appointed surgeon, remaining in that position until close of the war, when he came to Whiteville to practice medicine. He has met with unusual success, receiving a liberal and lucrative patronage. He is acknowledged throughout the section as one of the most able and popular physicians. In 1869 he married Miss Emma L. Cross, who was born in 1846. To their union three sons and four daughters have been born. Mrs. Rhea is a member of the Methodist Church and the Doctor of the Presbyterian. He is also a strong Democrat and was a Whig previous to the war.

Dr. John S. Robertson, a farmer and retired physician of Whiteville, was born July 7, 1819, in Wake County, N. C., the only surviving member of a family of nine children born to John and Mary (Barrham) Robertson. The father was a native of the same State and county as his son. The mother was born in Virginia, but immigrated with her parents when a small child to North Carolina, where she was married. Both were of Scotch-Irish extraction. In 1820 they moved to Madison County, Tenn., being among the first settlers west of the Tennessee River. They were not connected with any church, but were honorable and respected people. The father was a Whig; during his entire life was a planter and very prosperous. He employed a large number of hands. His death occurred in 1821, after which the mother lived with her family until 1852, when she departed this life. The subject of this sketch was raised on a farm and educated in the old field schools. About the time he attained his majority, he began the study of medicine; afterward took a course in the Ohio Eclectic Medical School at Cincinnati, where he graduated in 1844. He immediately began to practice in Henderson County, and in 1848 located in Hardeman County, three miles west of Whiteville, where he engaged in the exercise of his profession, and also agriculture, meeting with success in each. In 1870 he moved into the town, where he has since resided. For fifteen years he was postmaster, at same time keeping a drug store. After thirty-four years of active and profitable practice he retired from his professional duties in 1880, and since that time has been giving his attention to his plantations. He owns some 700 acres of valuable land. Before the war he was a Whig but since that time has affiliated with the Democratic party. In 1844 the Doctor married Miss Amanda M. Wood, born in Henderson County, October 1, 1826. To their union three sons and one daughter were born: Andrew L., who was in the army under Gen. Forrest's command, and was killed at the battle of Memphis; Eugenia C., Christopher W., also in Forrest's command, and John B. Mrs. Robertson was a true Christian woman, an earnest member of the Methodist Church. Her death occurred in 1860. Three years later the Doctor wedded Miss Nannie M. Carnes, who was born April 4, 1835. This marriage resulted in the birth of two children: Mary W. and Carnes. The Doctor and Mrs. Robertson are active and esteemed members of the Methodist Church.

Elder Wiley W. Sammons, a prominent farmer of the Cedar Chapel District, was born in Hardeman County, November 11, 1827. His parents were Allen and Sallie (Long) Sammons, both of whom were of English extraction, born in Sussex County, Va., the father in 1788 and the mother in 1795. They were married in 1811, remaining in their native State until 1827, when they came to Hardeman County, being among the early settlers. Eleven children blessed their union, of whom only two are living. Mr. and Mrs. Sammons were zealous Christians. For thirty-three years he was one of the most faithful and active ministers that the Primitive Baptist Church ever had. All his efforts in the noble work were given without price or money. In connection with his ministerial duties he engaged in farming and was one of the most prosperous agriculturists of the county. He was a fife major in the war of 1812. He was a strong, straight Democrat. He departed this life in 1862, and two years later the mother, too, passed away. The subject of this sketch was raised on a farm, receiving a fair education. He remained beneath the paternal roof until he attained manhood's estate, then began farming on his own responsibility, and met with unusual success. Twice he was financially wrecked—once by the war, and again by parties whom he assisted when they were embarrassed, and they afterward proved faithless. Being possessed of a brave heart and much determination, he was soon again in flourishing circumstances, and now owns 312 acres of valuable land. For twenty-six years he has labored as an elder without pecuniary considerations of any kind. Although he has ridden thousands of miles between North Mississippi, West Tennessee and western Kentucky, he has never served for a salary. In 1850 he married Miss Martha F. Wilkes, a daughter of Joseph Wilkes. Mrs. Sammons was born October 16, 1833. A true Christian woman, and member of the Primitive Baptist Church, she died in 1885. Of the ten children born of this union, three daughters and two sons are living. J. A., the eldest son, is a minister. Late in the year of 1885 he wedded Miss Susan A. Price, who was born October 22, 1843. For fifty-nine years Mr. Sammons has made Hardeman County his home and has seen the country change from a wilderness to a fine farming district. His family is one of the oldest, most useful and honored in the community.

Dr. J. D. Sasser, a respected resident and popular physician of Middleton, was born September 18, 1846, in Hardeman County. His parents, John and Mary Ann (Ewing) Sasser, were natives of North Carolina. The father was born in 1784, and immigrated to Tennessee at a very early day, settling in the Twelfth Civil District of Hardeman County, where he remained until his death in 1876. The mother was born about 1818, of Irish origin. She bore three sons and three daughters, all of whom with their aged and beloved parents are still living. The Doctor was brought up on a farm, and educated in the common schools. In 1872 he began the study of medicine under guidance of Dr. T. B. McKey, and entered the Medical University of Louisville September, 1874, graduating March 1, 1876, and returned to the old homestead where he commenced the practice of his chosen profession. In December, 1877, he moved to Middleton where he has since enjoyed an extensive and lucrative practice, in connection with which he is interested in merchandise business, the firm being known as J. D. Sasser & Co. He is a devout member of the Missionary Baptist Church, and belongs to the Masonic order and K. of H. He is a stanch Democrat. October 1, 1868, the Doctor married Rachel M. Grantham, whose father, Thomas G., was one of the pioneer settlers of Tennessee. To this union two children were born: Rachel Ann and Margaret Grantham. Mrs. Sasser died September 25, 1872. The Doctor married again January 23, 1878, to Isabella Swineboard of Bolivar, Tenn. There is no issue.

Dr. J. D. Sauls, a prominent resident and physician of Saulsbury, of English descent, was born October 18, 1833, in Hardeman County. His parents were Burrell and Jane (Mathis) Sauls. The father was born in North Carolina, August 17, 1800. He went to Alabama in 1819, and shortly afterward immigrated to Tennessee, locating in Hardeman County. He was a very prosperous and respected man. The town of Saulsbury was named in honor of him. He donated considerable property for a depot site, and did all in his power for the improvement of the place. The mother was born in Georgia in 1812, and departed this life April, 1886. The subject of this sketch was raised in Saulsbury. He began the study of medicine January, 1854. He entered the Jefferson Medical College at Philadelphia, Penn., October of 1854, and graduated at the University of Louisiana at New Orleans, in 1856. He returned to his native home where he has since resided, and enjoyed the benefit of an extensive and lucrative practice. He is a substantial and worthy citizen, esteemed by all who know him. He is connected with the Masonic order, and is a stanch Democrat. September, 1857, the Doctor married Diza Ann Jones, who died in 1873, without issue. He was wedded in 1874 to Mrs. A. M. Jones, whose husband died in October 1867 of yellow fever. She is a daughter of J. M. and S. E. Oliver, whose births occurred respectively in 1800 and 1806, and died in 1842 and 1869. To Dr. and Mrs. Sauls two children have been born: Diza E., who died in 1882, and Joseph. Mrs. Sauls has two children by her first union: Moses L. and Mollie V. Jones. The Doctor and wife are consistent and active members of the Cumberland Presbyterian Church.

Jefferson C. Savage, trustee of Hardeman County, was born May 27, 1820, in Monroe County, Ky. He is the only surviving one of a family of twelve children born to Hamilton and Elizabeth (Martin) Savage, both of whom were born, raised and married in North Carolina. Soon after marriage Mr. Savage moved to Kentucky, and about 1824 to Tennessee, locating in Hardeman County. He served in the war of 1812. He was a Whig before the civil war, and afterward a strong Democrat. He was a successful farmer. After the death of his first wife, he married Mrs. Paie. He was of English descent, and Mrs. (Martin) Savage, Scotch-Irish. Both were members of the Missionary Baptist Church. He died in 1865 at the age of eighty-four. The grandfather was a soldier of the Revolutionary war; by birth a Virginian. He lived to the remarkable age of one hundred and ten years. The subject of this sketch was raised on a farm. His educational advantages were very limited, attending school only about twelve months. He was an affectionate, dutiful son; devoted himself to his parents as long as they lived. In 1843 he married Miss Lucy Dean, who was born in 1811. To them six children were born—two sons and four daughters —two of whom are living: Giles M., and Eudora F., wife of W. F. Prewitt, a farmer of the county. In 1878 Mrs. Savage died. She was a member of the Missionary Baptist Church. Four years later Mr. Savage married Mrs. Sallie Black. There is no issue. 1862 Mr. Savage entered the army, first in Capt. Wilson's company, and shortly afterward was transferred to the company of Capt. Wiley Higgs of which he was made first lieutenant, serving in that capacity until close of war. During all of his active and gallant service he was neither wounded nor captured. After the restoration of peace he began farming, continuing until 1872 when he was called to his present position. He has discharged the duties of his office in such a satisfactory and creditable manner that he has been re-elected eight times in succession. He has resided in the county for sixty-one years. He began life as a poor man, but by honesty, industry and enterprise has accumulated nearly 900 acres of fine land and considerable means. He is a generous contributor to all charitable and religious institutions. He is an esteemed and worthy citizen. Mr. and Mrs. Savage are both consistent members of the Missionary Baptist Church.

Reuben S. Scott, farmer of Hardeman County and resident of Hickory Valley, is a native of Wake County, N. C., born February 23, 1825, son of Joseph and Susanna (Halliburton) Scott. The parents were both natives of Wake County where they were married and lived all their lives. The father was born in 1781 and was of Scotch descent. He was a planter by occupation; for a number of years held the office of magistrate and was at one time deputy sheriff of his county. He served as second lieutenant of infantry in the war of 1812 and died in his native county at the age of eighty-seven years. The mother was of English ancestry, born about 1786 and died in the ninety-fourth year of her age. Reuben S. is the eleventh of a family of twelve children and secured a good education. In 1849 he immigrated to Hardeman County, Tenn., and with the exception of two years has ever since made it his home. In 1862 he enlisted as first lieutenant in Company L, Thirteenth Tennessee Regiment (Infantry), was received in Cheatham's division and participated in the battles of Shiloh, Richmond, Perrysville and Murfreesboro, and on account of ill health was honorably discharged in 1863. In 1868 he purchased the farm thirteen miles southwest of Bolivar where he lived five years, but early in 1874 he moved to Hickory Valley and has since been one of its substantial residents. He owns upward of 400 acres of land, besides a town lot with sixty acres connected. May 23, 1850, Mr. Scott married Miss Eliza J. Perry, a native of Chatham County, N. C., born October 27, 1827. To this marriage have been born eight children, three of whom are living. Mr. Scott is a Democrat in politics and he and family are members of the Cumberland Presbyterian Church.

Squire Thomas Shea, a respected resident of Pocahontas, Hardeman County, was born February 1, 1844, in Kerry County, Ireland. He was the oldest of six children born to John and Bridget Shea; all are living. The father died December, 1880. Our subject with parents immigrated to America in 1852; they located in Memphis, Tenn., where they resided three years, then moved to Pocahontas where they have since made their home. Squire Shea entered the Confederate service in 1861, at the early age of sixteen years, in Company F, Ninth Tennessee Infantry. At Shiloh, April 7, 1862, he was shot through the left lung, the ball entering about the seventh rib, and coming out near the spinal column. This wound disabling him for active infantry service, he consequently joined the cavalry troops, remaining with them until the close of the war. He was captured May, 1863, near Tupelo, Miss., and imprisoned at Alton, Ill. He was soon afterward exchanged. He was again taken prisoner October, 1863, at Bolivar but made his escape. After the surrender he returned home and engaged in farming until 1878, when he embarked in merchandise, continuing in that line until February, 1886. He was elected magistrate of the Nineteenth District in 1876, and has served the people in that capacity up to present date. He is acting justice of the peace. October 1, 1865, he married Mollie E., daughter of Thomas H. and Helen E. Neese, *nee* Patterson. This union resulted in the birth of six children: John Neese, Clara E., Robert E., Mary Helen, Daniel O'Connell and James Mack. Squire Shea is a self-made man, and respected, worthy citizen. He has always been honest and industrious, by which means he has been enabled to accumulate considerable means and property. He is a devout and consistent member in good standing of the Roman Catholic Church, and a sound Democrat.

Benjamin A. Simmons, a prosperous farmer of the Fourth District, was born October 3, 1834, in Halifax County, N. C. He was the only son of James B. and Sarah (Worrell) Simmons, both of whom were born, raised and married in 1829, in same county and State that Benjamin was. They had four children. In 1853 the family moved to Hardeman County, where the mother, who was a Primitive Baptist, died in 1867. Mr. Simmons was of English origin. He was a strong Democrat, and served many years as magistrate, in his native State. By occupation he was a farmer, owning quite an extensive plantation. In 1883 he wedded Miss Clara Willoughby, and in 1886 departed this life. The grandparents on both sides were Virginians. The subject of this sketch spent his early life on a farm. He received an excellent academic education. He made his home with his parents until long after his majority. In 1861 he married a daughter of Thos. H. Harris, Miss Martha O., who was born in Hardeman County, September 20, 1844. Their union has been blessed with two sons and three daughters. In 1861 Mr. Simmons volunteered with the South. Shortly afterward he returned home and joined the One Hundred and Fifty-fourth Senior Regiment of Tennessee, serving until the close of the war. He was never captured, but received a severe wound at the battle of Jonesboro, Ga., and two others less serious. After the restoration of peace, he returned home and found all of his stock, provisions and household goods destroyed and gone. He began with absolutely nothing, but by industry and judicious management has met with great success, and now owns 1,400 acres of land. Thirty-three years he has lived in Hardeman County where he is universally and favorably known. He is very liberal to all churches, schools or beneficial enterprises.

Robert W. Smith, farmer and magistrate of the Ninth Civil District of Hardeman County, is a native of what is now Chester County, but at that time was a part of Henderson. He was born March 17, 1847, and is the fourth of six children, all now living born to Dr. John D. and Isabella (Dickson) Smith. They were married in Chester County about the year 1841. The father was a physician of large practice, and spent thirty years of his life in this profession. He was probably of English extraction; was a native of North Carolina, born in 1804 and died in Chester County, January 25, 1881. The mother was of Scotch-Irish descent, born in 1807, and died in Chester County in 1851. They were both influential members of the Missionary Baptist Church. Robert W. was principally educated at the college for gentlemen at Jackson, Tenn., and after completing his education he taught school for two years. In 1870 he formed a partnership with William G. Moore, and established a general merchandise store, which business he soon exchanged for the more congenial occupation of farming. In 1871 he took charge of the farm where he now lives, a portion of it coming into his possession by his marriage. He now owns 1,500 acres of land, six improved lots in the town of Henderson, and a steam cotton-gin and grist-mill. August 25, 1869, Mr. Smith married Miss Hattie A. Ham, daughter of Daniel and Harriett Ham. The father died June 1, 1871, and the mother is still living, making her home with her daughter. Mr. and Mrs. Smith have two children: R. Frank, born August 3, 1874, and Joseph Dickson Smith, an adopted son. Mr. Smith has held the office of magistrate for eight years, is a Democrat, and he and wife are members of the Missionary Baptist Church.

Elias B. Stewart, planter, is a native of Jefferson County, Ala., born November 3, 1832, the fifth of a family of nine children born to Elias and Elcy (Neighbors) Stewart. The parents were married in Alabama, and in 1835 came to Tennessee and settled in Hardeman County, where they spent the remainder of their lives. The father was born in 1801 in Middle Tennessee, was a farmer, and a Democrat, and died in 1854. The mother was a native of Jefferson County, Ala., and died in 1866. Elias B. secured good educational advantages in youth, and began farming at an early age. When an infant he came with his parents to Hardeman County, and has ever since made it his home with the exception of four years, when he was in the Confederate Army. In 1862 he enlisted with the South and was received into Forrest's cavalry, participating at Shiloh and Chickamauga and several other important engagements. He was honorably discharged in the spring of 1865 in Mississippi, and then returned home to resume farming. In 1873 he purchased the farm where he now lives, eleven miles west of Bolivar, and has made life a success, owning at present 1,280 acres of good land, besides owning a steam cotton-gin and grist-mill. January 27, 1859, Mr. Stewart married Miss Lucy M. Farris, a native of Hardeman County, born in 1836, and an estimable lady. They are the parents of eight children, six of whom are living. He is a Democrat in politics, and a member of the Methodist Episcopal Church. Mrs. Stewart and five children are members of the same church.

Thomas C. Stuart, a leading merchant of Whiteville, is the eldest of six children born to Arlington C. and Mary F. (Rochelle) Stuart. The father was of Scotch-Irish descent, born in Sussex County, Va., in 1816; the mother is of French origin, born in Southampton County, Va., in 1826. In 1844 they were married and moved to Haywood County, Tenn., spending a portion of their time in that and Madison County, until Mr. Stuart's death, which occurred in 1861. He was a Democrat. Although not a member of any church he was an honest respected and intelligent man. He and his wife were highly educated, and engaged in school-teaching many years, which profession Mrs. Stuart still follows. After her husband's death she and her children settled in Hardeman County, where she is generally known, and is an esteemed member of the Missionary Baptist Church. The subject of this sketch was born September 4, 1845, in Haywood County. He was raised on a farm, forming a taste for that sort of life; he began agricultural pursuits on his own responsibility at the age of sixteen. In 1863 he volunteered in Company K, Fourteenth Tennessee Cavalry, Confederate service. He soon became courier for the colonel of his regiment, so continuing until the close of the war. After the restoration of peace he resumed his farming, and in 1869 married Mrs. Henrietta C. Sammons, daughter of Joseph Wilkes. By her first marriage she had two children, and four by the union with Mr. Stuart. He is a member of the Missionary Baptist Church, and his wife belongs to the Cumberland Presbyterian. In 1879 Mr. Stuart moved into Whiteville; he was interested in various kinds of business. In

1884 he established a grocery store, since which time he has added a stock of dry goods, and is still engaged in farming. He has been a magistrate for the past four years, still holding that position. He has made his home in Hardeman County for a quarter of a century, and been intimately connected with the mercantile interests of Whiteville for several years. He is accounted a man of fine ability, and honorable and worthy citizen. He is a Democrat.

Dr. H. W. Tate, one of the leading physicians of Bolivar, was born March 14, 1840, in Burke County, N. C., and is a son of William Caldwell Tate, who was also a native of North Carolina. The father was of Irish descent and a graduate of the medical colleges at Charleston, S. C., and Philadelphia, Penn. He was a skillful physician and a prominent man. He married Mrs. Laura (Wilson) Polk, a widow with two children. By her union with Mr. Tate she became the mother of seven children—four sons and three daughters. The oldest son, J. W., is a grocery and commission merchant, and is doing a lucrative business. Robert A. is a practicing physician and J. K. a farmer. The mother was of English extraction and died in 1848. Her husband followed her in death in 1868. Our subject received a liberal education, completing the same at Davidson College, North Carolina. After a course of medical lectures at the University of New York he graduated at the Richmond Medical College of Virginia in 1861, and immediately afterward entered the Confederate Army as surgeon, in Stonewall Jackson's command, where he continued until the close of the war. In 1866 he came to Bolivar, where he has since resided, engaged in an extensive and lucrative practice. He is also the owner of some valuable land and considerable means. In 1867 he married Fannie, the daughter of Robert H. Wood, one of the leading lawyers of West Tennessee and the granddaughter, on the maternal side, of Maj. John H. Bills, who was one of the original settlers of this place. Mrs. Tate was born April 13, 1848, and by her union with our subject became the mother of two children: Mary Lucy and Robert Wood. She is a worthy member of the Presbyterian Church. Mr. Tate is a Democrat in politics and an excellent man.

Robert H. Walton, one of the old and most respected residents of Hardeman County, was born April 7, 1818, in Davidson County, Tenn. His parents were Mabrey and Martha (Exum) Walton, both of English origin and born in Virginia. They came to Sumner County, Tenn., when quite young; there they married and lived until about 1816, when they moved to Davidson County. In 1835 they settled in Hardeman County, where the remainder of their lives was spent. Their family consisted of nine sons and one daughter. Both parents were true members of the Missionary Baptist Church. Mr. Walton was a farmer by occupation. He met a sad and shocking death when about sixty-five years of age. He was standing by a chimney during a severe storm, the lightning struck it, killing him instantly. The mother lived to the advanced age of eighty-two. The grandfather Walton served seven years in the Revolutionary war, and the maternal grandfather procured supplies for the army. The subject of this sketch was the fifth child; he was raised on a farm, receiving his education in the old field schools. At eighteen he began life on his own responsibility. After keeping a toll bridge across Hatchie River, he volunteered in Capt. R. P. Neely's company, to remove the Indians to their territory. After his return he began farming, which has since been his occupation. In 1842 he wedded Mrs. Sarah Kearney, by whom he had three children, two of whom are living: Mary E., wife of D. E. Durrett, and Charles A. April, 1886, Mrs. Walton died, she was an exemplary Christian, and a member of the Missionary Baptist Church, a loving wife, a kind and affectionate mother, a useful and valuable member of society. Mr. Walton is also connected with the Missionary Baptist Church. He is a strong old school Democrat. For six years he was a magistrate, and coroner same length of time. As an agriculturist he has met with great success; having started in life with almost nothing, he has by judicious management and energy been enabled to purchase 500 acres of fine land. He has made Hardeman County his home for more than fifty years. He is well known as an honest man and worthy, upright citizen.

Andrew J. Walton, farmer, was born in Davidson County, Tenn., March 25, 1828, the ninth of ten children, three now living, born to Mabrey and Martha (Exum) Walton, both natives of Virginia and of English descent. They were married in Middle Tennessee and moved to Davidson County soon after. In the latter part of 1835 they came to Hardeman County and here spent the rest of their days. The father was born October 7, 1785, was a farmer, a Democrat and a member of the Missionary Baptist Church. His death was caused by a stroke of lightning July 15, 1851. The mother was born February 1, 1787. She was a member of the Missionary Baptist Church and died in Hardeman County May 16, 1868. Andrew J., at the age of seven years, came with his parents to Hardeman County and he has practically made this his home ever since. In youth he received a good education and decided to make farming his life occupation. In 1852 he purchased a portion of the old homestead and in a few years became owner of the whole tract and has now 370 acres of land in his county. In 1863 he entered the Confederate Army, enlisting in Company C, was received into Gen. Forrest's command and served under him until November, 1864, when by reason of ill health, he returned home. September 10, 1868, Mr. Walton married Mrs. Nancy (Marsh) Smith, a native of Hardeman County, born June 29, 1831. He is a Democrat in politics, and although not a member of any church, is a firm believer in the Bible and the Christian religion.

Alexander White, a well known resident of the Fifth District, of English origin, was born June 4, 1823, in North Carolina. His parents were natives of the same State. They were King and Telitha White. They moved to Tennessee and engaged in farming. The father died in 1838, after which Alexander took control of the homestead, which he is managing with success up to the present. He was married February, 1847, to Mary E., daughter of W. D. and Maria Simmons. Their union resulted in the birth of Maria Jane, wife of James Pirtle; George A.; James B.; Tabitha Ann, the wife of Wm. Pirtle; Mary Emma, widow of Walter Pirtle; John H., Mathias O. (deceased), Jefferson Davis, Sarah Ann, Lucie F. and Susie E. Mr. White is a self-made man, who has accumulated his possessions by industry, economy and judicious management. He is of good social standing and highly respected. Previous to the late war he was a Whig; since that time he has been a Democrat.

Rufus D. Whitley, one of the leading and well known farmers of Hardeman County, was born September 12, 1840, in Johnson County, N. C. His parents were Haywood and Esther (Gouringham) Whitley. Both were born, raised, married and died in the same State and county in which Rufus first saw the light of day. Each was of Primitive Baptist faith, although neither united with the church. They had two sons and one daughter. The father was a Democrat and farmer by occupation. He died about 1846. Mrs. Whitley married the second time to Henderson Graham, by whom she had seven children—three sons and four daughters. One of the boys, E. B., is a Methodist minister. The mother departed this life in 1861. The subject of this sketch was raised on a farm. His educational advantages were very limited. In 1861 he volunteered in the Confederate service, Company D, of the Third North Carolina Cavalry, in the division of Wm. H. Lee. During more than four years of faithful and active service he was never wounded. At Comeus Crossing, south of Pittsburg, Va., he was taken prisoner and retained at Point Lookout for eight months. While in confinement he learned to make horsehair watch-guards and thus earned the means with which he supplied himself with the extras of prison life. After the close of the war he returned financially ruined; he began life again by hiring on a farm and teaching school. In 1867 he started to Mississippi, but his means gave out, and meeting Martin Moore, he was induced to come to Hardeman County to work for him. In the fall of same year he married Miss Margie R. Hammond, who was born November 3, 1839, in Haywood County. Their union has been blessed with four children: William T., Jesse B., Rufus M. and Joseph A. Mr. and Mrs. Whitley and three older sons are members of the Methodist Church. In politics Mr. Whitley is an ardent Democrat but has never aspired to places of public trust, but by close attention to his affairs, industry and economy, has risen from a tenant to the proprietor of 360 acres of valuable and productive land as can be found in the county. He lends a liberal and helping hand to all churches, schools and good enterprises. No man is more respected or better known.

John A. Wilson, one of the leading merchants of Bolivar, was born May 27, 1832, in Hardeman County, a son of John and Mary C. (Stuart) Wilson, both of whom were natives of Kentucky where they were raised and married. They came to Hardeman County in 1824 before the days of Bolivar. Their family consisted of two sons and five daughters; three only are living. The father was an extensive planter. He was a strong Whig. He belonged to no church but was a good and noble man. His death occurred in 1837. He was of Irish origin, his father a soldier of the Revolutionary war. The mother was a true Christian woman and member of the Cumberland Presbyterian Church. She departed this life in 1872 after a lengthy widowhood. She was of Scotch descent. The subject of this sketch was raised on a farm and received a common-school education. From the age of sixteen until the outbreak of the war he managed his mother's farm. In 1859 he was married, in Marshall County, Miss., to Miss Ann E., daughter of Hardin Franklin, and granddaughter of Gov. Franklin of North Carolina, in which State Mrs. Wilson was born in 1838. The fruits of this union have been five children—three sons and two daughters. In 1862 Mr. Wilson entered the Confederate service, Company B, under command of Gen. Forrest. He served ten months, then was discharged. In 1866 he embarked in the mercantile business in which he has been successfully engaged since that time. Previous to the "late unpleasantness" he was a Whig and is now a stanch Democrat. For fifty-four years he has been a resident of Hardeman County; twenty years of that time he has been connected with the business interests of Bolivar. He is a man of ability and honor. He has never been insolvent nor sued. He is an exemplary member of the Cumberland Presbyterian Church and his wife of the Methodist.

Squire J. W. Wilson, a prominent resident of Middleton, was born March 23, 1834, in South Carolina. His father, Ashley H., was born in same State February 10, 1810. He immigrated to Tennessee in 1840 and one year later moved to Tippah County, Miss., where he still lives an old and respected man and extensive farmer. The mother, Martha P. (Janes) Wilson, was born in 1810 and departed this life in April, 1872. She was the daughter of John Janes, an Englishman. The paternal grandfather, Joseph Wilson, was a native of Ireland. The subject of this sketch was raised on a farm and worked at that occupation until 1854. He then taught school until date of the late war. He entered the Confederate service in 1861 in the Thirty-second Mississippi. He was appointed recruiting officer and returned to Mississippi where he organized a company, being elected first lieutenant of the same. They were called Company K, Tenth Mississippi Regiment. He was wounded September 20, 1863, at the battle of Chickamauga, receiving a shot through the right thigh which disabled him for further service and since that time for manual labor. After the restoration of peace he resumed teaching which, with the exception of two years in the drug business, he has followed altogether. He was married in November, 1862, to Martha A., the daughter of Joseph and Annie Janes. To the union six children were born, four of whom are still living: Cora, Maurice, John and Joseph Ashley. Mr. Wilson is a good man and respected citizen, a member of the Methodist Episcopal Church South. He is connected with the Masonic order and a true Democrat. In August, 1876, he was elected magistrate and has retained the office since that time. He is also notary public for this end of the county.

Squire J. W. Wilkes, one of the best known residents and natives of Hardeman County, was born September 17, 1835, the third of a family of three sons and six daughters born to Joseph and Naomi M. (Barnett) Wilkes. The father was of English descent, born in Davidson County, Tenn., in 1807, and raised in Humphreys County. His educational advantages were very limited. When only seventeen years of age he plied a flatboat on Hatchie River. Later he and his brother went to Haywood County, and for several years kept "bachelors' hall," and in 1826 he settled permanently in Hardeman County. In 1829 he married Miss Barnett, who was of Irish extraction, born in Kentucky in 1809 and died in 1847. His second union was with Mrs. Rebecca J. Kirkpatrick, by whom he had two sons and four daughters. The second wife died in 1875. Some time afterward he wedded Miss Ann Robley. He and each of his wives were members of the Cumberland Presbyterian Church, he having joined when a lad of twelve years. He was a stanch Democrat, and successful agriculturist. Having started in life a poor man, by hard work and good management he became owner of more than a thousand acres of land. He died March 3, 1881. The subject of this sketch was reared on a farm. After attending the schools in the vicinity he took a thorough course in the McLemoresville College, Carroll County, preparatory to the study of medicine, but failing health compelled him to abandon this desire, and he turned his attention to farming. In 1858 he married Emily J. Mitchell, who was born in Middle Tennessee November 17, 1838, a daughter of James and Mary W. Mitchell, a most highly respected family. The father was a native of South Carolina, and the mother of Tennessee. Squire and Mrs. Wilkes have two children: John W., Jr., and Emmett C. Mrs. Wilkes is a member of the Methodist Church, and Mr. Wilkes of the Cumberland Presbyterian. He is a strong Democrat. He was a stanch Union man, but when war became the last resort he went out, in 1863, in Company F, Fourteenth Tennessee Cavalry, Confederate service. During more than two years of active duty he was neither wounded nor captured. At the close of the war he returned home, and resumed farming with comparatively nothing, but by hard work, energy and judicious management he has accumulated considerable property, owning 1,100 acres of fine land. In 1866 he was made magistrate, giving so much satisfaction that he held the office for eighteen years, declining to serve any longer. He has been a resident of Hardeman County all his life, and no man in the community has a fairer name. He is charitable, and an honest, worthy citizen.

Charles Wood, a well known and enterprising farmer of Hardeman County, is a native of Virginia, born in Albemarle County, March 25, 1824, son of James and Frances A. (Allen) Wood, both of English descent and natives of Albemarle County, Va. They were married in Virginia in 1823, and in 1826 immigrated to Tennessee and settled in Hardeman County. The father was born February 22, 1797, was engaged in the mercantile business in Virginia, but after coming to Tennessee gave his attention exclusively to farming. He was a Democrat, and a member of the Presbyterian Church. He died in Hardeman County, February 7, 1867. The mother was born in June, 1804; is a member of the Presbyterian Church and is now living in Hardeman County. Charles received his education at Danville, Ky., and in 1846 settled on a farm six miles west of Bolivar, and has since been one of Hardeman County's substantial and worthy citizens. In 1872 he located where he now lives, and owns upward of 2,400 acres of land. June 22, 1858, Mr. Wood was united in marriage to Miss Blanche E. Wharley, a native of Michigan, born November 5, 1838. She is a lady highly esteemed by all and a member of the Episcopal Church. They are the parents of nine children—five sons and four daughters. Mr. Wood is a Democrat and a member of the Presbyterian Church.

John D. Woods, magistrate of the Second Civil District of Hardeman County, is a native of the county where he resides, born August 29, 1847. His ancestors were among the first settlers of Hardeman County. His grandfather, David Woods, who was a native of North Carolina and of Scotch-Irish descent, made a settlement in this county as early as 1824. The parents of the subject of this sketch were Samuel M. and Narcissa (Robinson) Woods. The father, who was a native of Orange County, N. C., born February 16, 1821, came with his parents, when an infant, to Hardeman County. He was a farmer by occupation, a Democrat in politics, and died in this county May 5, 1849. The mother is of Scotch-Irish-French descent, born in Hardeman County, March 29, 1824, and is now a resident of Tipton County, the wife of Joseph H. Shinault, to whom she was married in 1852. John D. is the elder of two children born to his parents, and received a good education in his youth, which has since been greatly improved by extensive and select reading. For several years he taught school, and in 1879 came into possession of the old homestead, and since then has been an active an enterprising planter. August 2, 1879, Mr. Woods married Mrs. Annie (McLarty) Hunt, a cultured lady, born in Hardeman County November 26, 1846. To this union two children have been born: David, born July 14, 1880, and Bessie, born March 2, 1883. In August, 1882, Mr. Woods was elected to the office he now holds, and for six years has been school director of the Second District, and being a man of liberal views he is a strong advocate of the free school system; has done much toward advancing the educational interests of the county. He is a Democrat, and though not a member of any church, is a firm believer in Christianity and is in sympathy with the doctrines of the Methodist Episcopal Church South, of which Mrs. Woods is a member.

R. M. Wright, a member of the prominent firm of Wright & Durden, of Saulsbury, was born December 3, 1834, in Madison County, Ala. His parents were John and Hannah (Moore) Wright. His father is supposed to have emigrated from Ireland to Virginia at an early day, and moved to Alabama, where he died about 1837. The mother was a native of Alabama and died when our subject was a very small child. R. M. worked on a farm until about nineteen years of age, at which time he obtained a situation as clerk in the drug store of W. B. Wright & Co. of Memphis. As he had almost no early educational advantages he had to work for his board and clothes half of the day and night, attending the public schools of the city the remainder of the day. Thus he struggled on, applying himself every spare moment to study, until he has acquired a valuable and practical store of information. September, 1857, he came to Saulsbury and engaged as a salesman for A. G. Dennis & Co., for the small amount of $150 per annum. This place he kept until the war. He entered the Confederate service in Company C, of the Twenty-second Tennessee Regiment. He was appointed sergeant by Gen. Bragg, which position he retained during the conflict. He participated actively in all the engagements into which his command was drawn, but met with no serious accident. After the surrender he returned to Memphis and clerked for Taylor, McEwen & Co. for a short time. August, 1865, he secured a place with W. W. R. Elliotte of Saulsbury. January, 1867, he formed a partnership with W. Durden and established a store, where they have since been engaged, and with no small amount of success. Mr. Wright is to-day one of the most solid and honored citizens in the community. He began life without capital and with little education, but had sufficient ambition and courage to overcome the difficulties with which he was surrounded. He is an elder in the Cumberland Presbyterian Church, a prominent member of the Masonic fraternity and K. of H. He is a stanch Democrat. August, 1865, he was married to Samuella Bunting, a daughter of Samuel and Eliza Bunting. This union resulted in the birth of four children. Mrs. Wright died August, 1874. January 28, 1875, Mr. Wright wedded Maggie Williams, a daughter of Joe C. and Mary Ross (Lake) Williams. This second union has been blessed with two sons and two daughters.

Hiram B. Wynne, a prominent merchant of Whiteville, was born February 16, 1851, in Humphreys County, Tenn. His parents were John W. and Frances S. (Traylor) Wynne. The father was born in Benton County, Tenn., in 1818, and the mother in Humphreys County, same year. John W. was a captain of flatboats, owning an interest in some of them. In his early life he was rather careless of his means, which rendered him an objectionable suitor, but he afterward settled down and became one of the best men in the community. Of the eight children born to their union, two sons and one daughter are living. In politics Mr. Wynne was a Jacksonian Democrat and a strong Union man. His wife was a true, good woman. She never united with any church. The subject of this sketch was raised and received an excellent education in his native county, remaining at home until 1878, when he began life for himself. In 1879 he married Miss Annie Sedden, born July 20, 1861. Their family consists of Willie B., Albert E. and Annie C. Mrs. Wynne is an estimable lady and sincere member of the Cumberland Presbyterian Church. The year of his marriage Mr. Wynne opened a first-class grocery store, and in June, 1886, he purchased a drug stock of Mitchell and another of Robertson. Both houses are in a flourishing condition and receiving an extensive patronage. He is also interested in farming. He is the postmaster of Whiteville, and well versed in law, practicing in the magistrate's office. He has been a resident of Hardeman County eleven years, and with the exception of a short period, closely associated with the commercial interests of the town in which he lives, and is regarded as one of the most substantial, enterprising and upright citizens. He is a stanch Democrat.

Alex. F. Yopp, sheriff of Hardeman County, where he was born January 10, 1846, is the eldest of a family of seven children born to Dr. Wm. T. and Elizabeth (Coleman) Yopp. The father is of English descent, was born in North Carolina in 1826, and the mother in Rutherford County, Tenn. Both came to the county when quite young, where they were raised and married. Dr. Wm. Yopp received his education in Memphis. For thirty-five years he was one of the most successful and popular physicians in the entire section. He retired from practice in 1883, and since that time has been engaged in agricultural pursuits. He and his wife are consistent and respected members of the Methodist Church. Our subject was raised on a farm and received his education in the common schools of the county. Before the age of fifteen, in 1862, as a volunteer, he entered the Confederate service, Company A, Fourteenth Tennessee Cavalry. During three years of bravery and active service he was but once taken prisoner; he was held about four months. At the battle of Franklin he received a wound in the face by a minie-ball. After the war he engaged in farming until 1876, when he moved to Bolivar. He held the position of deputy sheriff from 1872 to 1876. He was twice a candidate for the office of sheriff and each time defeated, but in 1882 was elected. He has given such entire and perfect satisfaction that he has been enabled to retain the place since that time. In connection with his official duties he deals extensively in horses. For eight years he has been a public servant, and has proved himself an efficient officer, an able and honorable man. In 1867 he was united in marriage to Miss Pattie Yoakum, who was born in 1847. To them have been born four children: Elmo, Neely, Ike and Harry. Mrs. Yopp is an earnest and respected member of the Methodist Church. Mr. Yopp has never united with any denomination. In politics he is a Democrat.

INDEX

Prepared By
Frances Maynard
Fort Worth, Tex.

Abernathy...807
Adams, F. L. 806
  G. G. 823,824,830
  G. W. 801
  L. B. 830, 836
  Mary 838
  Thomas B. 838
  W. C. 823
  William 808
Aggie (colored) 839
Aitken, John Hall 926
  Mary A. 924,926
Akin, Susan 905
Albright, Barbara E. 888
  G. N. 887
  James R. 887
  John 808
  Mollie 888
  Sallie 887
Alfred (slave) 826
Allen, D. J. 829
  Frances A. 960
  George 808
  Jesse 801,810
  R. C. 824
  T. D. 816
  Thompson 829
  Vincent 829
Allison, John 824
  R. D. 814
Amons, David 825
  R. F. 823
Alexander ...807
  A. R. 837
  Ann 837
  Cynthia 840
  Cyrus 813
  D. 837
  Easter 933
  Eliza 813
  J. H. 826
  James W. 813
  Jane A. 813
  M. P. 805
  Maggie N. 813
  Mary 813,837
  Mary B. 878
  Moses 813
  Nancy 860
  Samuel J. 840
  Uriah 813
  Wm. 832
  Wilson 813
Anderson...804,806,808
  Adelia A. 882
  Annie A. 861
  B. H. 823
  Benjamin B. 888
  C. H. 823,824
  Chamberlain H. 888
  E. R. 829
  Edward 941
  Elizabeth W. 888
  Fannie R. 941
  J. A. 816
  J. R. 941
  Lena G. 841
  Moses L. 841
  Nancy H. 888
  W. T. 828
Andrews, Alice P. 908
  Sallie 907
Appleberry, Abe 801
Applewhite, Sarah 860
Archie (slave) 826
Armistead, A. M. 830
  G. W. 828

Armour...804,827
Armstrong, Frances 867
  Frank 858
  L. 832
  Nettie 867
  Thomas 867
Arnett...830
Arnold, J. H. 824
  Wm. 829
Atkinson, Nathaniel 801
Atwood, Joe 827
  William 827
Austin, Alfred 808
Avent, Nannie P. 843
Avery, Nathan 827

Babbitt, Thomas 816
Bacon...804
Baggaly, Elizabeth 880
Bailey...804,806,807
  A. F. 830
  J. J. 832
  M. M. 830
Baird, Benjamin F. 842
  Callie V. 889
  Charles 842,889
  Emma H. 889
  Lamiza A. 889
  Nancy 842
  Nancy F. 889
  S. J. 813
  S. W. 806
  Washington L. 889
Baker, Sarah 863
Ballard, Blair 803
  Samuel O. 801
Ballentine...858
Barden, Jesse 925
  L. T. 910
  Mary A. E. 910
Barnes, Temperance 857
Barnett, Naomi M. 959
Barrett...827
  A. J. 889
  Anderson 890
  J. A. 889
  John 889
  Kindred 890
  Salina 889
  Thomas 890
  William 836
Barrham, Mary 947
Barry, Harry 826
  Valentine D. 802,824
  825,826,829
Bartholomew, Jacob 837
Barton, Roger 802,824,826
  William 802
Baskerville, G. B. 811
Bass, James 923
  James W. 843
  Mary O. 864
  Nannie P. 843
  Olivia Polk 923
  R. J. 806
  Thomas W. 843
Baugh, Wm. R. 806
Bayley, Agnes 886
  J. S. 831
Beatty, Arthur 813
  Lucilla 813
Beauford, M. 809
Beech, C. 829
Bejack, Samuel 807
Belcher, E. R. 823,839
Bell, Jas. G. 829
  John 799

Bell, W. A. 816
Bells, J. H. 822
Belvat, C. S. 809
  Charles 809
Benjamin...819
Bennett, G. L. 808
  George W. 808
  M. 890
  Thomas 809
  Thomas M. 822,823
  Stephen 824
Benton, Samuel 850
  David 832
Bethune, James 927
  Mary B. 927
Bickerstaff, James 809
Biddle, R. 829
Biggs, A. 890
  James William 891
  Luke 890
  M. 890
  Henry 803,890
  Wm. 824
Bill(s)...819,821
Bills, Clara 838
  Isaac N. 829
  John H. 800,820,821,
  823,824,827,828,829,
  839,955
  L. 840
  Leonidas 830,833,839
  Lucy A. 838
  Prudence 839
  W. T. 828
Birkhead, Salina 889
Bishop, Emily 882
Black, Ann E. 892
  Amos 891
  Editha 892
  Lucy 891
  Robert J. 816
  Robert R. 891
  Sallie 940,950
Blain, Sarah E. 863
Blair, Editha 892
  Elizabeth 892
  Nancy 892
  Minerva 893
  Thomas 892
  William J. 892
Blakeley, Drewry 879
  Laura 879
  Mary E. 879
Blalock, Annie May 893
  Jesse 893
  Katie 893
  Pauline 893
  Rosana 893
  William 893
Bland, Peter R. 812,838
Blanks, May R. 839
Blare, T. A. 879
Bolivar, Simon 820
Bomar, W. W. 839
Bonar(s)...819
Bond, George 809
  Thomas 832
Bone, R. H. 861,884
Boones...901
Booth, Thomas 809
  W. A. 805
Borroum, A. J. 931
Bosswell...804
Bostwick, Caroline 893,895
  906
  Fannie Guy 896
  Marie Louise 896

Bostwick, Mary Jane 906
  Luta Paulina 896
  Robert Graham 896
  Robert Montrose 893,895, 896
  William Merida 893,895, 906
Boswell, T. L. 841
Bounds, F. 809
Bouten, Annie 915
  E. J. 915
  R. L. 915
Bowdon, T. B. 925
Bowels, T. J. 943
Bowers, Ben 825
  Felicia 844
  George 798,803,808,809
  J. T. 806
  P. H. 804
Bowling, Alexander 843
  Elizabeth 843
  Felicia 844
  George W. 843
Box, Robt. 824,825
Boyd...804
  Cordelia 887
  E. W. 824
  Elisha 819,823,824
  Hadassah 887
Boydstun, Robt. 824
Boyle, Ada C. 943
Bradford...823
  Alex. B. 824
  Mary E. 931
Bradley, Bettie 913
Bragg, Elizabeth 887
Branch, Benj. 801
Brannam, A. J. 920
  Loudella D. 920
  Martha 920
  M. J. 920
Brantly, Mary P. 918
Brauer, Willimine 873
Brewer, Martha 905
Brightwell...822
Brock, Caleb 824,829
  Dicy 934
Brogden, Elizabeth E. 932
Brook(s)...807
  Henry 801,808
  Laura 844
  Robert 809
Brough, Margaret 928
Brown...806
  Aaron V. 863
  Ann 885
  Asa 836
  D. F. 827,829,839
  E. C. 813
  Eliza 885
  Elizabeth 910
  F. N. 831
  George 810
  H. B. 832
  H. C. 838
  J. 815
  James 798,808,809
  John 802,803,804,809,810
  L. M. 832
  Lawson 910
  Lou 856
  Maggie 910
  Malinda 813
  Mary 813
  Milton 802
  R. A. 856
  Samuel 813
  Thomas 885
Brownell, T. A. J. 816
Brownlow...940
  W. G. 873
Bruce, Elizabeth 880
Bryan(t)...806

Bryan, A. 809
  Dempsey 809
  Joseph 809
  W. A. D. 901
Bryant, Charles Wesley 902
  D. R. 830
  Elisha 901
  James Hart 902
  John Clark 902
  Jos. Johnson 903
  Leah 901
  M. A. 902
  Mattie McNeill 902
  Michael 901
  Nannie Taylor 902
  Sue Idella 903
  Susan E. 902
  Thomas Lafayette 902
  Virginia C. 902
  W. A. D. 901
  William S. 902
Buell, William P. 838
Buford, J. S. 831
  S. 813
Buizwell, Rebecca 878
Bull, Lugenia 851
  Rebecca 850
Bumpass, G. W. 804
Bunting, Eliza 962
  Samuella 962
  Samuel 962
Butler...819
  Charity 926
  John 926
  William O. 926
Burford, Jonathan 939
  Nancy 938
Burleson, Ed 824
Burnett, Callie E. 880
  Jeremiah 844,845
  Joshua 845
  Mary F. 844
  Wilson L. 844
Burns, Truman 826
Burt, L. 822
Burtis, Fannie 876
Burton, Horace 809
  J. W. 814
  Robert 809
  W. C. 816
  William 801

Cablier, Martin H. 801
Caldwell, D. 831
  Robert 801
Callahan, N. 833
Callender, J. H. 823
Campbell, A. J. 823
  A. R. 838
  A. W. 833
  Alex 837
  Alexander 812
  Andrew M. 803
  Fannie 928
  John 825
  Robt. 832
Cannon, Nora 811
  Robert 845
  William J. 845
Cargile...905
  Annie 903
  Elizabeth 903
  Francis Marion 903
  Ida 903
  James 903
  James Robert 903
  Mary K. 903
  Ruth 903
Cargill...832
Carlton, Ranie 926
Carnes, David B. 846
  Nannie M. 948
  Stephen G. 815,846

Carr. Anna 942
Carrington, L. M. 830
  Laura 830
Carter...822
  Daniel 808
  J. S. 804
Cartwright, Anna J. 849
  Ella 864
  Elizabeth J. 857
  Lizzie 930
  Love O. 857
  N. R. 857
  Peter 814
Caruth, George 895
Caruthers, Hugh 835
  John P. 802
  Wm. 834
Casey, L. D. 831
  R. D. 823
  Zadoc 832
Cash, Katie 893
Castleton, Sallie 871
Cater, Edwin 812
Cauley, Elizabeth 915
Chaffin, Nancy 939
  Nathan 832
  Jesse 832
Chalmers, James R. 935
Chamberlain, H. 812
Chambers. Amanda C. 848
  B. 825
  Barnabas 824
  Daniel G. 847
  Gools B. 847
  Green B. 825
  J. J. 925
  John M. 925
  Marcus L. 847
  Margaret L. 848
  Martha F. 848
  Thomas G. 848
Chamless, J. S. 832
  John C. 832
Chandler, Wm. 832
Chapman, C. F. 806
  Wm. 825
Charlie (slave) 826
Cheairs, Daniel B. 829
  Margaret 918
Cheatham...845,867
Chesire, W. D. 837
Chessman, C. F. 806
Chew, R. H. 811
Chillers, E. J. 815
Chisam, Jas. 825
Choat, Joseph 808
Christian...804
  Alcey B. 848
  Annie L. 848
  Carrie V. 848
  Eddie L. 848
  Joe D. 848
  Louis 848
  Mary E. 848
  W. 848
  Robert W. 848
Clanch, J. S. 836
Clark, Cornelius 904
  Jackson 904
  James 826
  Jewel E. 904
  Pearl T. 904
  Rogers 904
  Sallie 904
  Sarah E. 904
  W. H. 807
Clay, Annie O. 849
  James A. 848
  James N. 849
  John W. 848
  Maggie L. 849
Cleere, Ida 861
Cleft, Daniel 800

Clement, R. Alexander 825
Clift, Daniel 808
  J. 832
Cloyd, John 801
Coapwood, William 807
Coates, A. J. 826,827
  Mary A. 932
Cobb, Emma H. 889
  Louis T. 889
Coburn, Tabitha 945
Cocke, A. E. 865
  Amy E. 877
  J. H. 849,850
  Martha H. 862
  Mary J. 850
  Thomas J. 808
  Thomas R. 801,849
Cockerham, J. T. 827
  John G. 827
  John Y. 820,824
Cockran, W. S. 812
Cockroft, S. L. 802,824
Coe, D. H. 825
  Leven H. 803
Coffee...820
Coggins, Eliza J. 905
Coleman, Alfred 838
  Catharine 838
  E. G. 821
  Elizabeth 963
  John 807
  Wm. 838
Collier...804
  C. C. 821,936
  Carter C. 829
  Louisa 838
  W. C. 828
Compton, Mildred 860
Conrad...805
Cook, Ann E. 924
  Martha 924
  Thomas 809
  William 924
Coolidge...806
Coons, G. W. 838
Cooper, Bettie 846
  Henry C. 846
  J. C. 810
  John 804
  John B. 846
  John C. 801,804
  W. 810
Copeland, Rebecca 881
Copeman, Dora 859
Cosbey, Mary C. 937
Cossett, George G. 806,807
Cotter, Robert 809
Cotton, Robert 808
  Zarilda 940,941
Cousar, R. M. 802
Covington...804
  John 832
Cowan...806
  Alexander F. 850,851
  David P. 851
  E. P. 813
  John S. R. 807,850,851
  Lugenia 851
  Lulie 851
  Mary 813
  Sarah 906
  Walter B. 851
  William P. 851
Cox, S. J. 833
  Samuel 808,809
Craddock, Clifton 816
Craighead, T. B. 812
Crawford, David 813
  Edwin 834
  L. M. 830
  R. 824
  Samuel I. 849
  Sarah 813

Crawford, William M. 849
  W. H. 849
Crenshaw...804
  J. M. 806
Crisp, E. C. 823,824,829,
    834,839
  Eli 822
  Gilbert L. 825
Crisum, Catharine 930
Croft, Richard 826
Crossett...807
  Joseph 851
  Joseph I. 816,851
Cross, Eddie 904
  Emily 904
  Emma L. 947
  John B. 905
  Lizzie 905
  Mattie A. 877
  Napoleon B. 904
  Napoleon R. 905
  Richard D. 904
  Robert D. 905
  Sarah 904
Crook, James B. 840
  Mary 864
Crow, James 832
Culbertson, John 808
Cummings, Charles 812
Cunningham, Callie V. 889
Curls, Mary E. 847
Currie, Sarah A. 882
Curtis...806
Curtise, Winfield 807
Cuthbert, Dan 829

Dade...831
Dance, Nancy H. 888
Daniel, Dudley Dix 945
  M. E. 945
Dare, Thomas 824
Dashiell, R. R. 815
Davenport, Chancey 827
  W. G. 840
David, Ella 838
Davis...806,807
  G. 831
  M. L. 923
  Mildred 929
  Susan 854
  William 803
  William I. 852
  W. L. 807
  Young 852
Dawson, James 832
Day...815,823
  H. P. 805
  J. S. 806
  Martha 905
  William 905
Dean, Lucy 950
  Wiley 832
Deberry, J. 817
Dederick, David 804
Deming, J. W. 823
Dennis, A. G. 962
  Samuel 829
Denny...806
Derrett, C. E. 830
Devermeux, Thomas J. 809
Dickens...807
Dickinson, Cornelia 877
  E. 804
  Edwin 877
  Edwin D. 877
  Eva A. 877
  Fannie F. 877
  H. S. 804
  Isaiah W. 877
  John T. 877
  Mary M. 877
  Neal S. 877
  Sallie W. 877

Dickinson, T.L. 804
Dickson, Isabella 953
Dobbs, Nancy 865
Dodd, Elizabeth 923
Dodson...835
Dollor, Lucretia 886
Donoho, R. A. 856
Dorion, Maggie 830
  W. C. 823,824,828,830,
    832
Dortch, J. H. 802,803
  Josiah H. 853
  W. B. 803
  William B. 853
Dougan...840
Douglass, Burchet 803
  H. L. 815,832
  James 809
  Martha V. 865
Dow, Lorenzo 814
Dowdy...807
  B. F. 905
  Ernest 906
  Frank 906
  G. W. 905
  Joe 906
  Julius 906
  Laurie 906
  Mahala C. 868
  Mary Susan 906
  Nicholas 906
  Sallie E. 906
  Susan 905
  Theodore 906
Doyle, L. L. 942
  Mary 906
Drake, Edwin R. 906
  George W. 907
  James 817
  John 906
  John R. 907
  Mary 906
Duncan, Alice P. 908
  C. A. 907
  Hanery W. 907,908
  Margaret 908
  Mussie D. 908
  Nancy 907
  S. 824
  Sallie 907
  Stephen N. 908
  Thomas 907
  Thomas L. 826
  William B. 907
Dunden...830
Dunlap, W. C. 824,826,832
  Wm. C. 802
Dupree, Jesse 809
Dupuy...804
  J. J. 824
  John J. 802
Durrett, D. E. 827,828,922,
    956
  David E. 909
  Mary D. 909
  Mary E. 909,922,956
  Robert D. 909
  Edward Tucker 909
  Elizabeth 908
  M. E. 909
  W. 828,962
  Wiley 908
  William 908
  Willie Gwynne 909
Dyer, Beverly 807
  Beverly L. 816
  J. W. 807,866

Ealey, W. A. 805
East, John M. 823
Eastham, E. J. 804
Evans, Lawrence G. 800
Edgerton., John 809

Edmundson, John P. 803
Edwards...887
  Jacob 824
Elam, W. J. 811
Eldridge, J. W. 817
Elkins, J. 825
Elliotte, Alice B. 910
  C. G. 910
  Daniel F. 910
  Elizabeth 910
  Emily 910
  Fannie E. 927
  Francis 910
  Ida May 910
  Jemima W. 910
  John W. 910
  Lawson W. 910
  Lizzie J. 910
  Maggie 910
  Mary A. E. 910
  Sarah E. 904
  Virginia T. 910
  W. W. 904,927
  W. H. R. 830
  W. W. R. 910,962
  William 910
Ellis, Mary F. 844,845
Emerson...828
Estel, Thomas 809
Estep, E. L. 943
  Olivia 943
  Jennie 946
Estes, M. P. 815
  T. E. 815
Eubank, Julia 842
Ewell, R. H.D. 838
  R. S. 880
Ewing, Mary Ann 949
Exum, Martha 955,956

Fain, Hiram 804
Fairfield...806
Falconer, Kimlock 850
  Thomas A. 850
Falls, H. H. 806
Farley, Franklin B. 910
  John A. 853
  Mary 910
  Mary J. 911
  Thompson 853
  W. W. 823,829,831
  William E. 911
  William W. 910
Farmer, Virginia O. 924
Farrar, Girault 912
  Matilda 912
Farris, B. M. 812
  Lucy 873
  Lucy M. 954
  Sallie 873
Farson, Elias 826
Fate, Mark 809
Fenel, W. H. 829
Fenner, J. S. 815
Fentress...819
  Bettie 913
  Calvin 912
  David 825,826,827,911,
    912
  David W. 911
  Elizabeth 913
  Ethel 912
  Francis 824,826,838,911,
    912
  Frank 913
  James 798,802,820,824,
    826,838,911,912
  John 826
  Kate 911
  Louise 913
  Margaret 913
  Mary T. 912
  Mary W. 912

Fentress, Matilda 838,911,
    912
  Sallie W. 911
Ferguson, Daniel A. 913
  Frances E. 913
  G. T. 827
  James 913
  James R. 913,914,928
  Jemima 913
  Jemima W. 910
  Joel 826,913
  Mary Frances 913
  Mary L. 914
  Sarah 913
  W. O. 823,824,829
  Z. L. 914
Finley...805
Finney, John 803
  W. P. 802,803
Finnie...824
Fisher, George W. 803
Fitzhugh, Ann E. 839
Fleming, W. C. 823
Flippin, Thomas J. 802,803
    824
Floyd...832
Flynt, Sarah 913
Foote, John L. 801
  J. T. 806
Ford...804
  R. L. 810
Forrest, Frances 932
  N. B. 925
Forsyth, R. 832
Fort, Elias 825
  Tilghman C. 832
  William 824
Foster, Lucy 891
Fowler,..806,819,824
  D. T. 806
  J. C. H. 832
Fox, Timothy 829
Frasier, Jane 856
Frank, Tillie 922
  Wm. 806
Franklin, Ann E. 958
  Hardin 958
  J. B. 823
  Mary 910
  Ophelia 917
  Rebecca 931
  William A. 917
Freeman, Thomas J. 925
Fusch, Edmund 835
  H. J. 835

Gabbie, Mary 871
Gaines...816
Gaither...928
Galloway, Bunyan 914
  David 915
  Edgar 915
  James 809
  Kelcie 914
  Martha 914
  Nona G. 914
  Robert 914
  Sarah 914
  T. S. 803
  William D. 914
  Wilmer 915
Ganell, A. D. 815
Gannon, William 925
Garges, Job 809
Garnett, Eli 854
  Elmer 854
  John H. 854
  Mamie 854
  Mattie 854
  Minnie 854
Garrett, E. J. 915
  Elizabeth 915
  G. W. 915

Garrett, Georgie 915
  Hallie 915
  Henry 915
  Lloyd 915
  Minnie 915
  Ottie 915
Garrison, Sarah 882
Garthright, Mary E. 942
Garvin, Adelia 845
Gatley, Sarah 852
Gatlin, B. H. 903
  Elizabeth 903
  Mary K. 903
George (colored) 838
Gibbons, Joseph 806
Gibbs, George W. 802
Gibson, Elizabeth 915
  George S. 915,916
  Jesse 915
  Nancy 916
  W. E. 805
Giles, T. N. 827
Gill, David 855
  R. S. 813
  S. S. 854
Gilliam, J. M. 804
Glasscock, Laura R. 865
Glaster...806
Gleen, P. B. 810
Glenn, P. D. 803
Gober, Milton A. 803
Goodall...821
  J. D. 802
  W. G. 803
Golden, John 819
Gooden, Monroe 803
Goodlett, Austin 836
  Lorenzo 836
Goodman...850
Goodnight, David 832
Goodrich, H. 839
Goodwin, Arrozene 852
  John W. 806,807
  Letitia F. 924
Goosman, Emma L. 855
  F. 805
  Fred 855
  George F. 855
  Jennie C. 855
  Lillie B. 855
  Mary J. 855
  William H. M. 835
  Willie M. 855
Gordon, Rebecca 847
Gossett, David 824
  Elijah 824
Gouringham, Esther 957
Grace...822
Gracy, Mary 846
Graham, Caroline E. 906,
    893,895
  E. B. 957
  Esther 957
  George 893,894
  Henderson 957
  James 893,894,895
  John D. 820
  Joseph 895
  Leah 901
  Mary 895
  William A. 895
Granbery, Anna Cossie 857
  James H. 856
  John 856
  John W. 856
  Joseph 845
  Kate O. 857
  Langley 856
  Robert D. 856
  Roy 857
  Ruby E. 857
  Thomas N. 857
  William B. 856

Granbery, William R. 857
Granger, Nancy 881
Grant...816
   J. C. 817
Grantham, J. 832
   Joshua 832
   L. 832
   Rachel M. 949
   Thomas G. 949
Graves...928
Gray...806,835
   B. F. 810
   Benjamin 805
   G. C. 830
   George 806
   Nancy 907
   W. C. 840
   W. G. 810
   W. L. 810
   William S. 804
Green, Emily 904
   J. C. 831
   Thomas A. 904
Gregory, Katherine 865
Grider, Shadrack 809
   Tobia 809
   Zebra 809
Grier, Margaret R. 866
Griffin...807
   J. R. A. 809
Groomes, Wm. 825
Guthrie, J. M. 806
   James 835
   Mary 920
Guy, Esther 896
   Hester Ann 896
   J. H. 926
   Joseph A. 896
   Josie 926
   Martin Winston 896,897
   Ranie 926
Guynn, H. A. 925
Gwynn, Columbus 816
   James 817

Hackney...806
Hain, John 809
Holcomb...915
Hall, Ann E. 886
   C. H. 816
   J. J. 837
   Jesse D. 837
   Laurel 838
   M. 834
   W. W. 833
   William E. 886
Halliburton, Susanna 951
Haltom...806
Ham, Daniel 953
   Hattie A. 953
Hamblett, W. T. 805
Hamilton, James 812,837
Hammond, Margie R. 958
Hancock...830
   Ida Lee 857
   Irene 857
   Martha C. 857
   Mary B. 857
   Robert 857
   Sarah L. 857
   Thomas 833
   Wiley J. 857
   William F. 857
Hannah (slave of James A-vant) 826
Hannah, Eddie 916
   James 916
   Leean 916
   Margret 916
   Robert 916
Hannum, A. 817,833
   W. L. 810
Hardeman...833

Hardeman, May 839
   T. M. 839
   Thomas Jones 819,820,
     823,827,828,839
Hardin...828,917
   George 803
Hardy, Hester Ann 896
   R. S. 838
Harkins, Hugh, Sr. 909
   W. C. 829
Harner, M. J. 837
Harper, Samuel 801,806,808
   824,829
Harrell, J. C. 803
   James C. 857
   William 807,857
Harris...835
   A. B. 802
   Ann C. 917
   B. A. 831
   C. A. 923
   C. C. 803
   Calvin 803
   Charles H. 917
   E. W. 808
   Elizabeth 916
   Hardy 916
   Hudson 858
   Isham G. 856
   J. R. 823
   James B. 824,833,917
   John W. 802,803,824
   L. C. 815
   Lucilla W. 917
   Lula B. 853
   Martha O. 952
   Mary 917
   Mary E. 853
   Ophelia 917
   Orin 831
   Orris 916
   Patience 852
   R. R. 917
   Thomas H. 952
   Turner 858
   W. A. 805,853
   West 820,821,827
Harvey, M. W. 826
Harwell, Richard M. 816
Haskell, Joshua 802,824,
   826
Hasley...806
Hatcher, Nancy 875
Hatley, Joe 825
Hatton...830,857
Havens, Charles H. 859
   Henry D. 859
Hawkins...804,830
   A. G. 824
   H. H. 832
Haynes, Andrew 808,809
   J. 829
   Joseph 824
Head, Daniel 808
   Thomas 809
   William 807
Heaslett, James A. 801
Heartfield, Anson 837
Hecht...807
Hedge, Samuel 812,837
Hedges, James 827
Henderson, B. H. 810,812
   Littleton 827
   William H. 827
Hendon...804,805
Hendrix, A. T. 902
   Nannie Taylor 902
Henley, Moses 824
Henson, Jesse 865
   Nancy 915
Henry, A. J. 808
   B. A. 831
   C. W. 831

Hersh...804
Hess, W. R. 829
Hester, W. H. 801
Hickman, Wm. 832
Hicks...894
Higgasson, Amy E. 877
   Josiah 805,877
   Lizzie H. 877
   Lucy W. 853
Higgs, Margaret 918
   Mary P. 918
   Theophilus 918
   Wiley 833,950
Hill...804
   Allen 821,823,827,839
   Ann T. 845
   D. L. 817
   Elizabeth 944
   Jerome 911
   Mary (Clayton) 873
   Sallie W. 911
Hiller, J. S. 816
Hilliard...804
   J. W. T. 805
Hindman, J. H. 832
   John 831
Hinson, Martha J. 945
Hiram...804
Hobson, Horace P. 802,803,
   882
   Junius 802
   Sallie M. 882
Hodges, C. T. 806
   William F. 801
Holden, Catharine 871
Holland, B. H. 816
Holloman, J. C. 804
Holloway...804
Holman, Elizabeth O. 860
   Luther A. 860
   Newton A. 859
   Wilfred L. 860
   Wilson 859
Holmes, Thomas E. 801
Holt, Elizabeth 873
   J. B. 817
Hook, Ella A. 860
   Florence M. 860
   Jessie H. 860
   John H. 860
   Lovard 860
   Lovard E. 860
Hope, S. R. 838
Hotchkiss, E. B. 805
   Jerrod 801
House, Samuel 808
Houston, B. 806
Howard, John 808
Howell, F. M. 812
   R. B. C. 919
   Sarah 919
Hubbard, J. M. 828
Hudson, Benjamin V. 828,918
   Bettie 893
   Elizabeth C. 918
   I. C. 810
   J. 809
   J. C. 809
   Thomas C. 801
   Thomas W. 918
Hudspeth, Seton 801
Hughes, Wm. S. 826
Hull...804
   C. H. 833
Hullenn, D. W. 903
Hulum, Duke W. 836
Humphries(Humphreys)
   A. B. 803
   J. C. 802,803,824
   West H. 803
Hunt, Annie 961
   John 837
   Thomas 809

Hunter, A. G. 810
Hurlbut...816
Hurst...834
Hurt, C. L. 815
Hust, C. S. 815
Hutley...819

Ingram, George T. 828,919
  Mary 919
  Robert M. 803
  Thomas 919
  Virginia C. 902
  W. P. 902
Irby, H. C. 815
  W. D. 815
Irish...806
Irwin, T. R. 861
  Uriah A. 860
  William 860
Isbell, Geraldine 883
Isom, Robert 808
  Thomas 808
  William 808
Ivedell, Thomas 805
Ivy...884
  A. J. 861
  Charles P. 861
  Eliza L. 861
  Pearla T. 861

Jack, James 894
Jackson...798
  Andrew 818
  C. A. 811
  Mrs. Stonewall 895
Jacobs, J. G. 839
  Wm. R. 836
James (Colored) 838
James, Annie 959
Janes, John 959
  Joseph 959
  Martha A. 959
  Martha P. 959
Jansen, Lewis 839
Jarmon, Lizzie 905
Jarnigan (Jernigan)
  Arlington Lee 920
  Arthur A. 919
  David 800,801,808,809
  Hiram A. 920
  John 808
  Loudella D. 920
  M. H. 919
  Martha 920
  Mary Rosella 920
  Sarah 919
  Smithie E. 920
Jerman, Stephen 835
Jetton, Robert 798,820,826
Johns, W. M. R. 814
  William M. R. 876
Johnson...871
  A. 838
  Andrew M. 920
  Curtis 861
  Belle 921
  Daniel 798,800,801
  Henry M. 800,801,804,805,
    808,809
  George W. S. 861
  L. M. 833
  Lou 921
  Margaret 921
  Mary 920
  Mary Lou 874
  Myrtle 921
  Nettie 921
  Samuel 808
  Thomas I. 862
  W. B. 825
  W. P. 833
  William 862
  William M. 920

Jones...804,806,827
  A. M. 950
  Alexander W. 863
  Andrew 824
  Author 863
  C. P. 816
  Calvin 802,803,824,826,
    839,863
  Diza Ann 950
  E. M. 921
  F. B. W. J. 839
  J. H. 832,921
  James C. 822
  James M. 863
  Jennie M. 921
  Joel 801
  Mary 913,921
  Mary J. 849
  Mary K. 857
  Mollie F. 857
  Mollie 950
  Moses L. 950
  P. T. 805,821
  Paul T. 823,838,921
  R. A. 815
  Thomas C. 838,839
  T. P. 815
  Thomas 817
  Thomas W. 863
  W. A. 804
  W. P. 823
  W. T. 823
  Wiley B. 838
  Wilson 863
Jordan, O. S. 806
Joslin, Benjamin 902
  Susan E. 902
Joy, C. G. 829,830
Jurry,..810

Kahn...804,827
  Annie 922
  Claude Mellville 922
  Emma 922
  Harry 921,922
  Isaac 828,921
  Jacob 922
  Louise 921,922
  Marcus 922
  Samuel 828,921
  Tillie 922
Keady, William G. 838
Kearly, West 832
  Wm. 832
Kearney, Ann C. 917
  C. A. 923
  John H. 922
  M. L. 923
  Philip 922
  Sarah 922,956
  William R. 917,922
Kent, Joseph 923
  Olivia B. 843
  Olivia Polk 923
  Sallie R. 923
Kerr, Catharine 813
  Frances N. 813
  Henry M. 813
  Isabell 813
Kettle, Martha 886
Ketchum, Adrian W. 864
  Leon N. 864
  Levi 864
  Lucile W. 864
  Morgan C. 864
  William 864
Key...804
  Felica 844
  Felicia O. (Bowers) 844
Kidd, Ludwick 808
Kilpatrick, A. 825
  Eli 837
Kimbrough, James 809

King...806
  E. W. 802
  E. W. M. 824,826
Kinney, Frances M. 907
  George W. 923
  John W. 923
  Letitia F. 924
  Lucinda J. 923
Kirk, Henry 798,800,808,809
Kirkman, Mary 920
Kirkpatrick, Alex. 827
  E. 829
  Rebecca J. 959
Knox, James 894
  James G. 805,812
  Robert 808
Koonce, Amos 809
  J. 864
  Jarmon 801
  William A. 864

Lacy, Margaret 921
Lacey, Thomas 832
Lacy, William S. 812,813
LaFayette...797
Laird, David 827
Lake...804,827
  Mary Ross 962
Lakey, Wm. 832
Lamb, Allen 865
  Cleveland 865
  L. B. 865
  Levy Leroy 865
  Lowelle 865
  Paschal 865
  Robt. P. 865
Lambert, Samuel 836
Lambeth, A. M. 830
  Samuel 924
Lane, James 824
Langham, Joel 808
  Thomas 808
Lanier, J. J. 826
Lattin, John T. 803
Latty, W. S. 801
Lawrence...873
Leatherman, D. M. 802
Lee, Elizabeth 936,937
  H. D. 935
  Rosana 893
  Wm. H. 957
Leech...827
  W. H. 805
Lemay...873
Lenow, Joseph 814,822
Lensberry, A. J. 812
Lewis, Abner D. 801,803,806,
    865
  Charley 866
  Corbin 865
  E. E. 866
  Eliza 885
  Elton 866
  Kathleen 866
  M. A. 837
  Richard H. 866
  Sarah E. 866
  William 805
Lightfoot, R. L. 840
Limerick...837
Lipscomb, W. P. 806
Little, James 930
Livingston, Henry J. 802
Lloyd, Nancy 884
Locke, Margaretta L. 885
  Robert 806
Logan...816
Logwood, I. H. 833
  John E. 804
  T. H. 803,816
Long, John 809
  Nicholas 803
  Sallie 948

Longwell, J. M. 803
Loomis, Horace 809
Looney, Mary 867,946
  Robert F. 816,852,867
Louston...806
Love, Isaac 896
  J. B. 805
  William 819,825
Loving, William C. 801
Lowe, Ada C. 943
Low, Charity 926
  Cynthia A. 869
  E. E. 924,925
  John T. 924,925,926
  Josie 926
  Josie Irene 926
  Mary A. 924
  Mary E. 869
  Ranie Mary 926
  T. B. 925
  Thomas 925
  Willie Carlton 926
Lumas, Horace 804
Lumpton, H. J. 824
Lyle, Sallie 904
  W. J. 815
Lynn...806
  Charles 801,803
Lax, Ann E. 924
  Berryman 924
  Joseph L. 924
  Virginia O. 924

McAnulty, David W. 914,927
  Joseph S. 927
  Margaret A. 927
McCain, Joe 827
  John 827
McCalla, James M. 803
McCalpin, J. H. 815
McCammon, Elizabeth 914
  George 914
  Sarah 914
McCampbell, Andrew 802
McCarley, Mary 873
  W. W. 833
McCaskill, Cynthia 930
  John E. 929
  Nancy 929
  Taylor 929
McClaren...807
McClellan, Fannie M. 867
McClelland, Isaac B. 802, 804,866,879
McClellan, J. B. 809,810
McClelland, J. H. 928
McClellan, Margaret R. 879
  Mary C. 879
  Mattie B. 867
  Mollie L. 867
  Thomas G. 801,802,866, 867
McCoy, S. S. 813
McCree, Sarah M. 848
  William 895
McCrory, Martha 914
McCurley, S. 837
  W. 837
McDaniel, W. A. H. 835
McDonald, James L. 827
McDowell, Isabella 838
  J. B. 829
  L. B. 824
  Samuel 823
  T. B. 823
McElroy, J. H. 832
McEwen...962
McFadden, E. C. 813
  James C. 813
  Martha 813
  S. M. 813
  Thomas 813
McGee, William 812
McGehee, J. H. 864

McGlathery, F. M. 930,931
  Mattie E. 931
  Nancy S. 930
  Samuel E. 930
McHenry, Abner 813
  James 813
McINtosh, John 812
McKay, W. D. 827
McKean, J. M. 829
McKenzie, A. F. 947
  Alexander 808
  James 808
McKey, T. B. 949
McKinnie, Arthur 935
  Arthur S. 935
  Claude. S. 935
  Elizabeth C. 918
  H. D. 935
  J. 832
  J. A. 830
  Michael 825
  P. H. 935
  Mrs. S. F. 830
  Susan M. 935
  William H. 935
McKissack, Rebecca 863
McKnight, Mary 813
McLarty, Annie 961
McMillan, Wm. 825
McNamee, C. 866
  Emily 866
  Mattie C. 866
McNance, F. M. 806
  Fannie 806
McNannie...806
McNeal...821,827
  Albert T. 826,828,832, 839,840,911
  Clarissa 839
  E. 839
  E. A. 840
  E. P. 821,838,839
  Kate 911
  Thomas 819,821,824,825, 829
McNutt...804
McRae, Robt. D. 830

Maas, B. A. 807
  J. H. 807
Macbeth...806
Macon...828

  I. M. 831
  Mary 838
Malone, Ferd M. 835
Manning, Elizabeth B. 881
Manly, W. B. 832
Manson, F. E. 926
  Fannie E. 927
  Frank E. 927
  Grover Cleveland 927
  J. A. 926
  Joseph A. 927
  Mary B. 926
  Mary J. 927
  Minnie J. 927
March, Mary 934
Marie, William 803
Maris. William 811
Marsh, Daniel H. 934
  Margaret F. 934
  Nancy 957
Marshall...804
  Dixon 809
  Jas. 825
Martin, Eliza 935
  Elizabeth 950
  Susana M. 875
  William 798,820,826
Mask, Kate M. 857
Mason, J. M. 832
  Julia W. 891
Mathews, Ellen 928

Mathews, Fannie 928
  Isabell 839
  J. M. 815
  J. W. 837,838
  Jennie 928
  John 837,838
  Joseph A. 928
  Joseph C. 928
  Margaret 928
  William M. 928
Mathis, Jane 949
Maxwell, John 832
May...943
  Annie 929
  John 824
  Mildred 929
  W. C. 832
  William A. 929
Mayfield, Wm. 824
Mayo, F. A. 803
  Harriet A. 875
Mebane, J. W. 817
Melane, E. J. 815
Melroy, Isaac 824
Melton, N. 832
Menees, Elizabeth B. 881
Menifee, Sarah 938,939
Mercer, Catharine 930
  Lizzie 930
  Mattie E. 931
  Thomas B. 930
  Thomas E. 930
  W. A. 827,828,930
Meriweather...804
Meriwether, Minor 822
Metcalf, Rev. 813
  William 808
Meux, L. M. 875
Michaels, A. 806
Michaels, M. 806
Middleton, J. N. 830
Miller...819
  Austin 802,820,821,822, 824,826,828
  C. A. 828,830
  Calvin 816
  Chas. A. 826
  J. R. 931
  John 931
  John F. 931
  Joseph 821
  L. L. 830,942
  Martha B. 939
  Mary 942
  Mary E. 931
  Pitser (Pitzer) 821,822, 825,827,828,839,901
  Pleasant M. 802
  Rebecca 931
  Robert P. 931
  S. A. 867
  Simon 867
Milliken, W. A. 803
Mills, Jas. 831
  John 826
Mims, D. 827
Minor, Peter 824
Minter, T. S. 835
Mitchell,..807,963
  Emily J. 959
  Fannie 858
  H. H. 815
  James 959
  Julia 842
  Margaret A. 933
  Mary W. 959
  R. N. 920
  W. H. 802
Monroe...819
Montgomery, Sam 824
Montrose...893
Moody...806
Moore...937
  Benjamin F. 932

Moore, C. C. 803
  Elizabeth 874
  Elizabeth E. 932
  Frances 930
  George W. 932
  Hannah 961
  James 833
  Jamea A. 932
  James P. 925
  Margaret A. 933
  Martha E. 932
  Martin 932,958
  Mary A. 932
  R. M. 802
  T. C. 925
  W. H. 818
  William 823,932
  William A. 932
  William G. 953
Moorman, Annie E. 867
  Easter 933
  Frances B. 867
  Hiram C. 803,867
  M. C. 933
  Marion R. 867
  Martha A. 933
  Martha R. 928
  Mary L. 914
  N. T. 934
  R. A. 914,928,933
  Robert 867
  Robert M. 867
  Thomas A. 867
Morgan, A. P. 809
  Annie 929
  Martha A. 933
  Martha E. 867
  Mary E. 879
  Sarah 945
  W. N. 804
Morghis, Alex. 809
Morrow, Ellen 928
  Jane 934
  John T. 934
  Margaret F. 934
  William 934
Morse, Thomas E. 838
Morton, S. H. 801
Mosbey...804
Mosbey, Dewitt C. 801
  Joseph R. 803
Moss, Bartley H. 934
  Dicy 934
  Eli 934
  Eliza 935
Mullen, Adaline 936
  Alexander 935
  Edward A. 935,936
  Eliza 936
  Jane 935
Munroe, David W. 868
  William D. 868
Murray...835
  John 819
Myrick, Elizabeth 916

Nail, T. W. 815
Napier, R. L. 830
Neal, Ann L. 857
  Emma J. 857
  Thomas G. 857
Neeley, Charles 936
Neely, Bettie 913
  Elizabeth 838,936
  Francis F. 937
  J. J. 817,823,824,828,
    833,877,925
  James J., Jr. 937
  J. S. 832
  Jack 844
  Julia A. 937
  Louisa 838,936
  May B. 838

Neely, R. 839
  R. P. 823,831,832,913,
    956
  Rufus P. 852,936,937
  Thomas S. 937
  Wm. 828
Neese, Helen E. 952
  Mollie E. 952
  Thomas H. 952
Neighbors, Elcy 953
Neil, Joseph 808
  Thomas 808
Nelson...806
  A. G. 829
  Wm. 828
Nesbitt, Robert N. 801
Nevels, Cassandra 891
Newberger, Louise 921
Newbern...828,836
  D. J. 837
Newell, Jonah 809
Newland, H. G. 826
Newsom, E. R. 824
  Mary C. 937
  Michael J. 937
  T. M. 823
  Thomas M. 937,938
Nicholson, Nancy 942
Nooner...828
Norman, Mahala 872
Norment, Hamilton 940
  J. S. 831
  Jesse 826,828,939
  Jesse B. 940
  John S. 938,939
  Maggie 940
  Martha B. 939
  Nancy 939
  Nancy E. 940
  Nathaniel E. 938,939
  Sallie 940
  Sarah 938,939
  T. B. 831
  W. E. 819,825
  William M. 939
Nuckolls, Fannie R. 941
  John 827
  John W. 940
  Narcissa 940
  Noah 828
  Noah C. 941
  Priscilla 919
  Richard 940
  Starling 940
  Temperance 940
  William 829,940,941
  Zarilda 940,941

Oates, Fannie Guy 896
  Martin Guy 896
  William Leroy 896
Old...804
  Martha 867
Oldham, W. 809
Oliphant, M. 816
Oliver, A. M. 950
  J. E. 950
  James 832
  S. E. 950
Osborn, J. E. 806
Osborne, J. S. 831
  Sarah 865
Oswald, Ed 822
Otey, James H. 839
Oursler, Sophia M. 860
Outlaw...844
Owen...804
  John 807
  William 798,801,808,809

Paie...950
Paine, Robert 863,885
  Susan 885

Palmer...804
  C. R. 815
  Katherine E. 879
Pankey, W. R. 806
Parham, R. S. 803
  Richard S. 830
  Sarah A. E. 866
  T. S. 806
  William S. 866
Park, John S. 838
Parker...804
  R. A. 801,810
Parkinson, Wm. 832
Parks, Hugh L. 809
Parmley, Elizabeth 915
Parner, J. C. 831
Parr...807
  Mary 910
Parran, Anna 941,942
  David 941,942
  Maria 941
  T. A. 941
  Thomas C. 941
  Thomas O. 942
Parrish, M. R. 828
Parsons, Annie 903
Pate, Fannie 876
Patrick, J. G. 833
Patterson, H. J. 811
  Helen E. 952
  Joe 813
  John J. 808
  John T. 798,800,868
  Mary C. 868
  Robert G. 868
Patton, Thomas 813
Pauley...799
Payne, H. C. 809
Paine, James 812
Pearson, A. L. 869
  Samuel 869
Peebles, Andrew J. 802
  Edwin D. 870
  Elizabeth F. 881
  R. E. 815
Peete, Elizabeth 916
Pegram, S. G. 836
Perkins, Mary T. 912
Perry, Bettie 875
  Eliza J. 951
  Elizabeth W. 888
  Henry H. 803
  J. S. 801
Person...903
  Thomas 809
  William 836
Peter (a man of color) 825,
  826
Peters, G. B. 829
Pettigrew, Carrie B. 942
  Edna L. 942
  James C. 942
  James M. 942
  Joseph V. 942
  Nancy 942
  Nannie P. 942
  Samuel E. 942
Pettus, Dorcas 870
Peyton, T. B. 825
Phelps, C. W. 925
Phillips, J. W. 817,849
  Joseph W. 870
  Josie 849
  L. 832
  Pettus 870
Philpott, J. W. 893
Pickens, Israel 835
  Robert B. 801
Pickett, Courtney 839
  J. G. 839
Pierce, Cordelia N. 871
  William C. 871
Pillow, Abner 819

Pillow, Gideon 809
  Gideon J. 809
Pipkina, Elizabeth 869
Pirtle...835
  Jacob 824,825
  James 957
  M. H. 824
  Maria Jane 957
  Mary Emma 957
  Tabitha Ann 957
  Walter 957
  Wm. 824,834,957
Pitchford, J. 821
Pitkin, J. W. 831
  W. 832
Pitman, R, W. 811,816
Pledge, Archie 942
  Elvia J. 943
  Mary E. 942
  Joel A. 943
  Olivia 943
  W. A. 942
  William W. 943
Plummer, Philip B. 807
Pocahontaas 830
Poindexter, Wm. H. 829
Polk...819,909
  Ada C. 943
  B. 839
  C. P. 823
  Edwin 825,828
  Elizabeth 923
  Ezekiel 819,820,826,827,
    829,936
  Florence E. 944
  H. M. 828
  J. J. 943
  J. K. 923
  John J. 944
  James J. Jr. 828
  James K. 943,944
  Lousa 936
  Laura 955
  Lola M. 944
  M. T. 828,834
  O. B. 929
  Oscar B. 943
  Sallie R. 923
  Samuel 809,819,827
  Sarah T. 944
  Sophia 839
  Thomas 809,843
  T. J. 943
  William 809,819,823,824
  Willie 944
  Wm. 823,825,829
Pope, J. H. 830
Porter...821
  Charles B. 867
  Fannie E. 866
  G. C. 815
  Wm. 831
Potts, Mrs. William 895
Powell...892
Pratt, J. 809
Prewitt...830
  A. A. 919
  Bennona F. 945
  David 944
  Dudley 945
  Elizabeth 944
  Eudora F. 950
  G. R. 815
  J. A. 919
  James 944
  James H. 945
  Lee Roy 945
  M. E. 945
  Malcolm 945
  Mary 919
  N. H. 944
  Nathan 944
  W. F. 950

Prewitt, Thomas E. 944,945
  Thomas W. 945
Price, Edmund 808
  Henry M. 872
  James 872
  Lela V. 872
  Lucilla W. 917
  Lula O. 872
  Robert 827
  S. 917
  Susan A. 949
  Zula C. 872
Proudfit...806
Pruet, P. F. 837
Provine, Alex 801
Puckett, Eddie 916
Pugh, Joel P. 832
  W. C. 832
  William 831
Pulliam, Amelia 875
  Bettie 875
  J. L. 803
  Martha J. 945
  Sarah 945
  Silas 945
  T. P. 945
Purios, Jason 815
Purtle, Jacob 819

Quinn, Arthur J. 806
Quintard, C. T. 840

Ragan, A. P. 809
  Marcus 808
Ragland, Fred B. 803
  Milton 815
  Nathan 809
Raines, J. S. 832
  Jas. 832
Ramsey, A. M. 825
  John 833
  H. B. 803
  Sarah 922
  William 800,808,820,821,
    824,825,826,827,829
Randolph, M. 827
Ransey, Leean 916
Ray, Mathew 810
Rayner, J. T. A. 815
Read, John 824
Reader, Rebecca 869
Reagan, Crawford 822
  Jane 822
  John 824,825
  Martha J. 945
  N. 824
Reaves, Elizabeth C. 918
Redd, P. B. 911
  W. J. 828
Reed. R. C. 812
Reeves, Abner 872
  Geo. W. 802,824
  J. O. K. 801,803
  James O. K. 801,803
  John 801,805,873
  Mary A. 873
  Peter G. 836
  W. 809
  W. G. 802
  William C. 872
  Willis 873
Reichardt, August 873
  Carl August 874
  Edna Willimina 874
  Frederick Earl 874
  G. A. 873
  William Edward 874
Reid, Jane 934
Reynolds...827
  Benjamin 798,820,826
  Jennie 946
  Tabitha 945,946
  W. H. 828,830

Reynolds, William 945,946
  William H. 946
Rhea, M. 812
  Abraham 946
  Emma L. 947
  J. S. 811
  James I. 812
  Joseph 947
  Lucinda S. 867
  Mary 867,946
  Mat. 811
  Mathew 811,867,946
  Matthew 811,867,946
Rhodes...804
  Albert H. 874
  Benjamin 874
  Gaston Harvey 874
  Joe M. 874
  Thomas Whitson 874
  William 874
  William Albert 874
Richardson, Kate 830
  R. V. 802
Riddick, Amelia 875
  E. G. 875
  Harriet A. 875
  Harriet M. 875
  Joel P. 875
  Lucy T. 875
  T. K. 803,874
  Thomas K. 803,874
Rieves, D. N. 801
  W. C. 801
Rich, J. W. 817
Richardson...833
  J. M. 823,830,832,908,
    925
  N. O. 815
Richmond, N. O. 815
Ricketts, Bashaba 876
Ritchey, James 809
  Moses 809
Rivers, D. F. 803
  Martha 867
  W. J. 804
Rives, Sarah 866
Roark, Wm. 832
Robards, Nancy T. 889
  Nancy 842
Robb, Mary 917
Roberts...804
  Lena G. 841
  Wm. F. 831
Robertson...963
  Alex. 826
  Amanda M. 948
  Andrew L. 948
  Asa 824
  Carnes 948
  C. W. 805
  Christopher W. 948
  Eugenia C. 948
  J. C. N. 829
  J. R. 834
  John 825,947
  John B. 948
  John S. 947
  Julius C. N. 824
  Mary 947
  Mary W. 948
  Nannie M. 948
  Walter 824
  William H. 801
Robinson, Narcissa 961
  Rosanna T. A. 839
  Sallie 854
  W. B. 825
Robley, Thomas 822
  Ann 959
Rochelle, Mary F. 954
Roders, Willie 944
Rogers, W. E. 815
  C. J. 830

Rodgers, M. 832
  Martha L. 869
  W. J. 816
Rose, M. 835
  William S. 804
Rosenthal, Emma 922
Ross, C. W. 815
  F. M. 804
  H. 832
Rossen, William 819
Rosser, Robert 827
Rosson, John 824
Rousseau, John A. 855
Rucker, Henry T. 835
Ruddell, Margaret 908
  R. K. 908
Ruffin, James 823
  James F. 802,803
Russell...812
  J. P. 816
Russey, Elizabeth 872
Rutherford,..894
  Mary F. 926
  Samuel 926
Rutledge, Frances 854
  William R. 801

Sale, Dudley 875
  H. T. 816
  John D. 875
  Mancy 875
Salmon, Basdell 876
  Bashaba 876
  Sallie 884
  Sydner B. 876
Sammons, Allen 948
  Henrietta C. 954
  J. A. 949
  Sallie 948
  Susan A. 949
  Martha E. 930
  Martha F. 948
  Wiley W. 948
Sanders, C. A. 831
  J. L. 829
  John 825
  W. 832
Santa Anna 831
Sasser, Isabella 949
  J. D. 949
  John 949
  Margaret Grantham 949
  Mary Ann 949
  Rachel Ann 949
  Rachel M. 949
Saul...830
Sauls, A. M. 950
  Burrell 949
  Diza Ann 950
  Diza E. 950
  Elizabeth 908
  J. D. 830,949
  Jane 949
  Joseph 950
Saunders, Jemmima 913
Savage...828
  Elizabeth 950
  Eudora F. 950
  Giles M. 950
  Hamilton 950
  J. C. 828,833
  Jefferson C. 950
  L. 925
  Lucy 950
  Sallie 950
Scaller...804
Scott...831,846,894,943
  Eliza J. 951
  Hardy 836
  Jas. 825
  Joseph 951
  Maria 855
  Reubin S. 951

Scott, Susan M. 935
  Susanna 951
  W. T. 929
  Winfield 895
Scruggs, E. R. 803,816
  P. T. 803
Seabrook, James 815
Searcy, Granville 826
  Granville D. 803
Sedden, Annie 962
Sellars, Abe 836
Senter, N. A. 817
Sharpe, Esther 896
  James 894
  Mary 861
Shaw...804
  A. G. 823
  Ann L. 848
  A. M. 801,848
  Alsey M. 876
  C. A. F. 802
  C. A. S. 805
  Calvin A. S. 876
  Eva S. 876
  Fannie 876
  Henry C. 876
  Hugh 832
  J. D. 815
  John T. 876
  John W. 877
  Josiah 877
  Lizzie H. 877
  Pheraby M. 877
  Thomas 826
  Thomas I. W. 876
  Valerie F. 848
Shea, Bridget 951
  Clara E. 952
  Daniel O'Connell 952
  James Mack 951
  John 951
  John Neese 952
  Mary Helen 952
  Mollie E. 952
  Robert E. 952
  Thomas 951
Sheets, Daniel 826
Shelby, Isaac 818
Shelton, Bittie Winston 877
  E. H. 803
  George P. 806
  John W. 877
  Mattie A. 877
  Mattie Lee 878
  Ridley 878
  T. J., Jr. 803
  William D. 877
Sheppard...896
  John 839
Sherman...816
Sherrel, R. E. 812
Shinault, John 809
  Joseph H. 961
  Narcissa 961
  William 819
Shinaults, Wm. 824
Shinporch, George 806
Shoemake, David 827
  F. 821
  Francis 827
Shoffer...832
Shore, Wm. 829
Sills, Lemuel 832
Simmons, Benjamin A. 952
  Clara 952
  James B. 952
  Maria 957
  Martha O. 952
  Mary E. 957
  Mattie F. 855
  Sarah 952
  W. D. 957

Simms...806
Simpson...808
  James 808
  Jesse 809
  Joseph 808
  Wm. 824
Sims, J. B. 851
  Onora 851
Slinser, I. N. 816
Sloan...813,839
Small, W. A. 805
Smith...804,809
  Ada J. 878
  Arthur A. 878
  E. Kirby 856
  Frances E. 913
  Hattie A. 953
  Hattie M. 878
  Henry G. 803
  Isabella 953
  J. W. 830
  James 913
  Jasper 833
  John 830,878
  John D. 953
  John P. 832,878
  Joseph Dickson 953
  Julia A. 937
  Maria B. 842
  Mary 913
  N. K. 838
  Nancy 957
  Preston 833,887,896
  R. W. 806
  Rebecca 878
  R. Frank 953
  Robert W. 953
  T. R. 834
  Thomas 937
  Thomas R. 803
  W. J. 832
  W. R. 838
  Wade T. 839
  William M. 802
  Willie T. 878
  Zula W. 878
Sneed, J. L. T. 803
  John L. T. 802
  Samuel 801
Snow, Pamelia C. 852
Somers, Joe 815
  John 802
Somerville, J. H. 816,833
  Robert 798,803
Sparks...806
  J. L. 879
  James L. 879
  Margaret C. 879
  Mary C. 879
  Robert M. 879
  S. G. 805
  Samuel G. 879
  Samuel L. 879
Spence, John C. 804
Spencer, Amasa 809
Springfield, Sarah 904
Sprouell, Samuel B. 845
Spurlock, Mathew 809
  Nathan 808
Stafford, Jesse 806
Stainback, Ashley D. 879
  C. A. 803
  Charley A. 879
  Ingram M. 880
  Katherine E. 879
  Laura 879
Stall, H. B. 811
Stanfield, John A. 804
Stanley, Ellizabeth 869
  J. B. 815
  John D. 801
Stark, Joseph C. 889
  Lamiza A. 889

Steele...835
  N. 821
  Nathan 820
  Nathaniel 824,827
  Samuel 846
Steiger...807
  E. D. 803
  J. J. 803
  John J. 801
  R. E. 801
Stephens, Daniel 839
  M. E. 839
  Margaret 839
  Samuel N. 839
  Sarah H. 839
  W. H. 815,839
Stevens, Needham 827
  W. H. 876
Steve (colored) 838
Stevenson...880
Steward, Elizabeth 892
  Minerva 893
Stewart, Charles 825,827
  836
  Elcy 953
  Elias 953
  Elias B. 953
  Lucy M. 954
Stidham, Mary 862
  Sarah F. 872
Stinson...830
Stockton, Wm. 823
Stoddert, Wm. 829
Stone, K. T. P. 827
  Peter P. 832
  R. C. 811
Street, Mrs. L. M. 875
Stuart...842
  Arlington C. 954
  Henrietta C. 954
  Mary C. 958
  Mary F. 954
  Thomas C. 954
Sturm...807
Suggs, Nancy 892
Summers, Callie E. 880
  Eliza 936
  Elizabeth 880
  Hezekiah 880
  Julius A. 880
Summey, George 838
Surratt, Nancy S. 930
Suther, Caroline 848
Sutton, Cynthia 930
Swayne, J. T. 802
Swineboard, A. J. 830
  G. W. 836
  Isabella 949

Talbot, J. H. 824
Talley, W. F. 802
Tally, W. F. 824
Tarver, E. D. 823
  Edmund D. 800,801
  Edmund 808
Tate...937
  Fannie 955
  H. W. 955
  J. D. W. 825
  J. K. 955
  J. W. 830,955
  Joseph 827
  Laura 955
  Margaret V. 862
  Mary Lucy 955
  R. A. 830
  Robert A. 955
  Robert Wood 955
  Sam 822
  William Caldwell 955
Tatum, B. F. 817
  Bart F. 801
  E. W. 804

Tatum, Edward W. 801,880
  Elizabeth 880
  Elizabeth B. 881
  Elizabeth F. 881
  Henry 880
  Howell A. 829
  Rebecca 881
Taylor...814,821,962
  A. 829
  A. J. 824
  Abner 923
  Andrew 824,825
  Mary F. 848
  Willis 832
  Zachary 926
Teal, Matilda Ophelia 859
Teague, J. B. 831
  John 837
Tennyson, Smithie E. 920
Terrell...909
Terrence, Adelia A. 882
  Hugh 881
  James T. 881
  Nancy 881
Tharp, Hardy W. 801
Theobold, J. F. 829
Thomas...804
  A. 817
  A. N. 814
  D. W. 801,804
  F. M. 826
  J. E. 814,815
  J. J. 826
  John 824
Thomlinson, Ellen J. 844
Thompson...831
  Asa 809
  Barbara E. 888
  Elizabeth A. C. 851
  Geo. 836
  J. S. 831
  John 806,820
  Nancy J. 861
  W. H. 838
  William H. 801
Thomson, James 894
Thornton, Hamilton 798
  Charity 868
  Robert G. 798,800,808
  Robert S. 798
Thurmond, Gwynn 817
  Gynn 832,833,834
  M. M. 925
Tilghman, Arthur 825
  Benjamin 825
Timmons, Thomas 832
Tipler, W. F. 831
Tippett, Jas. 824,825
Tisdal, S. 824
Titus, James 808
Todd, Ann J. 873
  Emily 839
  Wm. 839
Tombers, J. T. 811
Tomlinson, G. H. 815
Toombs...806
  T. G. 806
Toone...831
  Ann E. 892
  James 836
Topp, A. F. 817,833
Totten, H. L. 840
Towles, Mollie W. 841
Traylor, Frances S. 962
Trent, I. 816
  W. C. 801,805
Trimble, Frank 804
Trotter, Benjamin 801
Truscott, J. B. 837
Tucker, Edmund J. 803
  Lucinda J. 923
  M. E. 909
Tunage, James 822

Tune, Wm. 832
Turley, W. B. 824,839
Turner, Elizabeth 859
  J. H. 817,833
  Sallie E. 859
  W. A. 803
Tyler, Ann J. 873
  H. Cockburn 829

Ussery, J. D. 925

Vandergriff, Joseph 837
VanDorn...858
Vaughan, A. J. 816
  E. 816
  James 826
Voss, W. J. 815

Wade, Fannie E. 847
Walden, Mollie 888
Walker, Georgie 864
  Iverson J. 882
  Job 882
  Lea E. 882
  Rachel 849
  Robert L. 838
  Sallie M. 882
  Sarah A. 882
  Simon H. 801
  Wilber I. 882
Walthall...850
Walton, Andrew J. 956
  Charles A. 922,956
  Elizabeth 844
  Mary E. 909,922,955,956
  Nancy 957
  Robt. 831
  Robert H. 922,955
  Mabrey 955,956
  Sarah 922,956
  Temperance 940
Ward, Pleasant 808
Warner, Amos 825
  John 831
  Joseph 819
Warr, A. V. 804,811
  Americus V. 882
  Emily 882
  James 882
Warren, Asbery 803
  Narcissa L. 887
  Sloan 829
Washington, J. S. 805
Waterhouse, Richard 814
Watkins, Benjamin 883
  Ethel 884
  Fannie Kent 884
  John T. 886
  Sallie 883
Watson, N. T. 934
Weatherby...828
Weber, A. 861,884,887
  Anna 884
  Catherine 884
  Clara 884
  Clara E. 884
  Elizabeth 884
  Fannie 884
  Isadora 884
  John A. 884
  M. F. 884
  May 884
  N. 884
  William A. 884
Webb, James Anna 855
  Jane 858
  Thomas 826
Welch, John, Sr. 839
Welkins, West 832
Wellens...830
  C. M. 830
  Charles 827
Wells, Allen 832

Wells, D. J. 829
  P. D. J. 829
Wendel, David 911
  Matilda 911,912
Wert...804
West, Jane 935
Westbrook, Adaline 936
  R. A. 831
Wetzel...805
Wharley, Blanche E. 960
Wharton, D. 866
  George 875
Wheeler...807
Whitaker, 819
  Isaac 874
  Julia 874
  Nannie 870
  Narcissa 940
  W. 825
White...840
  Alexander 957
  G. H. 815
  J. G. 826
  George A. 957
  James B. 957
  James L. 825
  Jefferson Davis 957
  John H. 957
  King 957
  Lucie F. 957
  Maria Jane 957
  Mary 870
  Mary E. 957
  Mary Emma 957
  Mathias O. 957
  May C. 839
  R. H. 817,833
  R. R. 833
  S. H. 832
  Sarah Ann 957
  Susie E. 957
  Tabitha Ann 957
  Telitha 957
  W. C. 839
Whitfield...901
Whitley, Esther 957
  Haywood 957
  Jesse B. 958
  Joseph A. 958
  Margie R. 958
  Rufus D. 957
  Rufus M. 958
  William T. 958
Whitly, Aaron 826
Whitlow, Frances 853
  Jesse 906
  N. C. 895
  Nicholas 906
  Sallie E. 906
  Sarah 906
Whitmore, C. H. 803,805
Whitsett, Sarah 813
Whitthorn, J. M. 825
Wiggins...804,832
Wiley, Nelson 832
Wilfong...804
  John 801
Wilkerson, W. D. 801,804
Wilkes, Ann 959
  Emily J. 959
  Emmett C. 960
  Henretta C. 954
  J. W. 959
  John W., Jr. 960
  Joseph 949,954,959
  Martha F. 948
  Naomi M. 959
  Rebecca J. 959
Wilkinson, W. D. 801
  William B. 884
  Wyatt 884
Williams, C. H. 831
  Charles 809

Williams, George 812
  I. B. 824
  Isaac B. 802
  J. 815
  J. J. 839
  Jane 858
  Joe C. 962
  L. M. 837
  Lewis P. 801
  Maggie 962
  Mary Ross 962
  Pheraby M. 877
  R. C. 814
  S. M. 837
  Samuel 813
  Samuel 812,813
Williamson, A. C. 815
  Alexander 885
  Ann 885
  Cordelia 885
  Cynthia 840
  J. M. 803
  James 863,885
  L. P. 803
  Mildred 863,885
  Nancy 884
  Orlando 885
  Robert 885
  Susan 863,885
  Susie 885
  Thomas 885
  W. C. 803
  William A. 885
Willis...839
  A. J. 827
Willoughby, Clara 952
Wilson...805,861,884
Wilson (slave) 826
Wilson, A. G. 839
  Ann E. 886,958
  Agnes 886
  Ashley H. 958
  Cora 887
  Cordelia 887
  David 886
  Elizabeth 886,910
  Eugenia 839
  Frank A. 886
  Hadassah 887
  J. A. 821,827,830
  J. W. 958
  James 813,886
  John 824,958,959
  John A. 958
  Joseph 959
  Joseph Ashley 959
  Laura 955
  Louis 809
  Lucretia 886
  Martha 886
  Martha A. 959
  Martha P. 959
  Mary 851
  Mary C, 958
  Maurice 959
  Sidney 886
  William H. 886
Winchester...820
Winfrey, Sallie 883
Wingfield, W. E. 816
Winston, John 808
  Laura J. 850
Wirt, Catherine 845
Wood, Amanda M. 948
  Blanche E. 960
  Charles 960
  D. W. 827
  Fannie 955
  Frances A. 960
  George 838
  J. W. 827
  James 960
  Jennie M. 921

Wood, John R. 838
  Maria 941
  Mary D. 909
  May 838
  R. H. 826,832,925
  Robert H. 955
  W. H. 839
  Walker 802
Woodfin, J. J. 804
Woods...819
  Annie 961
  Bessie 961
  David 961
  J. A. 816
  John D. 961
  Margaret A. 927
  Narcissa 961
  Samuel M. 961
Word, Benjamin 806
  Nat. 801
Worrell, D. 805
  J. J. 804
  Sarah 952
Worthy, Elizabeth 843
Wright...806,830
  Eldridge 817
  Hannah 961
  J. V. 816
  John 961
  John V. 845
  L. L. 817
  Maggie 962
  R. M. 828,908,961
  Samuella 962
  W. 829
  W. B. 961
Wyatt, Dickason 801
  Samuel 809
Wynn...805
Wynne, Albert E. 962
  Annie 962
  Annie C. 962
  Frances S. 962
  Hiram B. 962
  John W. 962
  Willie B. 962

Yancy...816
Yancey, Alexander L. 887
  Elizabeth 887
  Narcissa L. 887
  R. H. 879
  Robert J. 873
  Thomas B. 887
Yancy, Elvia J. 943
  John 809
  R. J. 805
Yansey, G. B. 805
  R. H. 805
Yoakum, Pattie 963
Yopp, A. F. 823
  Alex F. 963
  Elmo 963
  Elizabeth 963
  Harry 963
  Ike 963
  Neely 963
  P. E. 830
  Pattie 963
  Wm. T. 963
Young, N. T. 934
  Thomas 807

Zollicoffer...816

www.ingramcontent.com/pod-product-compliance
Lightning Source LLC
Chambersburg PA
CBHW020651300426
44112CB00007B/336